GENDER, CARE AND ECONOMICS

Gender, Care and Economics

Jean Gardiner

Senior Lecturer
School of Continuing Education
University of Leeds

First published 1997 by
MACMILLAN PRESS LTD
Houndmills, Basingstoke, Hampshire RG21 6XS
and London
Companies and representatives
throughout the world

ISBN 0–333–56310–7 hardcover
ISBN 0–333–66994–0 paperback

A catalogue record for this book is available
from the British Library.

This book is printed on paper suitable for recycling and
made from fully managed and sustained forest sources.

10   9   8   7   6   5   4   3   2   1
06 05 04 03 02 01 00 99 98 97

Printed in Great Britain by
The Ipswich Book Company Ltd
Ipswich, Suffolk

For Alice and Jack

Contents

List of Tables

Acknowledgements

I would like to thank all the friends and colleagues who encouraged me to write this book, the teachers and students who inspired me, the many feminist writers and activists whose ideas have helped clarify my own. I am grateful for the experience of working in a university adult education context which gave me the support and space to stand outside the narrow confines of academic specialisation. I am especially indebted to Peter Nolan, Elizabeth Silva and Bernard Campbell who read all the chapter drafts and gave me generous support and useful suggestions. I would also like to thank Sarah Benton, Jill Liddington and Katrina Honeyman. I am grateful to my editors at Macmillan for their patience and to Linda Auld for her careful editing. And finally I would like to thank Bernard, Jack and Alice for living with the book, and for their understanding and care.

Abbreviations

CI	Citizen's Income
CPS	Centre for Policy Studies
CSE	Conference of Socialist Economists
CSO	Central Statistical Office
ECCN	European Commission Childcare Network
EOC	Equal Opportunities Commission
ESRC	The Economic and Social Research Council
GCE	General Certificate of Education
GNP	Gross National Product
NEP	New Economic Policy
OECD	Organisation for Economic Cooperation and Development
OPCS	Office of Population Censuses and Surveys
TBI	Transitional Basic Income

1 Domestic Labour and Economics

> I turn the alarm off and I have about ten minutes of kind of free time while I'm lying there in bed. And during that time, I usually try to think of what I'm going to put in Brad's lunch (mother quoted in Devault 1991: 56).

All societies rely heavily on women's domestic labour in meeting the care needs of adults and children. Gender divisions in the social organisation of care are a central explanatory feature of the persistent economic inequality between men and women across societies. Paradoxically, economics has had little to say about either gender inequality or the social provision of care, over the period of more than two hundred years since Adam Smith published *The Wealth of Nations*. In industrial societies like Britain, the work involved in caring for people is organised through different combinations of household, market and state provision. Yet, whatever the combination of provision, households remain the basic unit of care and the most unresearched in terms of economic analysis. This book explores this history of neglect and offers a critical overview of the positive attempts by feminists, economists and other social scientists to refocus attention on household economic relations and gender divisions in the thirty year period from the mid-1960s to the mid-1990s. In the 1970s feminists placed domestic labour on the social theory and research agenda and the book sets out to explore and review the theoretical debates and empirical research that followed in the subsequent twenty year period and to offer a new political economy framework for analysing interrelationships between households, markets and the state in the provision of care in the contemporary British context.

Domestic labour is a concept that has been used by feminists and social scientists since the 1970s to refer to unpaid work that is done by and for members of households. This

1

introductory chapter explores the rationale for adopting domestic labour as the key concept for the book. This is followed
by a discussion of the significance of domestic labour in feminist and mainstream social science research. The next section
offers an overview of the political economy framework for this
study. Work that is not paid, which takes place outside the
framework of the market economy, is not easily defined.
Therefore, the next two sections offer a more precise and
technical discussion of the definitions of domestic labour and
of household units. The chapter finishes with an overview of
the structure of the book

1.1   WHY DOMESTIC LABOUR?

Domestic labour has been chosen as the central concept for
the book, in preference to a number of other options (domestic work, reproductive work, household labour, household
production, or household work). The use of 'domestic' emphasises that it is activities and processes internal to the household unit and outside the market economy that are being
considered. The term 'household work', for example, has
often been used to refer to all types of work, paid and unpaid,
carried out by household members, as in the expression
'household work strategies'. The household division of labour
is used to refer to the ways households divide all types of work
between members whereas the domestic division of labour is
understood to refer to the division of unpaid work in the
household.

The use of 'labour' in preference to 'work' is related to the
way the book is intended as a critique of economic theory in
particular. Economic theory generally conceptualises economic activity as 'labour' not 'work', whatever the school of
thought. Where references are made in economic research to
'work', invariably it is identified with employment, as, for
example in discussion of 'work incentives'. The choice of
'labour' locates the book within the tradition of political
economy with its recognition of 'labour processes', as opposed
to the neoclassical economic tradition in which household
production has become the favoured concept (see section 1.3
for further discussion of the distinctions between these two

traditions). Using 'reproduction' or 'reproductive work' also raises problems of definition and risks a too close identification between economic activities and biological processes (see chapter 5 for further discussion of 'reproduction'). Finally, linking 'domestic' and 'labour' establishes a connection between the current study and the 1970s domestic labour debate which is the subject of chapter 5. An important reason for writing this book was the perception that it was worth reflecting again on the outcomes of that debate and returning to some of the issues it had raised but not resolved.

Adopting 'domestic labour' also carries certain risks which it is helpful to identify at the outset. The term 'labour' may have various connotations for the reader which are not intended in this study. For example there is a tendency to perceive 'labour' in opposition to 'management', to see labour as execution, not conception, of tasks and, as physical rather than mental processes. This interpretation is contested in this study. Domestic labour includes the planning, management and execution of labour processes within the household, requiring the application of skills at different levels. A second risk is that 'domestic labour' will locate the study in too narrow a theoretical framework, either the Marxist feminism of the domestic labour debate, with its emphasis on capitalist exploitation, or the socialist feminist analysis of patriarchal exploitation. On the contrary, the aim of the book is to take a critical look at both these theoretical perspectives, as well as exploring the inadequacies of the neoclassical economic framework.

Nonetheless, the insights provided by Marxist and socialist feminists in the 1970s and 1980s, and their critiques of mainstream social science perspectives, provide a starting point for the book. Domestic labour was and is a concept with political, as well as an analytical uses, a concept created within socialist feminist discourse. This book owes its inspiration to that tradition and the powerful critique it provided of mainstream socio-economic research.

1.2   DOMESTIC LABOUR IN THE SOCIAL SCIENCES

In the 1950s and early 1960s all the social sciences virtually ignored housework and domestic caring work. Domestic labour neither existed as a recognised concept, nor as an area of study, despite the major way in which its organisation shaped most women's and men's lives throughout the world. Few social scientists at the time even questioned why this should be the case. Any who did would probably have offered one or other of the following explanations. Some would have suggested that domestic labour was a relic of pre-capitalist, pre-industrial society and that it was becoming less significant with industrial and economic development. Women were being drawn increasingly into production outside the home and home-based production was being drawn into the market. Labour saving appliances in the home were eliminating the physical drudgery with which previous generations of women had been burdened. Others might have argued that the private domestic sphere was separate from the public sphere, a realm of personal choice and moral imperatives, not one that was subject to social, economic or political analysis. The logical conclusion in either case was that there was no need to analyse domestic labour and no need for social and economic policies in respect of it.

Feminism in the late 1960s and 1970s challenged this complacency. Housework and childcare were central concerns in the 1970s feminist movement (Rowbotham 1990). Women's domestic labour was perceived to be a major material element of women's subordinate position in society. It was obvious from women's experience in the USSR and Eastern Europe that getting into paid employment did not and would not, on its own, solve the issue of women's economic inequality. It was also clear to women that domestic labour showed no signs of disappearing in spite of all the changes that had taken place historically concerning the unpaid work women did within the home. Moreover feminists in the 1970s disputed whether a society in which people paid others to do their housework and childcare was a desirable goal.

The intellectual debates about domestic labour which followed in the 1970s focused on the two questions: why had domestic labour not disappeared in industrial capitalist societies and why was it predominantly women who did it? The intensity with which feminists argued about whether the capitalist class or men benefited most from women's domestic labour may now appear misplaced. At the time it was undoubtedly an important and necessary process of grappling with the theoretical frameworks inherited from Marxism and emerging within feminism, which will be discussed in chapters 4 and 5. By the end of the 1970s the dual systems perspective which recognised interconnections between capitalist and patriarchal structures was emerging as an influential synthesis of the different positions (Hartmann 1979a and b, Sargent 1981). Within this perspective attention increasingly turned away from household relations to the interaction of patriarchy and capitalism in the labour market.

Whilst some discussion rippled on subsequently, the feminist debate about domestic labour effectively finished at that time. The focus of intellectual concern shifted to analysis of women's position in the wage labour force, segmented labour markets, occupational segregation and patriarchy in the workplace (Cockburn 1983 and 1985, Game and Pringle 1983, Walby 1986, Beechey 1987). There was a recognition that women's economic dependence in the family was directly related to their subordinate position in the labour market. Patriarchy was to be found in the workplace as well as the home. Although the inequality and dependence women experienced would not be solved solely by women getting into paid employment, at the same time they could not be tackled without women having access to paid jobs. In Britain particularly, the severe recession at the beginning of the 1980s created a real fear that women would have to struggle to retain their jobs and the limited rights at work which they had won in the previous decade. Moreover it was imperative for feminists to challenge the prevailing assumption in the social sciences that women were identified with the sphere of 'private' domestic family relations and men with the public sphere of the labour market and class relations (Siltanen and Stanworth 1984).

At the same time, the domestic labour debate seemed to have reached a dead end in both theoretical and practical terms. In retrospect this is understandable given the narrowness of the questions it posed and the limitations of the Marxist framework within which the debate was conducted. The hopes of some protagonists that Marx's labour theory of value offered a way of getting women's domestic labour acknowledged as an integral part of the economy were quickly disappointed. A few years of intense debate led to the conclusion that domestic labour, according to Marxist definitions, did not create value (Gardiner, Himmelweit and Mackintosh 1975). For many feminists this outcome merely confirmed their view that economic theory did not speak to the economic reality they experienced.

There were no agreed and obvious practical conclusions to be drawn from the debates about domestic labour at that time. The major campaign that was directly linked to them was that of Wages for Housework but this campaign was strongly opposed within the feminist movement (Malos 1980). Whilst childcare provision had been one of the original four demands of the Women's Liberation Movement in Britain in 1970, it was not one of the major campaigning issues amongst feminists in the 1970s and even in the domestic labour debate was given very little attention. The major feminist campaigns of the late 1970s were around abortion, domestic violence and equal rights at work.

However the feminist movement of the late 1960s and 1970s had a major impact on popular and social science definitions of work and created a new language to describe unpaid work and domestic labour. In the 1970s, space for research on gender divisions in the household and the labour market began to open up, particularly within the sociology discipline, where Ann Oakley's pioneering study of housework (1974) had a major impact. Sociologists were more receptive than economists to seeing work as a socially constructed category. They recognised that the definition of work could vary and change over time in popular consciousness and the social sciences (Wadel 1979). Sociologists began to take on board the feminist redefinition of work (Pahl 1988 and Roberts, Finnegan and Gallie 1985). Labour process theory began to recognise that separating analysis of the workplace from that of the household was problematic in the context of gender (Knights and Wilmott 1986).

Economics as a discipline was more resistant than other social sciences to acknowledging feminist redefinitions (Dex 1985: 9–10). Economists have rarely seen any need to define 'work' or 'labour'. Labour is the central concept used to refer to purposive economic activity but, at least in the second half of the twentieth century, the main economics textbooks did not perceive the need to define it. In the nineteenth century, on the other hand, considerable effort went into debating what was meant by 'productive' labour, although domestic labour was invariably excluded from this definition (see chapter 2). In the twentieth century it was generally assumed that labour should be restricted to those activities that are sold on the market for a wage, at least in industrial capitalist economies. Labour was treated as synonymous with paid employment. This definition of labour is linked to what Charlotte Perkins Gilman once referred to as a 'naively masculine' view of 'economic man' who would 'never do anything unless he has to; will only do it to escape pain or attain pleasure' (Gilman 1971: 36 cited Waring 1989: 26). The dominant philosophical tradition within economics perceived work to be necessary in a world of scarcity and only undertaken because of the extrinsic benefits derived from it. The goal of mainstream economics was to find the most efficient way of allocating scarce resources to meet competing material wants which could never be fully satisfied (see chapter 2). Mainstream economics deflected issues of social inequality, and of the control and use of resources outside the market, to other social science disciplines, thus disengaging with feminist critiques. In the period from the 1960s to the 1990s, few feminists, in Britain at least, managed or chose to pursue their research interests within the core economics discipline. Sociology, Social Policy, Development Studies, Geography, Economic and Social History, and Education offered more space for feminist research.

Within the framework of orthodox economic theory, however, there is a growing international literature which attempts to quantify the volume of domestic labour and the value of its contribution to the economy (Goldschmidt-Clermont 1982). A range of methods have been used to estimate the value of household production. These include different wage-based imputations for domestic labour inputs as well as price imputations for outputs. Although there are problems of measurement, the scale of the economic contribution made by domestic labour is undeniable. Most studies estimate the value of the economic contribution made by domestic labour in industrialised countries at between 25 and 40 per cent of Gross National Product (GNP) (Goldschmidt-

Clermont 1982: 1). In developing countries, with large subsistence sectors, household production for direct household consumption may represent even higher proportions of GNP. Estimates of the volume of domestic labour suggest that the number of hours devoted to it is of the same order as the number of hours devoted to employment, across industrial societies (Goldschmidt-Clermont 1982). This means that the working population as a whole spends roughly equivalent amounts of time on domestic labour and on employment.

Given the extent to which human resources are tied up with productive activities outside the market, measurement problems are not a valid reason for ignoring domestic labour (Waring 1989, Goldschmidt-Clermont 1990). The current development of environmental accounting demonstrates that non-market accounting frameworks can be developed once there is the political will to do so. Awareness of the economic significance of domestic labour has resulted in a growing literature that takes some account of it.

As well as the quantitative research already mentioned, there is now an extensive literature concerned with the New Home Economics (see chapter 3), the economics of the informal economy, especially in developing countries, and the self-service economy, notably the work of Gershuny (1983). Nonetheless mainstream economics in industrialised countries continues to regard domestic labour as outside the boundaries of the discipline. Whilst it is now possible to find introductory economics textbooks containing a short section on 'household production', usually within the consumer theory section, many standard texts continue to ignore this area altogether.

Some intellectual space for feminist economic research opened up in Britain during the 1980s, mainly within the study of labour markets, and there is an expanding research literature on gender in this field (for example Rubery 1988 and 1994, Humphries 1984 and 1992 and Joshi 1986 and 1991). However economics as a discipline, and the different schools within it, have been, at least in Britain, virtually untouched by feminism. Visits to the economics section of academic bookshops in Britain makes this apparent. Gender is still a long way from being theoretically integrated into the discipline. It is still largely treated as a sub-heading within a few

topics (employment, unemployment, wages) within a particular branch of economics (labour).

Although labour economics is the branch of economics
which has allowed space for research on gender, its boundaries and theoretical frameworks impose strict limits on how
that research has developed. Whilst the existence of labour
economics as a separate branch of economics offers recognition of the fact that labour is not just a commodity like any
other, in practice, labour economics is about labour that is
bought and sold and not labour performed outside the
market. Consequently 'labour supply' is defined as the supply
of labour to the market only, rather than the available labour
resources in the economy as a whole (Gershuny 1983: 123 and
Glucksmann 1990). It follows that female 'economic activity
rates' are normally lower than male and that women are
assumed to make a less significant contribution to the
economy than men. Yet, as discussed in chapter 7, most
women work longer hours than men when account is taken of
the time they spend on domestic labour. The different positions of men and women in labour markets cannot be explained without also analysing their distinctive patterns of
participation in domestic labour (Glucksmann 1990). Labour
should be considered a broader concept than employment.
Neither mainstream economics nor radical political economy
have seriously addressed this issue, with the result that gender
divisions remain of marginal concern within economic debate.

1.3 WHY POLITICAL ECONOMY?

Neither neoclassical economic theory nor the various alternative schools of radical political economy have responded adequately to feminist critiques of the social sciences. Neoclassical
economics, particularly in its New Home Economics formulation (see chapter 3), which takes the household as the decision-making unit, may appear to offer a more promising
framework for analysing domestic labour than political
economy with its focus on class and the institutions of the
labour market. What advantages, therefore, does a political
economy approach have over that offered by neoclassical
economic theory? The answer to this question lies partly in

the history of economic thought. The concerns of classical political economy, as developed by Smith and Ricardo in the late
eighteenth and early nineteenth centuries, were subsequently
separated out and divided between the two new social sciences, economics and sociology, that emerged as counter-
weights to the influence of Marxism in the late nineteenth
century. Markets and exchange became the central focus of
the new marginalist economics (see chapter 2). Within the
new disciplines, the economic analysis of markets was detached from the sociological analysis of institutions. At the
same time economics moved away from the notion that the
value of commodities, including labour, was based on their
costs of production. Thenceforth value was to be equated with
price and determined by the interplay of supply and demand
in the market. Labour became merely a factor of production,
devoid of its distinctive humanity, comparable only with the
other factors of production, capital and land. The distinction
between replaceable and irreplaceable physical resources,
capital and land respectively, was also ignored within the new
economic framework. Economics became a sphere of cultural
uniformity, based on universal assumptions and an ahistorical
concept of individualistic rationality.

Mainstream economics is still based on this inherited framework. Since, in the household economy, market exchanges are
not present, it is impossible to analyse domestic labour in abstraction from the social relationships to which it is linked, relationships between wives, husbands, mothers, fathers,
children and other dependent household members. Normal
economic assumptions about cultural uniformity are even
more obviously inadequate in relation to households than to
market production. The neoclassical New Home Economics is
inadequate to the task of exploring the complexities of household relationships and decision-making processes (see chapter
3).

Radical political economy represents a range of different
schools of economic thought with different emphases, including post-Keynesianism, institutionalism and Marxism (Sawyer
1989). In spite of the differences between these schools, there
are certain common themes which distinguish political
economy approaches from neoclassical economics and these
are summarised in Table 1.1. Political economy recognises

history and explores the institutional context for market forces. Conflict, inequality and cooperation are acknowledged as well as competition. The institutions of the state are generally recognised as having a role to play in the development of economies (Marquand 1988), as will be discussed in chapter 10. The next two sections discuss in greater detail the definitions of domestic labour and the household on which this study is based.

1.4   DEFINING DOMESTIC LABOUR

The boundary for market-based economic activity is normally defined by the exchange of money as payment for services rendered. Money clearly cannot provide a definition of which activities to include and exclude in the case of domestic labour. Another criterion is needed and the most commonly adopted is that an unpaid household activity is 'economic' if, at least in principle, it could be delegated to a third party and bought or sold in a market transaction. The definition of domestic labour in this book is based on Margaret Reid's definition of 'household production' as unpaid activities carried out by and for the members of a specific household which could be delegated and could produce marketable goods or services (Reid 1934: 11). This definition is in common use internationally within the research literature concerned with the measurement of household-based economic activity (Goldschmidt-Clermont 1982).

Outside the market framework, therefore, a productive or work activity is one that can be carried out by someone other than the consumer. Consumption or leisure activities are those that have to be carried out by consumers themselves (for example sleeping, eating, physical exercise). Production implies the possibility of a transaction and separation between producer and consumer. It is this separation that makes possible the development of markets, of a social division of labour and of specialisation.

Domestic labour is therefore defined as those unpaid household activities which could be done by someone other than the person who actually carries them out or could be purchased if a market for those activities existed. It can in this way

Table 1.1   A comparison of neoclassical economics and radical political economy

Neoclassical Economics	Radical Political Economy
1. Economics is about the alternative uses of scarce resources.	1. Political economy is about the production as well as the use of resources, about labour processes as well as market transactions.
2. Economics is about the exchange of goods and services, normally for money.	2. Political economy is concerned with the distribution of income and wealth as well as the exchange of goods and services.
3. Economics is about the market mechanism: the role of price in bringing about a balance between supply (sellers) and demand (buyers).	3. The economy is more than the market mechanism and is formed by a multiplicity of economic, political and social organisations and institutions.
4. The market is a democratic institution in which buyers and sellers have equal status.	4. Economic institutions, including markets, are typically characterised by inequalities in power and conflicts of interest.
5. The primary economic agent is the individual; households and firms act as if they were individual agents.	5. Economic agents are organisations, interest groups and classes as well as individuals and households.
6. Economics has universal applicability and can be applied to different societies and historical periods.	6. Economies evolve historically and hence there is no such thing as a universally applicable economic theory.
7. The main purpose of economics is to make valid predictions on how individuals and economies will behave.	7. Political economy is concerned with explaining why economies and individuals behave as they do.
8. Economic theory suggests that the economic role of the state should be minimal and that markets should be given the greatest possible freedom to allocate resources.	8. Historical experience suggests that economic success is based on an active partnership between the state and markets in which the state plays a developmental as well as a regulatory role.

be distinguished from personal care activities which people perform for themselves (eating, washing) and leisure activities which cannot be delegated to someone else (watching television or reading for pleasure). This definition of domestic labour is not based on whether the person doing it gains pleasure from the activity or exercises choice in the process. Contrary to the assumptions underlying mainstream economic theory, personal satisfaction and pleasure are often derived from labour, whether it is paid or unpaid. In both cases the degree of satisfaction derived from the work may be linked to whether or not tasks are routine and repetitive or not, the amount of skill involved, the degree of choice exercised in performing them and the social relationships within which they are carried out.

In the literature on measuring domestic labour there have been two slightly different interpretations of where to draw the dividing line between economic and non-economic activities in the household within the broad framework outlined above. Szalai (1972) and Hawrylyshyn (1976) drew a distinction between work, on the one hand and leisure/personal care on the other. Personal care (eating, washing, sleeping) could not be delegated to a third person, by definition, and leisure activities could not be delegated because they were a source of pleasure in their own right (creating direct utility for the person performing the activity), rather than a means to an end (where utility resided in the product not the process). A problem with this approach is that the work/leisure distinction relies on people's subjective interpretations of different activities. Although subjectivity is interesting in its own right, it provides an inadequate basis for economic valuation of household activities (Chadeau 1985: 241). For example men may perceive childcare as a leisure activity more often than women because of the different childcare tasks they perform. Women are more likely to be involved in basic routine care while men are more likely to play with children or take them out (Martin and Roberts 1984: 102) and this will influence subjective perceptions of childcare.

An alternative approach is to apply the concept of production (Hill 1979) and to distinguish activities where it is possible for the producer and consumer to be separate people

(productive activities) from those where production and consumption cannot be separated (non-productive activities).
Where production and consumption have to be done by the
same individual, delegation and market substitution are not
possible. The production approach has the advantage of not
being dependent on subjective perceptions. However its use
as a basis for assessing the economic value of domestic labour
is also problematic because of the lack of actual market substitutes, in many instances, for domestic labour activities
(Chadeau 1985: 241). Let us next clarify the household as a
unit of analysis since it defines the boundaries within which
domestic labour is carried out.

1.5 DEFINING THE HOUSEHOLD

The household rather than the family is taken as the unit for
analysis of domestic labour as it approximates more closely to
the notion of a domestic unit, being normally defined as an
individual or group of people who share living space and/or
take at least some meals together (Yanagisako 1979: 164,
Mackintosh 1988: 402). The family, on the other hand, is
defined in terms of marital and parental relationships rather
than co-residence. Since it is co-residence, and arrangements
for cooking and eating, which define the social relations of domestic labour, a household analysis is more appropriate than
one based on family relationships.

 The household is organised around a core of human needs
which have social, historical and cultural as well as physiologi-
cal dimensions (Harris and Young 1981: 124). These socially
constructed needs include food, shelter, sleep, cleanliness,
clothing, sex, reproduction, companionship, recreation. In
Britain data on households are collected using a definition
based on the way people are grouped around the basic human
needs of food, shelter and sleep. Household membership was
defined, prior to the 1990s, on the basis of a minimum
number of meals taken together and a minimum number of
nights spent in the common residence. But this definition
evolved as eating, sleeping and living patterns changed. For
example, in the 1950s and 60s, the National Food Survey
defined household members as individuals consuming at least

half of their meals in the household but, from 1972, the definition was amended to include any individual consuming at least one meal a day on four days a week and spending four nights at home (Ministry of Agriculture, Fisheries and Food 1974). The 1991 Census definition of a household was even broader and allowed for the possibility of households where no meals at all were taken together. Any group of people, living, or staying temporarily, at the same address, who shared common housekeeping, were treated as a household. Common housekeeping was interpreted as either a regular arrangement to share at least one meal (including breakfast) a day, or a shared living room (Office of Population Censuses and Surveys 1992b).

Official definitions sometimes embody universalistic assumptions about the nature of households and social relationships within them. For example, the 'head of the household' and the 'housewife' were defined as household members by the National Food Survey, from the early 1970s to the early 1990s, regardless of how many meals they took or nights they spent 'at home'. Prior to 1981, the Office of Population Censuses and Surveys (OPCS), used the following definition of a household in the General Household Survey and elsewhere: 'a group of people who all live regularly at the address...and who are catered for, for at least one meal a day, by the same person' (OPCS 1992a: 219). This definition ignored both the reality of single person households and the possibility of household catering being carried out by more than one person.

Although 'household', not 'family' is the appropriate unit for analysis of domestic labour, much of the literature on domestic labour, which will be reviewed in this book, focuses primarily on households which have a family structure based on a married couple, or a cohabiting heterosexual couple, with or without dependent children. There is relatively little data or research available on domestic labour in lone parent households, in gay and lesbian couple households, in single person households and in other types of household unit. It is to be hoped that, with increasing recognition of domestic labour as an area for serious socio-economic study, further research will be encouraged to take account of household diversity. Finally, it needs to be stressed that using the term 'household' incurs

a risk of cultural universalism. Even among married couple
households with dependent children, there will be fundamental differences related to class, income and employment, educational background, race, ethnicity, culture and religion.
Some of these differences are easier to identify in empirical
research findings than others, because of the questions that
social science research prioritises. This study cannot do full
justice to the social diversity of household experience but will,
at least, try to develop an analytical framework within which
diversity is recognised.

1.6   THE STRUCTURE OF THE BOOK

This book offers a critical review of the history of economic
thought from a feminist perspective and in chapter 2 discusses
how the classical political economists in the eighteenth and
nineteenth centuries defined the economy as a particularly
masculine terrain. Economics developed as the study of
market relationships and of trade between self-interested individuals. Efficiency was equated with narrow specialisation.
Household relationships were excluded, assumed to involve altruism and non-economic motivation and behaviour. Except
in the writing of John Stuart Mill, women were assumed to be
predisposed to serve the interests of their families, not to be
self-interested, and therefore not to be eligible for the individual freedoms being sought for men. With the pre-eminence of
marginalism from the 1870s, economics became even more
narrowly defined as the study of the rational individual
choices of buyers and sellers, interacting in markets, and
labour was reduced to a factor of production, paid in accordance with its contribution to production.

Marginalism provided the theoretical framework for the
mainstream neoclassical or neo-liberal economics of the
second half of the twentieth century. Within this framework,
as discussed in chapter 3, the New Home Economics developed from the 1960s to provide an economic explanation for
the rise in married women's employment and the maintenance of the domestic gender division of labour. It attempted
to integrate women and household relations into the theory
of rational choice, whilst preserving the household as a sphere

of altruism. Its characterisation of household relations and decision-making processes, and its assumptions about efficiency and specialisation, are highly problematic from a feminist perspective.

The major oppositional strand in the history of economic thought is discussed in chapter 4 which examines socialist and Marxist perspectives on household relations and domestic labour, focusing on the key nineteenth century writers and on debates about the socialisation of housework and childcare. The early socialist vision of sex equality as an integral part of economic transformation was not sustained and Marxism became virtually exclusively concerned with the class dimension of people's identity and interests and with the production relations between wage labour and capital. Attitudes to household gender relations in capitalist society were ambivalent but accompanied by an uncritical acceptance of the socialisation of domestic labour as a long term goal, driven as much by the goal of replacing private property with social ownership as by the objective of sex equality. In the 1970s socialist feminists challenged this Marxist orthodoxy and chapter 5 reviews the subsequent domestic labour debate. At the time it generated more criticisms than clarity for many who participated in it and observed it but, in retrospect, can be seen to have articulated some of the linkages and distinctions between the household and the capitalist or market spheres of production. It was an important and influential, if flawed, attempt to challenge the economic invisibility of household activity and relations.

The major feminist critique of the domestic labour debate coalesced around the proposition that it was through exploring patriarchal rather than capitalist relations that a satisfactory explanation for gender divisions of labour could be found. The debate about patriarchy is the subject of chapter 6. Feminists have used patriarchy in several different ways to explore domestic gender relations. Sometimes the focus has been on the marriage relationship, sometimes on the control of jobs and access to earnings in the labour market, sometimes on the relations of human reproduction. The most powerful critique of the feminist theory of patriarchy is made by black women who offer instead an analysis of gender relations based on a matrix of elements including race and class. The conclusion that is drawn is that for patriarchy to be a useful

analytical concept it needs to be historically grounded in particular household social relationships of production, human
reproduction and care, rather than used to describe more
diffuse social relationships between men which contribute to
the economic marginalisation of women.

Teasing out the linkages between gender inequality and domestic labour in Britain in the latter part of the twentieth
century requires an examination of the changing nature of
domestic labour and shifting patterns of employment.
Chapter 7 discusses the evidence on trends in domestic labour
and the interrelationships between patterns of women's
employment and the gender division of domestic labour. The
different opportunities and constraints for women in heterosexual couples associated with full-time employment, part-time
employment and full-time housework are explored.
Opportunities and constraints are shaped by different political
and economic contexts. Analysis of the strategies of households and individuals concerning labour market and domestic
labour choices needs to take account of all these factors. The
interaction of labour market conditions and the social organisation of care in the British context of the 1980s and 1990s
meant that most women were offered a limited choice
between traditional masculine career-centred work patterns,
combined with domestic care responsibilities, and traditional
feminine home-centredness, involving increasingly a combination of part-time employment and a traditional domestic
gender division of labour. By the end of the twentieth century,
full-time domestic care and housework was more likely to be
associated with poverty and dependence on state welfare
benefits than with male affluence and patriarchal household
relations.

Domestic labour and its gendered nature have proved remarkably resistant both to household technological innovation and to the market substitution which neoclassical, Marxist
and post-industrial theories predicted in the 1960s and 1970s.
Chapter 8 discusses alternative explanations for this. In the
British context there were particular configurations of labour
market conditions, consumption patterns and demographic
trends which militated against major reductions in domestic
labour time through the expansion of marketed services or
the application of household appliances. By the 1970s the dif-

fusion of household technology had begun to reduce time spent on the physical tasks involved in routine domestic work, but this was associated with a refocusing of domestic labour towards other activities, particularly shopping and the inter-personal work of caring for children.

Chapter 9 discusses childcare as one of the major keys to understanding domestic labour and its gendered nature in the contemporary British context. Children and childcare have been problematic for feminism and marginalised by the British state which defined social 'care' to exclude children except where parenting had failed. Domestic childcare is a skilled, complex, gendered and largely unacknowledged labour process and one that increasingly emphasised mothers' responsibility for their children's emotional and intellectual development in the latter decades of the twentieth century. The absence of a public childcare policy to support parental employment and equality of opportunity encouraged a po-larised pattern of female labour force participation and child-care provision to support it. Increasing numbers of women with young dependent children were in employment in the 1980s. Career aspirations and opportunities drew the educa-tionally qualified into employment. Pressures to take low paid, usually part-time, jobs to contribute to family income encour-aged an increased market labour supply among other groups of mothers. The relatively better paid mothers were forced in-creasingly to look to the market for childcare services (private nurseries, childminders and nannies), whilst those in low paid jobs relied on the informal care provided by fathers and other relatives.

Chapter 10 examines the childcare policy context in Britain and discusses the preconditions for the development of a public care policy and alternative strategies for doing so. Inadequate policy and the lack of a strategy for social care in Britain have perpetuated poverty, gender and class inequality and poor educational and economic performance. In the post-Second World War settlement, Britain became a welfare state rather than a developmental state, recognising some re-sponsibility for alleviating poverty but retaining its neo-liberal aversion to coordinating and promoting economic develop-ment. British public policy for care in the second half of the twentieth century was within this welfare tradition and em-

bodied a conservative gender contract in which men were
breadwinners and women were carers first and workers
second.

The final chapter provides an overview of the book's critique of neoclassical, Marxist and feminist theories and suggests a review of the scope and assumptions of mainstream
economic theory to encompass households, markets and
states. Alternative conceptualisations of human behaviour,
households and the capitalist economy are called for.
Households and markets are interrelated but distinct sectors
of the economy. Attempts to measure the value of household
production are helpful in demonstrating the scale of domestic
labour but risk submerging these distinctions. Households are
also highly differentiated, embodying diverse care and gender
relations. Strategies for changing these relations require
choices being made and action taken at the three key levels of
economic decision-making, namely households, employing organisations and government. An egalitarian feminist economic strategy would require a redefinition of the British
political and economic culture away from its emphasis on the
short-term cheapening of the costs of reproduction of labour
towards the development and full utilisation of society's
human resources. It would also involve major shifts in household relations and gender identities. Economics is about social
as well as individual choices. Social choices set the boundaries
within which individual choices are made.

2 Founding Fathers

> In truth, the system of the most enlightened of the school of
> those reformers called political economists, is still founded
> on exclusions. Its basis is too narrow for human happiness
> (Thompson 1825: xiv).

The history of economic thought over the period since the
publication in 1776 of Adam Smith's *Wealth of Nations* is a
history from which gender and domestic labour have been
largely excluded. This chapter explores how and why domestic
labour received so little attention either from the classical political economists, such as Adam Smith and David Ricardo,
writing in the latter eighteenth and first half of the nineteenth
centuries, or from the marginalists, like Alfred Marshall and
Stanley Jevons, who wrote in the latter part of the nineteenth
and beginning of the twentieth centuries. It was marginalism
that became the framework upon which mainstream economics in the latter years of the twentieth century was based. The
only writer within these two schools who explored gender divisions in a critical way was John Stuart Mill who, in association
with Harriet Taylor, brought a feminist perspective to his political economy. The chapter examines how domestic labour was
marginalised within the classical and marginalist schools and
also discusses Mill's and Taylor's perspective on gender and
domestic labour.

2.1 SMITH, RICARDO AND THE CLASSICAL SCHOOL
OF POLITICAL ECONOMY

The origins of modern economics are to be found in classical
political economy, which set out to provide an explanation of
the workings of the emerging industrial capitalist system in
Britain in the eighteenth and early nineteenth centuries. The
classical school was founded by Adam Smith, and quickly established itself as the most influential school of economic
thought in Europe until it was displaced from the 1870s

21

onwards by the marginalist school on the one hand (see section 2.3) and Marxism on the other (see chapter 4).

The two major concerns of the classical economists were the expansion of wealth (and how a stationary state of zero growth could be avoided) and the distribution of income between the major social classes (landowners, capitalists and labourers). Social and economic reality was being transformed by the rise of industrial capitalism and economic activity was becoming increasingly conterminous with industry and the market. It is not surprising that Smith identified specialisation and exchange as central to the new economic theory, since these were two crucial modernising forces at work in the emerging industrial capitalist economy.

Exchange was, of course, not a new phenomenon. Aristotle, over two thousand years previously, had distinguished between householding and money-making in the introductory chapter of his *Politics*, and argued, contrary to the views of his tutor, Plato, that men should concern themselves with politics and making money and women with household responsibilities (Steuernagel 1990: 170). However prior to the development of industrial capitalism, exchange had not been the major principle regulating human behaviour and socio-economic relationships (Polanyi 1957: 54). Historically, householding relationships had been central and were to remain an important aspect of economic life but one that was to be excluded from consideration within the emerging discipline of economics.

For the theorists of the capitalist system, household-based economic activity was interpreted either as irrelevant and anachronistic or was taken for granted as an unchanging given. Industrial capitalism produced a redefinition of public and private spheres. The commercial world of the market economy was detached from the domestic morality of the family (Rendall 1987: 45). Subsequently a dualistic theory of human behaviour in the household and the market became dominant in which it was assumed that the household was a sphere of morality and altruism whilst self-interest ruled in the market (Folbre and Hartmann 1988). Classical political economy embodied both a focus of interest and specific assumptions about work processes and human behaviour which inevitably marginalised household economic activity. On the one hand, productive activity was viewed as the outcome of people's propensity to trade and the pursuit of individualistic self-interest. On the other hand, efficiency was assumed to be based on specialisation of labour. Households were the major sector of the economy where production, although subject to a domestic gender division of labour, was not organised on the principles of a social division of labour and of specialisation, nor based on exchange.

The classical school was concerned with the production, distribution and exchange of wealth. For Adam Smith wealth consisted of tangible material goods, not the provision of services. Smith defined labour as 'productive' only if it added value to a material object or resulted in a tangible, storable commodity (Smith 1976: 330). Hence only labour producing goods, not services, was deemed to be productive. The motivation for the accumulation of wealth was assumed to be self-interest. Accumulation of wealth depended on increasing the efficiency of labour in the production process. The major stimulus to increased efficiency was assumed by Smith to come from trade between producers and specialisation within production processes. Individualistic self-interest was assumed to be a natural human characteristic and to act like an 'invisible hand', stimulating efficiency, trade and the expansion of wealth (Smith 1976: 27).

Domestic labour could be of little interest or relevance within this analytical framework. Even in the nineteenth century a large part of domestic labour was concerned with the provision of services for the household rather than the production of material goods. Moreover the motives and methods involved in the accumulation of wealth were contrary to those assumed to characterise activities internal to the household. Within the household altruism and morality, not self-interest, were assumed to motivate behaviour and there was neither trade nor specialisation.

Smith believed that the major stimulus for improved efficiency (reducing labour time per unit of output) came from the social division of labour, whereby different producers specialised in the manufacture of different products and from specialisation of labour between different tasks within each production process. Smith argued that specialisation improved efficiency for three reasons. First, constant repetition of specific tasks, he assumed, led to increased dexterity on the

part of the worker. Second, he believed that time was saved by
not having to switch from one task to another and that a
variety of work made the workman: 'almost always slothful and
lazy, and incapable of any vigorous application even on the
most pressing occasions' (Smith 1976: 19). His objection to allowing workers to vary tasks can be contrasted with the view of
Mill and Taylor (described below in section 2.2). Smith's third
argument was that dividing labour processes into specialist
tasks encouraged mechanisation and consequently further increases in labour productivity.

Mainstream economics inherited from Smith a presumption
about the efficiency gains of specialisation which some critics
have suggested were unwarranted, even in Smith's day. For
example Marglin (1978) argued that in the early days of the
industrial revolution the breaking up of the production
process into fragmented specialist tasks came about because it
enabled the entrepreneur to gain control of the production
process from the skilled workforce, not because of its superior
technical efficiency. Specialisation did not necessarily imply
any change in techniques of production but it required the
presence of the capitalist to orchestrate the process in a way
that non-specialised pre-capitalist production processes did
not. Management of labour processes gave capitalists control
over how much human effort went into production and over
the distribution of the product. It facilitated the expansion of
profit relative to wages and to workers' consumption. In turn
the reinvestment of profit promoted further increases in
labour productivity and enhanced economic growth.

Domestic labour processes were not amenable to a social division of labour, by definition, and therefore specialisation was
precluded. If subjected to Smith's efficiency criteria, domestic
labour would have been found wanting. However Smith actually believed that society needed a sphere of social relations
which were guided by morality not efficiency criteria. It was
the household, and particularly women's role within it, that
provided the necessary counterbalance to the individualism
and materialism of the market. There is a tension between
Smith's economic liberalism, the doctrine of the invisible
hand, expounded in *The Wealth of Nations*, and patriarchal political philosophy as outlined in *The Theory of Moral Sentiments*
and reflected in his references to women in *The Wealth of*

Nations (Pujol 1992: 22). Women were not intended to be guided by self-interest. Education for girls in the middle and upper classes was to be geared to preparation for marriage only. For Smith, unlike John Stuart Mill, the tenets of liberalism were not to be extended to women.

Smith acknowledged, but did not explore, the essential contribution of women in bearing and rearing children to become the next generation of productive workers: 'It is the sober and industrious poor who generally bring up the most numerous families, and who principally supply the demand for useful labour...the dissolute and disorderly...seldom rear up numerous families; their children generally perishing from neglect, mismanagement, and the scantiness or unwholesomeness of their food.' (Smith 1976: 872). This implicit recognition of the role of domestic labour led to some ambiguity in Smith's treatment of the concept of productive labour. As already explained, labour was only deemed productive if it produced goods not services. However he also defined as productive the labour which increased the value of capital and included a 'human' component in his definition of fixed capital, namely, the 'acquired and useful abilities of all the inhabitants or members of the society'. Hence he included investment in education as part of the national capital. However he failed to make any link between 'human' capital and domestic labour.

Apart from John Stuart Mill, the other classical economists made no reference to women's domestic labour. Women appear only as biological reproducers in Malthus' theory of population. Malthus adopted Smith's definition of productive labour as labour which produces material wealth, and also his inclusion of labour involved in education and the acquisition of skill, without attempting to incorporate domestic labour into this. Other economists in the classical tradition opposed Smith's distinction between goods and services and prepared the ground for its subsequent rejection within both the marginalist and Marxist schools. Say and Lauderdale argued that all labour was productive which produced 'utility', whether in the form of goods or services. McCulloch regarded all labour which added to economic growth in the form of exchangeable value as productive. Services should be included in this, because they represented either an investment in human capital or an economic stimulus to those who wished to afford them (O'Brien 1975: 234).

Smith had been optimistic that, with the freeing of market forces, the economic system would tend towards permanent expansion. This led him to conclude that the social inequality inherent in the market system, would be politically acceptable in the context of growth of incomes in general. David Ricardo, who published his third edition of *The Principles of Political Economy and Taxation* in 1821, was more pessimistic and believed that industrial capitalism would tend towards stagnation as profits were squeezed between wages on the one hand and rent paid to landowners on the other (Ricardo 1966). Ricardo believed that there was a 'natural price' of labour, based on the historical costs of reproduction of labourers' families which would vary between countries and over time in accordance with 'habits and customs' (Dobb 1973: 91). This set a limit below which wages could not be reduced without adversely affecting fertility rates. Ricardo recognised that the reproduction of the worker's family was an essential part of the reproduction of capital but he identified this reproduction process with the wage goods consumed by the workers family and ignored the domestic labour component of the reproduction of labour (Picchio 1992: 28).

Given the natural price of labour and the scarcity of land, Ricardo believed that capitalist accumulation would falter as profits were squeezed by higher rents going to landowners as economic growth brought less and less productive land into production. The Ricardian framework also highlights a potential conflict between profits, which feed accumulation, and the costs of reproduction of labour. The conflict between profit and the costs of reproduction of labour comes into play in periods of economic stagnation when growth will only be renewed provided there is a downwards readjustment in the historical costs of reproduction. The capitalist labour market with its inherent insecurity for the working population is one of the major ways in which adjustments in capitalist profitability can be brought about. What is clearer now than was the case in Ricardo's day is that adjustments are also facilitated through the attempts made by women to cushion their families from the adverse conditions of the labour market. Ricardo's approach at least recognised that the reproduction of labour was a social process rather than treating labour merely as a factor of production, as is the case within contemporary mainstream economics (Picchio 1992). However consistent with the classical school as a whole Ricardo's political economy was gender blind. Within that school only John Stuart Mill attempted to integrate contemporary feminist thinking into his writing on political economy.

2.2 JOHN STUART MILL AND HARRIET TAYLOR

John Stuart Mill argued against the exclusion of women from the new liberal economics and rejected the assumptions on which the patriarchal philosophy of other classical economists was based. His theory of gender inequality was developed in close collaboration with Harriet Taylor who was the primary author of an essay published in 1851, 'Enfranchisement of Women' (Rossi 1970: 41) and greatly influenced and contributed to the *Principles of Political Economy*. Mill and Taylor were close associates from 1830 to 1858 and married in 1851. Taylor's contribution has been underplayed by most writers on Mill's work despite the fact that, according to Mill himself, during the years of their collaboration 'all my published writings were as much hers as mine' (Mill 1935: 204–5 cited Pujol 1992: 44). Mill was influenced by Taylor's socialism as well as her feminism. However it is also clear that Mill had developed a feminist perspective under the influence of utilitarianism prior to meeting Taylor (Boralevi 1987: 171).

Mill and Taylor sought to apply the principles of liberalism to women alongside men in a way that the other classical economists had been unable or unwilling to envisage. They believed that patriarchal institutions and laws were the remnants of an obsolete feudal order and impeded economic and social progress. Unlike their contemporaries who, in the tradition of Hobbes and Locke, believed in a hierarchical model for marriage and the family with authority vested in the husband/father, Mill and Taylor argued for marriage to be a relationship between equal partners in which decisions were taken democratically and neither partner was forced into economic dependence on the other (Krouse 1982: 160). Mill identified the interconnections between the subordination of women within marriage and the restrictions on their access to employment in a way that prefigures contemporary feminist debate about gender divisions in the labour market (see chapter 6). Restrictions on women's employment were perpetuated by men's fear of women rejecting marriage as their primary vocation and also by their fear of losing their power over women within marriage. 'I believe that their disabilities elsewhere are only clung to in order to maintain their subordination in domestic life; because the generality of the male sex cannot yet tolerate the idea of living with an equal' (Mill 1970: 181).

Conversely, the legal subordination of women within marriage was the basis of women's subjection in the political and economic spheres. For example, one explanation for women's low pay was: 'custom; grounded either in a prejudice, or in the present constitution of society, which, making almost every woman, socially speaking, an appendage of some man, enables men to take systematically the lion's share of what belongs to both' (Mill 1865: 242).

Hence reform in the laws affecting the status of married women was an essential first step in achieving sex equality. Women should have the same rights as men over property and ownership of earnings and the same opportunities to take decisions about their lives. If women were allowed to be autonomous individuals, they would reject their role as domestic drudges:

> If women had as absolute control as men have, over their own persons and their own patrimony or acquisitions, there would be no plea for limiting their hours of labouring for themselves, in order that they might have time to labour for the husband, in what is called, by the advocates of restriction, his home. Women employed in factories are the only women in the labouring rank of life whose position is not that of slaves and drudges (Mill 1865: 579).

Educational reforms were also needed: 'All women are brought up from the very earliest years in the belief that their ideal of character is the very opposite to that of men: not self-will, and government by self-control, but submission, and yielding to the control of others' (Mill 1970: 141).

Although it was men's fear of women ceasing to provide them with domestic services that perpetuated resistance to feminist reforms, society as a whole would ultimately benefit from sex equality. For Mill an important aspect of social progress was the development of 'equal association' and its 'morality of justice' in place of relationships of command and obedience and the 'morality of submission' (Mill 1970: 173). Hence all legal restrictions on women's employment should be abolished. However there was a need for the state to regulate children's employment and for legal restrictions on the length of the working day for all adult workers (Mill 1865: 578–582).

Mill and Taylor had different views on the compatibility of marriage/motherhood and employment for women and on the related question of whether the marriage partnership could be an equal one if wives were financially dependent on their husbands. The differences between them appear as points of tension in their collaborative work, as, for example, in this passage from the *Principles of Political Economy*:

> ..even when no more is earned by the labour of a man and a woman than would have been earned by the man alone, the advantage to the woman of not depending on a master for subsistence may be more than an equivalent. It cannot, however, be considered desirable as a permanent element in the condition of the labouring class, that the mother of the family (the case of single women is totally different) should be under the necessity of working for subsistence, at least elsewhere than in their place of abode (Mill 1865: 242).

The second sentence in this passage was deleted, apparently under the influence of Taylor in the 1852, 1857 and 1862 editions but reintroduced in the later editions of 1865 and 1871, following her death in 1858 (Pujol 1992: 45). Taylor herself was explicit about the crucial role of women's access to earnings from employment as a basis for equality in marriage: '..a woman who contributes materially to the support of the family, cannot be treated in the same contemptuously tyrannical manner as one who, however she may toil as a domestic drudge, is a dependent on the man for subsistence' (Taylor 1970: 105).

Taylor's insistence on the compatibility of marriage and employment for women was a radical stance, even amongst the feminists of the day, and one that was shared by Barbara Bodichon, another nineteenth century feminist writer on women and economics who wrote: 'It is a mistake to suppose that marriage gives occupation enough to employ all the faculties of women' (Bodichon 1859: 29).

Mill, on the other hand believed that, once women had the freedom to take decisions about their lives and marriage became an equal partnership, most women would opt for either motherhood or employment rather than attempt to combine the two. The wife's responsibility for childbearing and for the care and education of children as well as 'the careful and economical application of the husband's earnings to the general comfort of the family' seemed to Mill to constitute 'not only her fair share, but usually the larger share, of the bodily and mental exertion required by their joint existence' (Mill 1970: 178). For married women to have paid work as well would involve them in an excessive double burden and prevent them carrying out their domestic responsibilities properly. Mill made no reference to the possibility that aspects of women's domestic labour might be socialised to relieve the burden upon them although ideas about communal living and housekeeping arrangements were being put forward at the time by groups like the Fourierists and by feminists in the United States. In common with virtually all nineteenth century feminists, neither Mill nor Taylor considered that men might take joint responsibility for domestic labour (Hayden 1982: 298).

Mill considered teachers and physicians to be productive labour because of their role in the education and health of the labour force. Although he also went further than any other classical economist in recognising the economic contribution made by women through domestic childrearing, he continued to exclude domestic labour from his definition of productive labour: 'To the community at large, the labour and expense of rearing its infant population form a part of the outlay which is a condition of production' but 'for most purposes of political economy, need not be taken into account as expenses of production' (Mill 1865: 25).

Mill's vision of social progress set him apart from other classical economists in a number of respects. He envisaged that machinery would be used to lighten drudgery rather than to stimulate economic growth (O'Brien 1975: 222). He looked forward to a future in which women and the working class would benefit from population control and the higher wages that they assumed would follow. He also argued that excessive population growth resulted from restricting women to an exclusively reproductive role and that a decrease in fertility would necessarily follow the emancipation of women, a view shared by other feminists like Charlotte Perkins Gilman (1898), whose ideas will be discussed in chapter 4.

Mill also questioned Smith's assumption that narrow specialisation was necessarily more efficient than work processes involving a variety of tasks:

> Women are usually (at least in their present social circumstances) of far greater versatility than men;...The occupations of nine out of every ten men are special, those of nine out of every ten women general, embracing a multitude of details each of which requires very little time. Women are in the constant practice of passing quickly from one manual, and still more from one mental operation to another, which therefore rarely costs them either effort or loss of time (Mill 1865: 79).

This insight prefigured late twentieth century debates about human resource management. The motivation and training of workers was perceived to be more important than the organisation of the labour process in determining the efficiency of production and the influence of gender within production processes was acknowledged in a way that was unique among economists of the time.

With the subsequent development of marginalism as the dominant school of economic thought, there was a shift away from the classical interest in the organisation of production, economic growth and the distribution of income towards a focus on exchange and the price mechanism. Again domestic labour was to be excluded from the mainstream.

2.3   THE MARGINALIST SCHOOL

The early 1870s marked the ascendancy of marginalism within European economic thought, with the publication of works by Jevons and Menger in 1871 and by Walras in 1874. Alfred Marshall's *Principles of Economics*, first published in 1890, represented a further development and became the most influential marginalist text in the English speaking world. In essence marginalism reduced economics to the study of the interaction of market demand and supply. The focus of attention shifted from relationships between social classes to relationships between individual sellers and buyers. Hence domestic labour and women's position in the economy were now marginalised because of the focus on markets and on price as a measure of value. Labour became a mere factor of production, its price divorced from social and historical processes and institutions, instead based on supply and demand forces in the labour market. Some of the leading marginalists were however particularly explicit in maintaining the patriarchal political philosophy of the classical school, identifying women's self-interest with the family and advocating a somewhat inconsistent combination of *laissez-faire* economics and patriarchal institutions. For example Marshall advocated restrictions on women's employment to ensure their primary commitment to marriage and motherhood.

For the marginalists, 'utility' rather than the accumulation of wealth was the goal of economic activity. Whilst for the classical economists wealth comprised labour embodied in tangible, durable form, for the marginalists, utility existed wherever people were willing to pay a monetary price. A commodity could be: 'any object, substance, action or service, which can afford pleasure or ward off pain…Utility is that property of a commodity which produces pleasure and prevents pain…Anything which an individual is found to desire and to labour for must be assumed to possess for him utility' (Jevons 1965: 38).

For the marginalists therefore, utility, not labour, was the source of value. But utility could not be directly measured. As Joan Robinson was to point out: 'Utility is a metaphysical concept of impregnable circularity; utility is the quality in commodities that makes individuals want to buy them, and the fact that individuals want to buy commodities shows that they have utility' (Robinson 1964: 48).

Within this framework no rational person would spend their income on a particular combination of commodities if a different combination could provide them with greater benefit or satisfaction. Moreover increasing the quantity of any commodity purchased must increase the utility associated with it, albeit at a diminishing rate. Rational behaviour, in economic terms, meant that more consumption was always preferable to less. For the marginalists, economics was concerned with the problem of how to satisfy wants to the greatest extent with the minimum effort. Labour was defined as: 'any painful exertion of mind or body undergone partly or wholly with a view to future good' (Jevons 1965: 168). A few hours work per day might be agreeable but, beyond that, people would only work if the end-result was sufficient to compensate them for their efforts. 'It would be inconsistent with human nature for a man to work when the pain of work exceeds the desire of possession' (Jevons 1965: 173). Hence work was defined as those activities which no one would perform unless paid to do so.

Although Marshall did consider a broader definition of labour as: 'any exertion of mind or body undergone partly or wholly with a view to some good other than the pleasure derived directly from the work' (Marshall 1959: 54), he subsequently argued that labour should include only those activities which were a source of income. Hence the work of domestic servants was classed as labour and evaluated by the total remuneration received in money and in kind, whilst unpaid domestic work did not count as labour. The inconsistency 'in omitting the heavy domestic work which is done by women and other members of the household, where no servants are kept' was recognised but not addressed further (Marshall 1959: 67). There was a class as well as a gender bias implicit in including production within middle and upper class households in the national income whilst excluding the value of the services of working class women for their families (Pujol 1984: 229).

Although he rejected the notion of including unpaid domestic labour in the national income, Marshall recognised that the prosperity of the economy rested upon women sacrificing their own material self-interest. Parents' commit-

ment to childrearing and the education of the next generation could not be explained by self-interest since it was their
children and their employers, not them, who benefited from
this investment (Pujol 1984: 220). For Marshall, women's domestic labour was the most important component of investment in human capital. 'The most valuable of all capital is that
invested in human beings; and of that capital, the most pre-
cious part is the result of the care and influence of the
mother, so long as she retains her tender and unselfish instincts, and has not been hardened by the strain and stress of
unfeminine work' (Marshall 1959: 469).

The implication was that women were assumed by nature to
put the interests of their families first. Marshall's recognition
of the importance of women's domestic labour led him to conclude that women's employment and wages should be exempt
from the principles of the free market. Women's altruism
needed reinforcing through state regulation of the labour
market. Marshall advocated a family wage for all male workers
and argued that the necessary minimum wage required for
the reproduction of unskilled labour should include sufficient
to support a housewife (Marshall 1959: 58). He supported restrictions on women's and children's employment through the
Factory Acts and argued that one of the major advantages a
son of a skilled worker experienced over that of an unskilled
worker was that: 'his mother is likely to be able to give more of
her time to the care of her family' (Marshall 1959: 469). A rise
of women's wages relative to men's would be detrimental: 'in
so far as it tempts them to neglect their duty of building up a
true home, and of investing their efforts in the personal
capital of their children's character and abilities' (Marshall
1959: 570).

Skilled domestic labour was deemed to reduce the level of
pay required to sustain a working class family whilst unskilled
domestic labour was blamed for the high rates of infant mortality in the poorest homes: 'a skilled housewife with ten
shillings a week to spend on food will often do more for the
health and strength of her family than an unskilled one with
twenty. The great mortality of infants among the poor is
largely due to the want of care and judgement in preparing
their food' (Marshall 1959: 163). Hence women's education
must be geared, first and foremost, towards motherhood and a

knowledge of nutrition, household economy and healthcare (Pujol 1984: 222). Consistent with this view Marshall opposed the granting of degrees to women in a submission made to the Cambridge Senate in 1896 (Pigou 1956: 72, cited Pujol 1984: 222), despite the fact that throughout his career he benefited from the support and assistance given to him by his wife, Mary Paley Marshall who taught economics to women at Oxford and Cambridge.

The need for state intervention to maintain women's role as housewives and mothers continued as a theme in marginalist writing through to the twentieth century. Pigou, in the *Economics of Welfare*, argued that impoverished women, especially mothers, should receive a state benefit to enable them to perform their domestic work adequately rather than having to seek employment. The state should also fund training of girls to become competent housewives and mothers (Pujol 1992: 170).

The marginalists justified giving money the central role in economics because it was: 'the one convenient means of measuring human motive on a large scale' (Marshall 1959: 18). The study of non-monetised economic activity was sacrificed in the interests of making economics into an 'exact' science. There were however to be exceptions to the exclusive focus on monetary transactions, for example imputed rent accruing to owner occupiers from their property. There was also some recognition of the arbitrary nature of the line that was drawn between the 'services that a man obtains from a house owned and inhabited by himself' which were assessed in monetary terms and included in national income, and the services provided by women for their families which were not included (Pigou 1929: 34).

Marshall was also concerned that production, valued at market prices, would not necessarily provide an accurate measure of economic welfare. Because of income inequality it could not be assumed that the pursuit of individual self-interest would lead to the greatest welfare for society as a whole: 'a stronger incentive will be required to induce a person to pay a given price for anything if he is poor than if he is rich. A shilling is the measure of less pleasure, or satisfaction of any kind, to a rich man than a poor man' (Marshall 1959: 16). If the marginal utility of each commodity fell as more was consumed it followed logically that the marginal utility of income must also fall, the higher the income.

Not all marginalists shared Marshall's social concerns. Edgeworth argued in 1881 that greater equality in the distribution of income and work would not bring greater social welfare because the greater economic privilege of some groups over others was linked with their greater capacity for pleasure: 'the privilege of man above brute, of civilised above savage, of birth, of talent, and of the male sex' (Edgeworth 1881: 77). Inequalities of class, race and gender were thus legitimised.

Vilfredo Pareto, in his *Manual of Political Economy*, first published in Italian in 1906, suggested an alternative solution to the moral dilemma confronting marginalist economics by arguing that interpersonal comparisons of utility were not possible. If utility could not be directly measured, then the utilities of different individuals could not be added up, nor could a rich man be said to get less utility from spending a dollar than did a poor man. Hence it could not be proved that total utility would be increased by transferring income from rich to poor. All that could be said was that social welfare could be increased as long as greater utility for one person did not mean less for another. The Pareto optimal solution, in which no one can gain without another person losing, was to become the lynch-pin of mainstream welfare economics in the twentieth century.

2.4   FROM MARGINALISM TO NEOCLASSICAL ECONOMICS

In the 1930s and 1940s marginalist theory began to be referred to as 'neoclassical economics' (Aspromourgos 1986: 268). This term became widely adopted in the 1950s and 60s and since then has been commonly used to refer to the mainstream economic paradigm based on marginalist theory. In the 1930s, economists shifted their attention away from attempting to measure utility directly, instead concluding that quantities of actual commodities purchased, valued at the prices actually paid, revealed the preferences of consumers (Routh 1989: 265). Labour that was not purchased and which did not produce for the market continued to have no obvious place within this conceptual framework. Following Pareto, income distribution was taken as a given and economic welfare was assumed to be maximised with the greatest possible production of commodities, valued and coordinated through the operation of the market mechanism.

Neoclassical economics has hovered between the individual and the household as the key consumer decision-making unit. This shifting conceptual framework reflects a failure to come to terms with gender. Whilst individual maximising behaviour has normally been used to explain male economic behaviour, such as the supply of labour to the market, the notion of the household as a maximising unit has usually been introduced where there is a need to explain female economic behaviour. Economic explanations that appear valid, in the sense of providing accurate predictions, for male behaviour, do not necessarily work for female behaviour. The New Home Economics, which will be discussed in the next chapter, was developed initially to explain what neoclassical economists perceived as the paradox of rising labour force participation rates for married women in the context of rising real income.

The New Home Economics would also explore the possibility that market concepts could be applied to activities internal to the household. This possibility was occasionally raised by earlier neoclassical writers. For example Wicksteed defined economics as the study of: 'acts of administration that directly involve exchange, and acts of administration dealing with exchangeable things. For instance, the housewife's administration of her stores amongst different claimants at home is not a series of acts of exchange, but is a series of acts relating to exchangeable things' (Wicksteed 1910: 160).

Within this tradition the household is perceived as a harmonious, rational and ahistorical unit. Economists only concern themselves with the economic benefits of the unit for its members in terms of pooled resources and shared consumption. They leave other social sciences to explore the way in which people organise themselves into different household units and distribute consumption, work and leisure between them: 'The theory as we shall present it takes the consumer unit as given' (Laidler and Estrin 1989: 7).

Economics in the twentieth century became increasingly restricted to a theory of rational choice in the context of scarcity
(Nelson 1993). Just as it abstracted from the social dynamics
underlying how decisions were made within households it
avoided addressing the implications of unequal access to resources. The lack of a moral perspective separates twentieth
century neoclassical economics from both Smith and
Marshall. Feminist economists have been key critics of the individualism and absence of an ethical dimension within mainstream economics (Ferber and Nelson 1993).

2.5   CONCLUSION

The work done by feminist scholars in the last two decades of
the twentieth century makes it possible to review the history of
economic thought in a new critical light. It is possible to identify the arbitrary nature of some of the boundaries economists
have drawn around their subject and to question the premises
that have underpinned different schools over the last two
hundred years. The feminist political economy of John Stuart
Mill and Harriet Taylor is now rightly acknowledged.

Classical political economy, for all its limits, may provide an
analytical framework which is more conducive to feminist perspectives than the marginalist framework. Within classical political economy labour was not treated purely as a commodity
and wages were not just determined in the market by the
forces of supply and demand. The reproduction of labour was
acknowledged as a social and historical process. The next
chapter explores the New Home Economics which was to be
the major initiative taken from within neoclassical economics
to widen the boundaries of the subject to take account of
economic activity outside the market.

3 The New Home Economics

> Recognition of the family context of leisure and work choices, and of the home-market dichotomy within the world of work, is essential for any analysis of labor force behavior of married women, and perhaps quite important for the analysis of behavior of other family members including male family heads (Mincer 1980: 44)

By the 1960s neoclassical economics had consolidated itself as the dominant theoretical school and was in the process of converting the discipline of economics into one that was defined less by its empirical subject matter and increasingly by a particular explanatory approach to social phenomena and way of viewing the world (Nelson 1993: 25). Economics in the capitalist industrial world was becoming a theory of autonomous, self-supporting, self-interested agents trading with each other to maximise utility or profit (Strassman 1993: 54). It was now 'the science which studies human behaviour as a relationship between ends and scarce means which have alternative uses' (Robbins 1962: 16). This focus on the study of rational choice informed the American economists who developed the New Home Economics (Mincer 1962 and Becker 1965) as a framework for analysis of female labour supply and the household division of labour. This chapter examines the development of the New Home Economics and discusses the feminist critiques that have been made of it, both within the neoclassical tradition and from outside that tradition.

As discussed in chapter 2, the economics discipline had evolved in a way that by the end of the nineteenth century domestic labour was definitely excluded as an area of concern. Consistent with the views of economists, women working at home were for the first time classified as 'unoccupied' in the 1881 British census (Higgs 1987: 70). In the USA, the decision taken for census purposes by 1900 to define married women without paid jobs as economically inactive 'dependants' had propelled the few scholars who were interested in domestic labour outside the narrow confines of economics to establish a new discipline of home economics (Folbre 1991: 483). Margaret Reid's pioneering study, *Economics of Household Production*, which was published in 1934 had little impact on economics at the time. Reid developed a definition of household labour which was subsequently adopted by economists in studies of domestic labour from the 1960s onwards (Goldschmidt-Clermont 1982: 4). 'Household production consists of those unpaid activities which are carried on, by and for the members, which activities might be replaced by market goods or paid services, if circumstances such as income, market conditions and personal inclinations permit the service being delegated to someone outside the household group' (Reid 1934: 11).

Thirty years later, in the 1960s, household production began to emerge as an area of legitimate concern among mainstream economists. The main reason for this new interest was that women, especially married women, were becoming more visible in the labour market. Economists needed to explain why increasing numbers of married women were entering the labour market at a time of rising household income when they had previously assumed that labour supply would decrease as incomes rose. The search for an explanation for this apparent paradox led to the development of the New Home Economics.

3.1 THE RISE IN FEMALE LABOUR FORCE PARTICIPATION RATES

The neoclassical theory of labour supply (in the sense of the hours individuals chose to work in paid employment) was based on the theory of consumer choice. Up to the 1960s it had been assumed that the choice was between work and leisure. According to the established theory, changes in the level of wages would affect hours worked in two opposite ways. On the one hand there would be a tendency for people to increase their working hours with an increase in wages, substituting work for leisure as the opportunity cost of leisure rose (the substitution effect). On the other hand an increase in wages implied increased income which would result in increased consumption and hence a desire for more leisure (the income effect). Hence the effect of an increase in wages might be either a rise or a fall in hours worked, depending on whether the substitution or income effect was dominant. But the conclusion drawn from empirical research, prior to the 1960s, had been that the income effect was generally stronger than the substitution effect, as evidenced by the historical decline in the working week and the inverse relationship between husbands' incomes and wives' labour force participation rates (Mincer 1980: 42). This had given rise to the notion of a 'backward-bending' supply curve of labour (Begg 1994: 182).

The fact that the labour force participation rate of married women in the USA had risen from 5 per cent to 30 per cent during the period from 1890 to 1960, when real income per worker had tripled, appeared to contradict the conclusion that economists had previously drawn about the relative impact of the income and substitution effects (Mincer 1980: 42). It seemed that the theory required further elaboration in order to provide a satisfactory explanation for the secular rise in married women's labour force participation. Moreover it was apparent that, because of the time married women spent on the production of goods and services for the home and family, their labour supply choice was not simply between work and leisure. Taking account of household production led to a more complex range of possible effects on household labour supply of variations in both household income and female wages.

First let us consider the household income effect. According to neoclassical theory a rise in family income would be expected to reduce the total number of hours worked by household members as higher income enabled them to afford increased consumption and leisure. But within the household a reduction in working time overall might not be distributed equally between household and market production or between different members of the household. For example an increase in one person's income might result in a decrease in another person's hours of work. Or a rise in family income might lead to a decrease in hours of work in the market offset by an increase in household work in response to an increased demand for home goods and services from household members. A third possibility was that higher income facilitated the substitution of household technology or domestic servants for household labour and market-produced goods for household goods. The greater the substitutability, the more hours of work in the home would be reduced relative to hours of work in the market as incomes rose. Where substitutability was assumed to be low, for example where young children were present and alternatives to domestic childcare unavailable or unpopular, a rise in family income would be likely to reduce hours worked in the market relative to hours worked at home (Mincer 1980: 45). Hence the income effect assumed a complexity which was absent from the traditional neoclassical theory and its impact on the distribution of total working hours between the household and the market and between household members would need to be explored by empirical research.

In relation to the substitution effect the relevant variable is the female wage rate rather than household income. Whilst an increase in the wage rate had traditionally been interpreted as a rise in the opportunity cost of leisure, in the case of married women it also represented an increase in the cost of home production relative to market goods and services. Hence a rise in the female wage rate would encourage women to reduce the time they spent on household production and leisure and increase their working hours in the market (Mincer 1980: 48). Whether an increase in women's wages would result in a rise or a fall in the supply of female labour to the labour market would therefore depend on how the income effect impinged on market work relative to household work as well as on the relative strength of the substitution effect.

Mincer suggested that for married women the substitution effect was likely to be stronger than in the traditional male model because wage goods might be more substitutable for home production than for leisure (Mincer 1980: 48). This would provide a possible explanation of the evidence that female labour supply had increased historically in response to rising female wages whilst there had been a reduction in male labour supply over time as incomes rose.

Most empirical research undertaken in response to Mincer's hypothesis found a strong positive relationship between women's labour supply and their wage rate and therefore supported his conclusion that for women the substitution effect was stronger than the income effect (Blau and Ferber 1986: 95). Subsequent research in the UK, the USA and other industrial capitalist economies confirmed that there is a difference in male and female labour supply responses to variations in real wages (Begg 1994: 183). In fact this evidence suggests that, contrary to popular assumptions, changes in real wage rates have almost no effect on the quantity of male labour supplied, suggesting that, for men, the substitution effect and the income effect cancel each other out. However for women the substitution effect appears stronger than the income effect since higher real wages encourage women to work longer hours (Brown 1980 and 1988).

The conclusion drawn by Mincer is open to varying interpretations which have not always been addressed within the confines of neoclassical economics. One issue is the uncritical acceptance of the gender divisions revealed in the analysis of labour supply. Implicit in the theory is the notion that men make choices between work and leisure whilst women make choices between working in the home (and leisure) and working in the market. Men are able to gain free time for themselves as their wages rise whilst a rise in women's wages prompts women to swap one type of work for another. The implicit inequality revealed in the analysis is not explored and the household is taken to be a single harmonious decision-making unit. The distribution of consumption is left outside the analysis and placed in the 'black box' of 'tastes'. 'We take it as self-evident that in studying consumption behaviour the family is the unit of analysis. Income is assumed to be pooled, and total family consumption is positively related to it. The distribution of consumption among family members depends on tastes. It is equally important to recognise that the decisions about the production of goods and services at home and about leisure are largely family decisions' (Mincer 1980: 44). Yet if the household is a single decision-making unit why should the choices open to husbands and wives be different? In the next section Becker's subsequent answer to the question of why women specialise in household production will be explored.

A second issue raised by Mincer's analysis of female labour supply is to what extent is it valid to interpret increased female employment as a substitution of market for household production. The assumption that there were market substitutes for home production and that households could make flexible choices about the extent to which needs were met through the market or through household production was essential to the new theory of labour supply. The evidence on the degree to which goods and services purchased by employed women are substitutes for household production is mixed but points to fairly limited substitution taking place. Some evidence of substitution of market services for household production has been found (Silver 1987) but there is also considerable evidence that full-time housewives and employed wives use similar techniques in running their homes and that relatively few purchased goods and services are used to replace the domestic labour time of employed women (Vickery 1979, Strober and Weinberg 1980 and Horrell 1994). The nature of industrial development in the second half of the twentieth century was such that increased employment for married women involved them substituting market work for leisure time as much, if not more than for domestic labour (Vickery Brown 1982).

The process of industrialisation of consumer products can be divided into two phases, the first involving a substitution of factory for home production (such as textiles, clothing, food) and the second involving the production of goods and services that had never been produced in the domestic economy (such as motor transport, electrical goods, medical care). In the second stage of development there is little scope for substitution between household and market production since the goods and services characteristic of this phase can only be acquired through the market or state provision (Vickery Brown 1982: 156). By this stage of development household products are primarily services and the extent to which markets or governments are able or willing to develop substitutes depends on the economic and political context, as will be discussed in chapters 8 and 10.

The assumption that a substitution of market for household production underlay the secular growth of married women's employment, enabled neoclassical theory of labour supply to avoid exploring the alternative less positive scenario of women sacrificing leisure for more work. If this alternative possibility were to be explored seriously it would be hard to avoid addressing the implicit gender inequality dimension of the analysis. Most economists preferred not to consider the possibility that economic growth might have given men greater leisure and women more work. Nevertheless when the New Home Economics moved on to the question of the household allocation of time an explanation of the gender division of work was needed.

3.2   A THEORY OF THE ALLOCATION OF TIME IN THE HOUSEHOLD

Gary Becker first proposed a framework for analysing the allocation of time by married couples in 1965. He argued that time was a scarce resource for all families and that consumption was not a timeless act but rather one in which time inputs needed to be combined with purchased goods and services. Hence consumption commodities were redefined as combinations of market goods and time inputs. The cost of these commodities to a household consisted of the cost of both types of input. Initially Becker did not distinguish between work within the household and leisure time spent consuming purchased goods and services. Visiting the theatre and sleeping were early examples given of consumption activities (Becker 1980: 54). Time spent eating a meal was included alongside the time spent preparing it and clearing it away.

However Becker recognised that, within a household, one person's consumption might depend on another person's time input. He took the household not the individual as the decision-making unit and assumed that households conformed to the model of rational choice, maximising 'joint utility', subject to the constraints of income and time. The time of adult household members could be measured and valued by its opportunity cost, namely the income foregone by the household in using time for household consumption instead of for market production.

The traditional gender division of labour within the household was explained as a rational economic response to market valuations of people's time which in turn were assumed to reflect the productivity of individuals in the market. As long as women's potential earnings were lower than men's, women's time would have a lower relative value and the use of that time in 'consumption-orientated' activities would lower the cost of household consumption relative to what it would be if men, rather than women, took responsibility for domestic labour. 'Members who are relatively more efficient at market activities would use less of their time at consumption activities than would other members'(Becker 1976: 108). Hence the shift away from the traditional gender specialisation of labour within the household (male breadwinner and female house-wife) was explained by increased female earnings in the market. Becker also argued that increased female employment and earnings reduced the gains from marriage and led to a rise in divorce rates.

Becker's influential analytical framework (1965, 1976, 1981, 1985) is based on the following propositions:

(i) Households make choices about the allocation of time which maximise joint utility. It is assumed that they allocate their time efficiently to maximise family welfare, defined as the total consumption of goods and services. Welfare, in the neoclassical tradition, is assumed to be maximised if no individual can consume more without another consuming less. Intra-household distributional issues are not considered (Becker 1976: 209).

However it is unclear how the choices of individual members are coordinated into household choices since, unlike the market, there is no explicit system of exchange to provide a coordinating mechanism for the different choices of self-interested individuals. To resolve this problem Becker (1981) introduced his 'rotten kid' theorem in which, even a selfish 'rotten' child or spouse would be brought into line, provided household decisions were taken by, and household resources controlled by, an altruistic head of household. The household head would act as a 'benevolent dictator' in the household, acting on 'his' interpretation of the best interests of household members. The critique of this device for constructing the household as a unified decision-making unit is discussed in section 3.3.3 Although Becker later referred to the possibility of husbands exploiting wives (i.e. taking all household output above a 'subsistence' amount given to women) his view was that 'exploitation' would not affect the main thrust of the argument that gender specialisation must be based on comparative advantage. For men would have an even stronger interest in maximising household output if they benefited disproportionately from this (Becker 1985: 41). It would still only make sense for husbands to get their wives to specialise in household production if they were more efficient at doing it than men. The working model continues to assume that household resources and decisions are controlled by an altruistic head.

(ii) All work is assumed to be a means to the end of higher consumption. The possibility that work itself, or certain types of work, might be satisfying in their own right or convey intrinsic benefits to the individual worker is not considered.

(iii) Markets coordinate the actions of individuals and households and provide shadow prices for people's time and for goods and services not exchanged in a market, enabling households to make informed and rational choices about how they allocate the time of their members.

(iv) Certain aspects of childcare and other consumption 'commodities' requiring 'altruism' for their production are assumed to be more efficiently produced in households than in the market because individual behaviour is assumed to be altruistic in the household and self-interested in the market (Becker 1981). Feminists have on the other hand argued that this dualistic model of human behaviour is implausible (see section 3.3.3).

(v) Initially Becker (1965 and 1976) argued that there were intrinsic differences in productivity between men and women which explained why household specialisation was invariably gender based. Although the explanation of gender divisions in the household and market is still based on the view that men have a comparative advantage in market production and women in the household, it no longer assumes this advantage is grounded in natural attributes. The pattern of comparative advantage which encourages men to specialise primarily in market production and women in household activities may be socially constructed rather than biologically determined. Discrimination is even acknowledged as a possible contributory factor. For example, if young men and women start out being equally productive in both spheres of production, dis-

crimination in the labour market (which reduces the earnings
of women below their market productivity) will lead to women
taking a larger share of household work and men taking a
larger share of market work. The next two assumptions
provide a basis for the conclusion that specialisation will subse
quently result in the establishment of a real difference in com
parative advantage in the two spheres between men and
women (Becker 1985: 42).

(vi) There are increasing returns to specialised human
capital investment in both household and market production
In other words, acquisition of specialist skills and expertise in
the two spheres results in increased productivity over time
Therefore even if there are no intrinsic differences in produc
tivity between men and women initially, if individuals make
different amounts of specific human capital investment in the
household and market production their respective productiv
ity in the two sectors will diverge over time. The plausibility of
this assumption is discussed in section 3.3.2

(vii) A further implicit assumption is that skills and exper
tise are not transferable as between the household and the
market. It is assumed that there is no interplay or transferabil
ity between the two different types of human capital invest
ment and that the key skills in each area of production are
specialist not generic.

(viii) In more recent formulations women are assumed to
allocate more energy per unit of time, as well as more time, to
household tasks than men and, conversely less energy to
market jobs. Hence women are assumed to opt for market jobs
which are less 'energy-intensive' and consequently lower paid
than those done by men (Becker 1985: 52–53). This proposi
tion is used to explain why gender differentials in pay have no
narrowed to the extent that neoclassical theory would have
previously predicted as a result of women's increased labour
force participation and investment in human capital in the
market. Empirical studies, such as Bielby and Bielby (1988)
do not support Becker's proposition that women's jobs are less
energy intensive than men's.

(ix) Even though it is now accepted that discrimination
may exist in the labour market, the New Home Economics
approach still asserts that differences in men's and women's
pay are primarily based on real productivity differences, al

though these are mainly produced by differences in human capital rather than inherent differences. Gender differences in employment patterns are explained as the result of the cumulative effects of men and women individually and in household units responding rationally to the way the market signals their comparative advantage in the different spheres of production.

In the later formulations of the New Home Economics, Becker concludes that, however insignificant the original differences in productivity between household partners may be in the two spheres of production, once specialisation is in place, an irreversible widening of relative comparative advantages takes place. It follows that specialisation of different members of the household as between market and household production will not necessarily remain in the future along traditional gender lines since comparative advantage is no longer assumed to be based on biological differences between men and women. However the view that specialisation between household and market production is the most efficient arrangement for households members remains a central tenet of the theory.

3.3   FEMINIST AND OTHER CRITICAL PERSPECTIVES ON THE NEW HOME ECONOMICS

From the early days of the New Home Economics feminists questioned the validity of the theory's assumptions and conclusions (Bell 1974, Ferber and Birnbaum 1977 and Sawhill 1980) and these criticism's developed over time into a larger critique of the neoclassical economic paradigm (Folbre 1988 and 1994 and Ferber and Nelson 1993). The major criticisms that will be reviewed here concern the circularity of the argument, the overestimation of the benefits of specialisation, the inadequacy of the benevolent dictator model of household decision-making, the failure of human capital theory to provide an adequate explanation of gender differences in earnings and, at a more general level, the questioning of the key assumptions of neoclassical economics, particularly its focus on rational choice as an explanatory approach to all economic questions.

3.3.1   The circularity of the argument

As stated above the New Home Economics rests on two inter-
connected propositions. First women invest less time and
energy in market production than men and hence receive a
lower return than men in terms of wages. Second households
take decisions about the allocation of members' time based on
opportunity cost estimates of time spent on household production. The problem is that, however accurately these statements may reflect the status quo, they do not provide a
satisfactory explanation since the argument they construct is
circular (Ferber and Birnbaum 1977: 20). Women earn less in
the market because they specialise in household production
and they specialise in household production because they
earn less in the market. The theory merely articulates and ra-
tionalises the vicious circle within which women find themselves. Households may be behaving rationally but within the
context of structural constraints which preclude genuine
choice.

3.3.2   The overestimation of the benefits of specialisation

Given the structural constraints discussed above, it appears rational for women to specialise in household production, for
example to withdraw from the labour market during the years
of early childrearing. However critics have argued that even
this is based on a very short term calculation. When account is
taken of the way in which temporary withdrawal from the
labour market tends to reduce women's earnings for the re-
mainder of their working lives, relative to those of women who
remain in paid employment through the early years of childrearing, the decision for women to specialise in household
production no longer appears so rational. Given that the economic value of household production to the family (for
example measured in terms of the market cost of services produced by women at home), reaches a peak when young children are present and subsequently declines as they start
school and grow up (Ferber and Birnbaum 1977: 23), it would
normally make economic sense, over the lifetime of the family,
for the wife to maintain or acquire market skills during the
years of early childrearing and for husbands to sacrifice some

leisure to enable wives to have paid employment. Household specialisation cannot therefore be satisfactorily explained in terms of economic rationality, even from the point of view of the household as a unit. Still less is it rational for women as individuals when account is taken of probabilities of marital breakdown and the risk that women may have to rely on their own earnings at some stage in their lifetime and lose entitlement to a share in their husband's pension.

The assumption that there are increasing returns to specific human capital has also been questioned. It is likely that the regular repetition of activities is more important in developing specialist skills than the total amount of time spent on those activities. There is evidence that decreasing returns to specialisation in household production are more likely than increasing returns with the onset of a Parkinson's Law effect (Owen 1987: 162). Moreover the increased demand for a flexible labour force which is able to switch between different productive activities suggests that narrow specialisation may be a less and less effective form of human capital investment.

The emphasis placed on specialisation as the most efficient strategy for organising labour processes reflects a lack of recognition of the transferability of major skill areas. Specifically the failure to explore the relationship between household and market skills and expertise reflects the general social devaluation of skills acquired through domestic labour or voluntary work. It is now well established that skills acquired in unpaid work are transferable to paid work situations. Some attempts have been made to analyse the competencies acquired in unpaid work and accredit these by direct comparison with vocational training competencies (Leigh and Butler 1993). It is likely that skills acquired in market production are also transferable to the household. Employed women are under particular pressure to find the most efficient domestic labour methods because of the limited time they have available. This could be described as a reverse Parkinson's Law effect (Owen 1987: 163).

If the transferability of skill between the household and the market is recognised it follows that, in place of the traditional specialisation of men and women, a work profile that included household and market production experience for men and women would maximise skill development for both. This recognition challenges the dualistic way in which the New Home Economics has characterised the separate spheres of altruistic household and self-interested market behaviour.

3.3.3   The problem of household decision-making

Becker's particular solution to the question of how the household unit formulates its preferences, as discussed above, was to posit an altruistic head of household who had control over resources and acted in the interests of the household as a whole. This conceptual device has been characterised as the 'benevolent patriarch' and criticised on the grounds that it ignores the dynamics of conflicting interests, negotiation and power relations within households (Folbre and Hartmann 1988: 189, England 1993: 47 and Strassman 1993: 58). Wives and husbands normally have different preferences and are known to behave differently when they make consumer choices as couples rather than as individuals (Menasco and Curry 1989). Where there are differences, joint decisions are reached by a process of negotiation ending somewhere on the scale between compromise (partners share equal influence) or capitulation (one partner is dominant and their own individual preference shapes the decision). The resolution of difference or conflict will depend on the relative bargaining power of the partners. Market income strengthens bargaining power more than the imputed value of household services and this provides women with an incentive to increase their market earnings (Folbre and Hartmann 1988: 199).

Some critics of Becker's characterisation of the household have looked to bargaining models to provide an alternative theoretical framework. The bargaining power of partners is assumed to depend on the level of well-being they could each attain if their relationship ended: their 'fall-back' position (Seiz 1991: 24). Fall-back positions depend on individual skills, income, wealth, pension entitlement and access to support from the state or relatives. Sen has provided a helpful formulation of the household as an arena of 'cooperative conflict'. On the one hand, partners have an interest in cooperating to increase their standard of living above what it would be in the absence of the other partner. On the other hand, conflict of interest arises over how the consumption gains from cooperation are distributed and on the way work is allocated. Conflict is resolved by a process of bargaining which will be resolved in favour of the partner with the higher fall-back position (Sen 1984: 374). An example of a formalised feminist bargaining model is provided by Ott (1992) who found that women had greater bargaining power if they had higher education qualifications and an income of their own and less bargaining power the higher their husband's income and if children were present.

3.3.4 Human capital theory and the labour market

The New Home Economics relies on human capital theory as the major explanation of gender differences in earnings. However empirical studies have demonstrated that returns to human capital investment are consistently lower for women than men and that gender alone, as well as motherhood, accounts for a major part of the difference in earnings between men and women (Joshi 1991 and England 1992). According to human capital theory a free labour market allocates society's human resources efficiently from both a social and individual perspective. This assumes that the labour market is a self-clearing mechanism and a neutral meeting point where the demand for and supply of labour are equated. If, on the other hand, as radical political economists would argue, the normal state of affairs is a surplus of actual or potential labour supply over labour demand (Sawyer 1989), other factors besides efficiency criteria need to be taken into account in analysing differences in pay between jobs. Labour markets are segmented and access to jobs depends only in part on human investment but also on the social and institutional processes of labour recruitment and retention. Labour markets are not simply divided into a primary sector, operating closed internal labour markets and a secondary sector operating in a competitive external labour market, as suggested by dual labour market theory. Even for lower paid jobs, where firms have access to a reliable supply of workers and skills, they may operate an extended internal labour market based on informal networks rather than open competition for jobs (Manwaring 1984). In these circumstances a hierarchy of disadvantage based on race, gender, class and social networks is maintained and wage differences reflect the differences in bargaining power and access to jobs at different levels of the hierarchy as much as in productivity between workers (Craig et al. 1982).

3.4   CONCLUSION

The New Home Economics represents an important and influential stage in the development of neoclassical economic theory with its recognition of the need to theorise the household and production within it. It acknowledged that gender divisions had an economic dimension rather than a primarily biological or cultural basis. The recognition that time was a resource with an economic cost that was capable of being quantified outside the context of market based activity was a major step forward. Almost unwittingly it provided an analytical framework which acknowledged the different choices open to men and women in labour supply decision-making processes and initiated a discourse within which feminist economists could legitimately engage with mainstream economic theory. Its emphasis on the rational and economic nature of women's actions in the labour market and the household made it possible for gender to be treated as an economic as well as a social and cultural issue.

Although the New Home Economics set out to explain gender divisions in the labour market and the household by means of rational choice, it inspired its critics to articulate the structural constraints imposed on different groups of women by the workings of the labour market. Nancy Folbre (1994: 51) coined the term 'structures of constraint' to refer to the ways in which race, class, age, sexual orientation and gender set 'boundaries of choice'. The New Home Economics itself failed to explore the inequalities and conflicts of interest within households. It avoided addressing the possibility that economic growth might have brought more work not more leisure for many women. It overestimated the efficiency of specialisation within the household and ignored the differences in bargaining power associated with market and household production.

In recent years many feminist economists have gone beyond specific criticisms of the New Home Economics to question the neoclassical economic framework in a more fundamental way. Nelson calls for a refocusing of economics away from its preoccupation with rational choice and towards 'the provisioning of human life' as an area of study (Nelson 1993: 32). Neoclassical economics has been constructed around the concept of self-interested, self-supporting economic agents who are faced with an array of options from which to choose within the limits of the resources available to them. This concept may have continuing appeal to the white, male, middle class men who dominate the economics profession but appears much less relevant as an explanation of the economic reality experienced by others who find it androcentric and steeped in Western cultural traditions (Strassman 1993: 61). For feminists equity is a central economic issue and economists should at least demonstrate awareness of the different distributional implications of alternative patterns of resource allocation. They reject the neoclassical assumption that interpersonal comparisons of utility cannot be made (England 1993: 42). Empathy and cooperation is possible in the market just as self-interested behaviour and conflict is a feature of the household.

4 Socialism and Marxism

> While the men are invigorated by the fight in the world outside,....we sit at home and darn stockings (Jenny Marx writing to Wilhelm Liebknecht in 1872, cited Kapp 1979: 41).

The earliest critics of classical political economy were socialists, like Fourier, Thompson and Owen, who advocated in the early years of the nineteenth century an economy based on cooperation rather than competition and the transfer of responsibility for housework and childcare from private households to the collective economy. The early socialists were committed to a transformation of sexual relations and the ending of patriarchal marriage and family relationships. Although they believed that the oppression of working class people and women would only be overcome by a reorganisation of the economy, they placed great emphasis on culture, ideas and morality as agents for social change. The critique of political economy based on a structural analysis of the capitalist economic system that was to be developed by Marx and Engels in the middle and latter years of the nineteenth century was to have a much greater impact on economic thought than the early socialists. This chapter starts with a brief discussion of the treatment of domestic labour by the early socialists and then examines in more detail the place of domestic labour in the development of Marxist theory. The Bolshevik revolution is then discussed as a case study of the application of Marxist theory in the early twentieth century. The concluding section offers a critical consideration of the contribution of socialism and Marxism to an understanding of domestic labour.

4.1   THE EARLY SOCIALISTS

Socialism and feminism initially developed together as part of a radical political and philosophical movement in Europe in the early nineteenth century. Twentieth century feminists have played an important role in highlighting this tradition within the history of socialist thought (Rowbotham 1974, Hayden 1982, Taylor 1983, Folbre 1993).

In France, Charles Fourier, beginning in 1808 with the publication of the *Theory of Four Movements*, argued that social progress could be measured by the degree of women's emancipation and that a society which condemned women to domestic labour and economic dependence was inferior to the new society he envisaged in which men and women would share equally in the full range of human activities. His follower, Hugh Doherty, called the new society 'socialism' (Rowbotham 1974: 42). It was Fourier who described in greatest detail the way in which cooking, housework and childcare could be collectivised in communities called Phalanxes or Associations. He believed that work should become a freely chosen and varied activity in the context of the new cooperative morality and that no one should have to spend more than a couple of hours on any task. Since he believed that housework, cooking and childcare would be more efficiently organised, he envisaged that it would be done with only a quarter of the labour required by isolated households and that sufficient women and men would freely choose to do this work in the new communities (Coole 1988: 175). Fourier's ideas about socialising housework and childcare were to be highly influential within socialist thought for over a century. His belief in the close link between freedom of sexuality and women's equality gained less support and was not to be taken up again by socialists until Alexandra Kollontai called for sexual freedom in the early years of the Bolshevik revolution.

William Thompson, inspired by Anna Wheeler, both Irish protestants, wrote the *Appeal of One-Half of the Human Race, Women, against the Pretensions of the Other Half, Men, to Retain them in Political, and hence in Civil and Domestic, Slavery* in 1825. In this he argued that women would always be at a disadvantage in an economy based on competition and in which wages were the only source of income. Women's economic dependence on men through marriage should be ended and society should take responsibility for the care of children. Domestic labour involved drudgery, inefficiency and isolation and family-based childcare was more likely to imbue children with competitive than with cooperative values. For all these reasons, and to free women from dependence on marriage, housework and childcare should be collectivised and paid for by the community (Coole 1988: 156).

Robert Owen believed that marriage and the family were wasteful of labour and breeded ignorance and selfishness. He expressed these ideas in his lectures *On the Marriages of the Priesthood of the Old Immoral World* in 1835. Owen advocated co-operative communities of 2000 people in which cooking, eating and childcare were organised collectively as well as educational, recreational and productive activities. However in the Owenite communities that were established, housework was arduous and remained a predominantly female task (Taylor 1983: 248). Given the difficult working conditions in communal laundries and kitchens, it is understandable in retrospect that shared housework and childcare proved unpopular with the women who found themselves responsible for it. Contemporary critics of women's attitudes in Owen's journal *The New Moral World* were less appreciative of the pressures on women. One man argued in 1836: 'Women....are attached to their own notions about comfort and privacy – and cannot easily admit that residence in community, without individual property, individual staircases and individual washtubs...can be consistent with domestic happiness' (cited Taylor 1983: 250).

The ideas of Fourier and Owen had less practical impact in Europe than in the USA where Owen inspired about fifteen model communities from the 1820s and about thirty Fourierist Associations were established from the 1840s onwards (Hayden 1982: 35). The experiments were short-lived since islands of cooperation inspired solely by a new morality lacked any strategy to withstand adverse external political and economic conditions or to combat deeply ingrained concepts of gender identity. The early socialists were however an important influence on the developing feminist movement, especially in the USA, where there were numerous further attempts, as the nineteenth century proceeded, to design homes in which domestic labour could be collectivised (Hayden 1982). Liberal feminists as well as socialist feminists were influenced by the collectivist ideas about housework and childcare.

For example Charlotte Perkins Gilman, the leading American feminist who published *Women and Economics* in 1898, argued that women could only be equal with men if they had the economic independence of work outside the family and if cooking, childcare and housework were professionalised. She argued for families to have the opportunity to live in kitchenless houses or apartments connected to central kitchens, dining rooms and childcare centres. Gilman was not a socialist or a believer in cooperation but rather believed that new forms of housing, childcare and domestic service should be developed by enlightened feminist entrepreneurs (Hayden 1982: 195).

The fragile alliance between middle class feminists and socialists broke down in the second decade of the twentieth century. Both the middle class women and the socialist men wanted to delegate their domestic work to paid employees. Because neither group considered the possibility of men taking their share of domestic labour, anti-feminists were able to drive a wedge between Gilman's followers and the working class women they planned to employ as domestic workers (Hayden 1982: 201). There was a race as well as a class dimension to the political divisions surrounding domestic labour. In 1900 one third of all domestic servants were black Americans. Subsequently the predominance of black women in domestic service work became even more pronounced as white women gained access to alternative employment denied to black women (Hayden 1982: 170).

In Europe in the middle years of the nineteenth century Marx and Engels were influenced by some of the early socialists' ideas, including their belief in the link between sexual equality and the collectivisation of housework and domestic labour. However they recognised that capitalism was too powerful a system to be challenged by a moral crusade. A more sophisticated analysis of the structure and dynamics of the economic system was needed. In the process the early socialists' commitment to an integrated reform of production and reproduction was abandoned in favour of an almost exclusive focus on the relationship between wage labour and capital. The primacy of sexual relations and moral and cultural concerns were to recede within the socialist tradition as the class relations between wage labour and capital assumed centre stage.

4.2 MARXISM

The development of Marxist theory in relation to domestic
labour can be traced through several key texts: Marx's *Capital*,
Volumes I–III (first published in German between 1867 and
1894) and *Theories of Surplus Value* (first published by Kautsky
in 1905–10), Engels' *The Condition of the Working Class in
England* (first published in German in 1845) and *The Origin of
the Family, Private Property and the State* (first published in 1884).
Here Marx's analysis of the capitalist mode of production as a
historical stage of economic development is first discussed.
This is followed by an examination of Engels' theory of the
family in capitalist society and a discussion of Marxist perspectives on women's employment and domestic labour.

4.2.1 The capitalist mode of production in Marx's theory

Unlike both the classical and marginalist economists, Marx
argued that production and exchange relationships were historical rather than universal relationships. Capitalism was perceived as a specific mode of production defined by a
particular form of exploitation based on the sale of labour
power and on capitalist control of production processes.
Marx's analysis focused on the internal workings of the capitalist mode of production. Domestic labour was to be marginalised within this context. It was neither wage labour nor an
integral part of the circular flow of exchange value and
capital.

For Marx the essential difference between various types of
society, such as feudalism, slavery and capitalism, was the particular form of exploitation, the way in which surplus labour
was extracted from the producers (Marx 1969: 217). Different
forms of exploitation were used by Marx to define the different modes of production dominant at different stages of
history. The labour time of producers could be divided into
necessary labour time (the average amount of time needed to
produce their means of subsistence) and surplus labour time
(the extra time spent working beyond what was necessary for
their own consumption needs to be met). Surplus value for
Marx was the form taken by surplus labour in the capitalist
mode of production. The value of labour power, was the

average labour time embodied in commodities required for the reproduction of the labouring population (Marx 1969: 193). Variable capital was that part of capital required to meet the consumption needs of workers through payment of wages. Constant capital referred to the capital advanced to pay for non-human inputs into the production process, like materials, fuel and instruments of production (Marx 1969: 209). Surplus value represented the difference between the total working time of the labouring population and the value of labour power.

Marx argued that exploitation in the industrial capitalist phase of history was rooted firmly in the capitalist labour process and in the ability of the capitalist class to utilise labour power however it chose during the hours it was at its disposal. This was in contrast with merchant capitalism where peasants and other nominally independent commodity producers were typically exploited through unequal exchange in the market (Rowthorn 1974). Hence the degree of exploitation would be affected by class struggle around living standards and within the capitalist labour process itself and would depend on the following three factors:

● the accepted standard of living of workers;
● the productivity of labour in those sectors producing goods and services that entered directly or indirectly into workers' consumption;
● the duration and intensity of labour.

Contrary to the popular meaning attached to exploitation, those who worked the longest hours for the lowest pay were not necessarily, on Marx's definition, the most exploited. If their productivity was low because of relatively backward technology, the rate of surplus value extraction might be lower than that produced by relatively highly paid workers in advanced technology sectors.

Marx considered that, apart from the pre-industrial phase of primitive accumulation when profits from slavery and indentured labour were important, the major source of surplus value in capitalism was higher labour productivity. Subsequently certain Marxists, notably Rosa Luxemburg in *The Accumulation of Capital* (1913), were critical of Marx's neglect of the role of imperialism and of profits from outside the industrial capitalist system in supporting the capital accumulation process.

For Marx, a unique feature of capitalism was that market competition made different types of labour with different degrees of skill comparable with each other and hence reduced concrete labour to units of general abstract labour time which could, in theory, be quantified as value. The operation of market forces within the capitalist mode of production forced firms to minimise their costs of production and converted actual labour time into abstract labour and measurable value (Elson 1979). Hence within the capitalist mode of production, unlike previous economic forms of society, qualitatively different types of labour became comparable and quantifiable and Marx believed it was technically possible to measure the rate of exploitation. He also believed that market prices could be derived from values. His attempt to do so was, however, flawed because he failed to recognise that the profit rate and relative prices of goods were determined simultaneously (Kurz 1994: 464). For a discussion of the relationship between the value of labour power and the level of wages see Green (1991).

Marx's definition of productive labour was linked to his concept of modes of production. He distinguished two types of productive labour, namely labour that was productive 'in the general sense' and labour that was productive within the context of the capitalist mode of production. Productive labour in the general sense was any labour that produced goods and services that were socially useful (use-values). Productive labour from the point of view of capital was labour that produced commodities with exchange-value, whether goods or services, that could be sold at a profit. An example of labour that was unproductive from a capitalist viewpoint was paid domestic service since this was labour paid for out of the personal income of the capitalist class for the purpose of consumption rather than for profit: 'the cooks and waiters in a public hotel are productive labourers, in so far as their labour is transformed into capital for the proprietor of the hotel. These same labourers are unproductive labourers as menial servants' (Marx 1969: 159).

Marx was therefore critical of Adam Smith's identification of productive labour with labour producing tangible goods.

Whether labour was productive or not depended solely on whether it was exchanged with capital to produce surplus value, not on the nature of the labour itself or of the product (Gough 1972 and Harrison 1973a).

Those who trained or maintained labour power, like the doctor and the school-teacher were also defined by Marx as unproductive from a capitalist viewpoint on the grounds that they did not themselves 'directly create the fund out of which they are paid, although their labours enter into the production costs of the fund which creates all values whatsoever– namely the production costs of labour power' (Marx 1969: 167-168).

Although distinguishing between labour that was productive for capital and labour that was productive for society, Marx focused almost exclusively on capitalist production relations rather than production in the general sense of socially useful work. Unpaid domestic labour, as well as paid domestic service, were both marginal in Marx's economic theory. Paid domestic servants were not productive from a capitalist perspective because they were not paid out of capital and produced neither commodities nor surplus value for their employer. Unpaid domestic labour was also outside the circuit of capital and unproductive for capital. But there was an additional problem in the case of unpaid domestic labour which made Marx's framework inappropriate. Unpaid domestic labour could not be compared in the way that other types of concrete labour could be through competitive forces operating in labour and product markets. There are a few occasions only when he acknowledges the role of domestic labour but then proceeds to ignore it. For example he states in a footnote that when: 'certain family functions, such as nursing and suckling children, cannot be entirely suppressed, the mothers confiscated by capital, must try substitutes of some sort. Domestic work, such as sewing and mending must be replaced by the purchase of ready-made articles. Hence the diminished expenditure of labour in the house is accompanied by an increased expenditure of money. The cost of keeping the family increases, and balances the greater income' (Marx 1961: 395).

Elsewhere, in *Theories of Surplus Value*, he comments that the unpaid domestic labour of the working class appeared as 'unproductive labour'. The working class 'can only cook meat for itself when it has produced a wage with which to pay for the meat; and it can only keep its furniture and dwellings clean, it can only polish its boots, when it has produced the value of furniture, house rent and boots. To this class of productive labourers itself, therefore, the labour which they perform for themselves appears as "unproductive labour". This unproductive labour never enables them to repeat the same unproductive labour a second time unless they have previously laboured productively' (Marx 1969: 166). Marx did not acknowledge that wage labour depended on domestic labour just as domestic labour depended on wage labour.

Rosa Luxemburg was to comment in 1912 on the way the Marxist definition of domestic labour as unproductive highlighted 'the crudeness and craziness' of the capitalist economy. The housework done by working class women:

> is not productive within the meaning of the present economic system of capitalism, even though it entails an immense expenditure of energy and self-sacrifice in a thousand little tasks….This sounds crude and crazy but it is an accurate expression of the crudeness and craziness of today's capitalist order (Luxemburg 1976: 215).

Marx occasionally offered insights that indicated a potential for understanding the economic nature of domestic labour. He looked beyond monetary transactions to the social relationships through which production was organised. These relationships were not those of equal individuals exchanging resources in the market but of classes with unequal power, some able to appropriate the labour of others within the production process itself. These relationships and the different contributions to production made by different groups could not be understood by looking only at monetary payments. For example:

> In slave labour, even that part of the working day in which the slave is only replacing the value of his own means of existence…appears as labour for his master. All the slave's labour appears as unpaid labour. In wage labour, on the contrary, even surplus labour, or unpaid labour appears as paid (Marx 1961: 539).

Apart from minor references, Marx ignored the role of household productive activity in the reproduction cycle of labour power. Marx chose not to investigate the process within the working class household in which commodities purchased with family wages were converted by domestic labour into renewed labour power which could be sold for wages on the market. Here he appeared to slip into an ahistorical, naturalistic conceptualisation of domestic relations: 'The maintenance and reproduction of the working class is, and must ever be, a necessary condition to the reproduction of capital. But the capitalist may safely leave its fulfilment to the labourer's instincts of self-preservation and of propagation' (Marx 1961: 572).

Marx abstracted from the problem of domestic labour by assuming, in the same way as Ricardo, that the capitalist sector provided everything required to reproduce labour power and only consumption of commodities, not production, took place in the household. The value of labour power was determined by the value of the commodities entering into the historically determined subsistence level of the workers (Marx 1961: 170). Domestic labour was not amenable to inclusion in Marx's theory. The key features that Marx identified as specific to the capitalist economic system did not apply to domestic labour. Because domestic labour was not subject to market forces, it could not be conceptualised as abstract labour. It was outside of the circuit of capital in the sense of not being labour power purchased by capital and hence not 'productive' for capital. It was not labour subject to direct capitalist control and hence to the intensification and pressure for enhanced productivity that was a central feature of the capitalist production process.

4.2.2 The patriarchal family and the development of capitalism

In their earliest writings Marx and Engels had recognised that the family and relationships surrounding human reproduction were social not merely biological relationships and had evolved historically. In 1845 they wrote in *The German Ideology*: 'The production of life, both of one's own in labour and of fresh life in procreation, now appears as a twofold relation: on the one hand as a natural, on the other as a social relation'

(Marx and Engels 1976: 43). However Marx subsequently focused his attention on the production of commodities and surplus value whilst Engels was to devote more attention to the 'production of life', culminating in *The Origin of the Family, Private Property and the State,* first published in German in 1884.

> According to the materialistic conception, the determining factor in history is, in the final instance, the production and reproduction of immediate life. This, again, is of a twofold character: on the one side, the production of the means of existence, of food, clothing and shelter and the tools necessary for that production; on the other side, the production of human beings themselves, the propagation of the species. The social organisation under which the people of a particular historical epoch and a particular country live is determined by both kinds of production; by the stage of development of labour on the one hand and of the family on the other. (Engels 1972: 71)

In their early writing, Marx and Engels had emphasised the property relationship aspect of the family arguing that its main purpose was to transmit private wealth between generations. In 1845 they even argued that the family no longer existed in the working class which, by definition, owned no property (Marx and Engels 1976: 180). In this context men's control of women, patriarchy, meant husbands controlling their wives' sexuality and fertility in order to ensure undisputed heirs.

Engels' later writing continued to highlight the transmission of property as a key factor in the development of the family: 'Monogamy arose from the concentration of considerable wealth in the hands of a single individual – a man – and from the need to bequeath his wealth to the children of that man and of no other. For this purpose, the monogamy of the woman was required, not that of the man' (Engels 1972: 138).

However he also recognised men's control of women's labour power in the monogamous family, here identifying patriarchy with 'domestic slavery'. 'In the old communistic household, which comprised many couples and their children, the task entrusted to women of managing the household was as much a public, a socially necessary industry, as the procuring of food by the men. With the patriarchal family, a change came. Household management lost its public character. It no

longer concerned society. It became a *private service*, the wife
became the head servant, excluded from all participation in
social production' (Engels 1972: 137).

By 1884 the growth of women's employment in capitalist industry was perceived to be undermining patriarchy within the
working class family: 'And now that large-scale industry has
taken the wife out of the home onto the labour market and
into the factory, and made her often the breadwinner of the
family, no basis for any kind of male supremacy is left in the
proletarian household, except, perhaps, for something of the
brutality toward women that has spread since the introduction
of monogamy' (Engels 1972: 135).

However Engels recognised that capitalism, by drawing
women into factory employment, had a contradictory effect
on the working class family. On the one hand, it provided the
basis for greater equality between the sexes by drawing women
out of the home into social production. On the other it prevented women carrying out domestic labour without providing any substitute for their traditional role within the family:
'Not until the coming of modern large-scale industry was the
road to social production opened to her again – and then only
to the proletarian wife. But it was opened in such a manner
that, if she carries out her duties in the private service of her
family, she remains excluded from public production and
unable to earn; and if she wants to take part in public production and earn independently, she cannot carry out family
duties' (Engels 1972: 137).

In his earlier writing, *The Condition of the Working Class in
England*, which was published in 1845, Engels had been even
more critical of the impact of capitalism on the family and on
women's domestic labour and skills. He commented that
where wives and husbands both worked twelve or thirteen
hours a day, children grew up 'like wild weeds' poorly super-
vised by lowly paid childminders and highly prone to acci-
dents. Infant mortality was high in industrial districts and
women were unable to breastfeed their babies properly, often
returning to the mill three or four days after confinement
(Engels 1969: 171). He wrote that factory girls were 'wholly in-
experienced and unfit as housekeepers. They cannot knit or
sew, cook or wash,...and when they have young children to
take care of, have not the vaguest idea how to set about it'

(Engels 1969: 175). This perspective had led him to conclude in 1845 that married women should be excluded from factory employment.

Marx incorporated this critical perspective on women's employment into his study of capitalism (Beechey 1987: 65). He argued that the employment of women enabled capitalists to extract larger profits from working class families than would be possible with an individual (male) family breadwinner:

> The value of labour-power was determined, not only by the labour-time necessary to maintain the individual adult labourer, but also by that necessary to maintain his family. Machinery, by throwing every member of that family on to the labour-market, spreads the value of the man's labour power over his whole family. It thus depreciates his labour power.....Thus we see, that machinery, while augmenting the human material that forms the principal object of capital's exploiting power, at the same time raises the degree of exploitation. (Marx 1961: 395)

Another effect of female employment was to erode male workers' resistance to capitalist production relations, by undercutting domestic craft production: 'By the excessive addition of women and children to the ranks of the workers, machinery at last breaks down the resistance which the male operatives in the manufacturing period continued to oppose to the despotism of capitalism' (Marx 1961: 402).

August Bebel took up a similar theme in *Woman Under Socialism*, first published in German in 1883, quoting evidence from the USA of large numbers of men in factory towns who were 'housekeepers', out of work because employers preferred to hire women at lower wage rates. 'Whoever calls shortly before noon will find them, with aprons tied in front, washing dishes. At other hours of the day they can be seen scrubbing, making the beds, washing the children, tidying up the place, or cooking' (Bebel 1971: 170). He went on to criticise the 'unwomanly' work that many women in Germany were doing in the latter years of the nineteenth century in areas like housing and railroad construction.

> It is, accordingly, easy to understand that, considering the extent to which female labour now prevails, and threatens

to make still further inroads in all fields of productive activity, the men, highly interested in the development, look on with eyes far from friendly, and that here and there the demand is heard for the suppression of female labour and its prohibition by law (Bebel 1971: 180).

These passages illustrate the ambivalent attitudes that were present amongst Marxists in the nineteenth century towards women's employment and reflect the belief that the traditional gender division of labour was a natural one. Domestic role reversal meant turning this natural order upside down. The idea that men should get involved in domestic labour to relieve the burden on working class women in capitalist society was not considered. Role reversal was strongly attacked for overturning what was assumed to be the natural division of labour between the sexes:

> In many cases the family is not wholly dissolved by the employment of the wife, but turned upside down. The wife supports the family, the husband sits at home, tends the children, sweeps the room and cooks. This case happens very frequently; in Manchester alone, many hundred such men could be cited, condemned to domestic occupations. It is easy to imagine the wrath aroused among the working-men by this reversal of all relations within the family (Engels 1969: 173).

At the time around 10 per cent of married women factory workers in Lancashire were family breadwinners. It was accepted that men's desire to re-establish their patriarchal position within the family was a legitimate working class defence against capitalist super-exploitation. If contradictions existed these were the product of capitalism not of divisions within the working class.

An overall assessment of Marxist writing in the nineteenth century suggests some ambivalence regarding the effect of women's employment on the well-being of the working class. For working class men as a class, unless they welcomed greater sex equality, there was nothing to gain and much to lose. They lost the domestic services of their wives, their wages declined and alternative non-capitalist sources of livelihood were undercut. For women the position was more complex. They

gained a measure of economic independence as joint or sometimes sole breadwinner and some freedom from the patriarchal control of the family. However they were overburdened
by the demands of domestic labour as well as wage labour and
unable to provide the care their families needed. In the long
term, the overall income of their families did not rise as their
earnings were offset by lower male wages.

Marx did not explore satisfactorily either the overall impact
of women's employment on the working class family or the differential impact on men and women. Whilst acknowledging
the sensitivity of the value of labour power of adult male
workers to the employment structure of the working class
family, he did not pursue this (Marx 1961: 519). He assumed
instead that the male worker supported a wife and children,
none of whom were wage labourers, despite, at the same time
excluding domestic labour from his model. Humphries, criti-
cising Marx's failure to pursue these issues, concluded that the
survival of the working class family in the nineteenth and
twentieth centuries was the result of working class struggle to
defend its own interests and minimise overall exploitation by
the capitalist class (Humphries 1977: 244). The sensitivity of
male wages to the employment structure of the family unit
provided the working class with a strong motive for defending
traditional family structures. Barrett and McIntosh (1980)
were critical of Humphries for not addressing either the tensions within the working class family between men's and
women's interests or the implications of reliance on a family
wage system from which many men were always excluded and
which placed mothers without husbands in poverty.

Alexandra Kollontai, writing in the early years of the twentieth century had a different explanation for the persistence of
the patriarchal working class family. She argued that, although
capitalist states were providing primary, secondary and higher
education and even playgrounds, kindergartens and playgroups,

> bourgeois society was afraid of going too far towards
> meeting the interests of the working class, lest this con-
> tribute to the break-up of the family. For the capitalists are
> well aware that the old type of family, where the woman is a
> slave and where the husband is responsible for the well-

being of his wife and children, constitutes the best weapon in the struggle to stifle the desire of the working class for freedom and to weaken the revolutionary spirit of the working man and working woman (Kollontai 1977a: 257).

Marx and Engels had argued that women would not gain equality with men until after the socialist revolution, when housework and childcare would become a collective social responsibility: 'With the transfer of the means of production into common ownership, the single family ceases to be the economic unit of society. Private housekeeping is transformed into a social industry. The care and education of the children becomes a public affair' (Engels 1972: 139).

Bebel was more optimistic than Marx and Engels about the possibility that capitalism could be reformed by electoral means. He believed that the historic role of capitalism was to bring about a technical revolution that would create the conditions for a future socialist society. He argued that domestic labour was already being transformed by technological progress: 'we are in the midst of a new industrial revolution, whereby the individual kitchen and other housework will become as superfluous as labor by manual tools became superfluous by the introduction of modern machinery' (Bebel 1910: 237 cited Diamanti 1993: 9).

Bebel also acknowledged more explicitly than Marx or Engels the active role played by men in maintaining women's oppression: 'The large majority of men believe in all seriousness that, mentally as well, woman must ever remain subordinate to them, and, hence, has no right to equality. They are, accordingly, the most determined opponents of woman's aspirations' (Bebel 1971: 187).

Alexandra Kollontai, writing in 1920, rejected Bebel's positive perspective on the scope for change within a capitalist economic framework because of the subordination of production to profit: 'under capitalism only people with well-lined purses can afford to take their meals in restaurants, while under communism everyone will be able to eat in the communal kitchens and dining-rooms' (Kollontai 1977a: 255). The Bolshevik revolution in Russia in 1917 was to provide the first practical opportunity for these ideas to be applied and tested out across a whole society.

4.3   THE SOCIALISATION OF DOMESTIC LABOUR IN THE USSR AFTER 1917

It can be seen from the writings of leading Bolsheviks in the early years of the revolution that there was a commitment in principle to finding social alternatives to domestic labour. This was recognised both as an essential precondition for women's emancipation and as a desirable economic goal. Domestic labour was viewed as oppressive, degrading, wasteful and inefficient. Clara Zetkin recorded a conversation with Lenin in 1920 in which he reported, 'We are organising community kitchens and public dining-rooms, laundries and repair shops, creches, kindergartens, children's homes and educational institutions of every kind' (Lenin 1965: 115). Lenin argued that sex equality would follow from the socialisation of domestic labour but also expected the work of organising these institutions to fall mainly to women (Lenin 1965: 70).

Major differences of view emerged, however, about the extent and speed of change that was thought desirable or practical. Inessa Armand and Alexandra Kollontai (the first two directors of Zhenotdel, the women's section of the Communist Party) argued that women's liberation and the socialisation of domestic labour had to be incorporated into the construction of socialism right from the start (Buckley 1989: 45). Others argued that the material basis for women's liberation had first to be built. Whilst the Bolshevik Party programme of 1919 advocated communes as supplementary institutions freeing women from the burden of the 'outmoded' household economy, a minority trend, including Kollontai, argued for communes as alternatives to the family.

Differences of viewpoint were related both to wide variations in attitudes about sexuality and gender and also to conflicting assessments of the political and economic context. In the early 1920s the Soviet Union was a backward, largely agricultural country which had suffered the social and economic disruption of several years of civil war. There were millions of homeless children and a high level of juvenile delinquency (Heitlinger 1979). The New Economic Policy (NEP), inaugurated in 1921, which partially restored private enterprise and ended labour conscription, led to a sharp rise in unemployment, particularly amongst women. It also forced the government to reduce public investment and after 1922 the number of homes for mothers and children declined (Farnsworth 1978: 141). By the mid-1920s Kollontai was politically isolated and in effective exile as a diplomat in Norway because of her support for the Workers' Opposition. Her proposals for housework and childcare to be collectivised were opposed both by the Right, who were against any increase in the tax burden on the peasantry, and by the Left, who were arguing that priority had to be given to rapid industrialisation not social innovation and that new ways of living could not, in any case be imposed from above.

Kollontai articulated more clearly and radically than any other communist in the early twentieth century a Marxist feminism based on the theories of Marx and Engels but which also linked back to some of the ideas of the earlier socialists, including the commitment to freedom of sexuality espoused by Fourier. However for Kollontai it was the state that should take over the responsibilities of the family, not the small cooperative community. Although deeply committed to sex equality and the need for women to become organised, her views on domestic labour aroused opposition from women as well as men. In much of her writing it is her critique of the family as both inefficient and anti-socialist that comes across more strongly than her feminism. The context in which Kollontai wrote was one in which there were deep political divisions between socialists and liberal feminists and 'feminism' was perceived to be concerned with advancing women's interests within capitalism, a political philosophy from which socialists like Kollontai and Zetkin were at pains to distance themselves (Holt 1977: 36). In 1921 Kollontai wrote:

> The family economic unit involves (a) the uneconomic expenditure of products and fuel on the part of small domestic economies, and (b) unproductive labour, especially by women, in the home – and is therefore in conflict with the interest of the workers' republic in a single economic plan and the expedient use of the labour force (including women) (Kollontai 1977b: 226).

Just as the state did not need the family, because it 'distracts the worker from more useful and productive labour' individuals were also assumed not to need the family either, 'because the task of bringing up the children which was formerly theirs is passing more and more into the hands of the collective' (Kollontai 1977a: 258). Mothers had a responsibility to society to bear healthy babies and breastfeed their babies. Society was responsible for ensuring support for women during pregnancy and childbirth and for providing care for babies and children, although it was women who were expected to do this work (Kollontai 1977e: 144) whilst men should be free to chose whether or not to share parental responsibilities with mothers (Kollontai 1977b: 228). Marriage was equated with prostitution: 'it is not important whether a woman sells herself to one man or to many', neither the prostitute nor the legal wife who stays at home does any 'useful work for the society' (Kollontai 1977c: 267).

It was this view of domestic labour which was implicit in the first marriage code enacted by the Bolsheviks in 1918. The 1918 code made divorce much easier but gave no property rights to divorced spouses. Because most subsequent divorces were initiated by men and most ex-wives had no independent income the effect was to make many women destitute. In response to lobbying from women workers, a further marriage code in 1926 provided for equal division of property acquired by spouses during marriage in the event of divorce. The economic contribution of women's domestic labour to the family unit was thus recognised in a way that ran counter to Kollontai's views.

The debate that led up to the new marriage code centred on the issue of whether men should be made financially responsible for their children. Kollontai's view was that the state, not fathers should support divorced mothers. She argued that the concept of alimony was demeaning to women as it forced them into dependence on former husbands and that even in a transitional society there should be a commitment to collective support for motherhood. She proposed that alimony should be replaced by an insurance fund, financed by a new graduated tax on all working adults. Single mothers who were unable to work and their young children would be supported by the fund (Kollontai 1977d: 308). These proposals were opposed by the Commissariat of Justice which argued that husbands, including common-law husbands, should be forced to take responsibility for their children, even though in a future communist society, there would be communal rearing of children (Farnsworth 1978: 147).

A number of urban communes were set up in the large cities in the early 1920s in converted houses. They were managed by elected committees which looked after housing needs and sometimes organised food stores, bakeries, laundries and recreational facilities. Some communes were for students and some for families (Heitlinger 1979: 81). Families, and particularly women, appear to have found these communes oppressive because the houses were small and overcrowded. The women always did the cooking and were unwilling to share it with each other. This led to congestion and disputes in the shared kitchens (Smith 1928: 149). Some leading Bolsheviks, like Trotsky, argued that new ways of living should be encouraged but not imposed and, in line with this thinking, in 1924 there was legislation to support the establishment of voluntary housing cooperatives (Heitlinger 1979: 82).

Subsequently Soviet architects organised design competitions for the dom-communa, or purpose-built communehouse, of which the first opened in 1929. Some of its residential units were without kitchens and served by a communal dining-room but after only two years the dining room and other communal facilities were subdivided to make further flats for individual families (Heitlinger 1979: 83). During these years of Stalin's First Five Year Plan, with its forced collectivisation and rapid industrialisation, there was a massive movement of population into the cities with very little additional housing provided. In these circumstances, communal housing became associated with overcrowding and a lack of privacy rather than a means of reducing women's domestic workload.

Once Stalin had consolidated his position, the idea of urban communes was abandoned as a futile attempt to introduce the communist future into the present and the traditional attitudes about the family and women which Kollontai had contested in the early 1920s provided the framework for state policy (Farnsworth 1978). The women's section of the Communist Party was abolished, abortion was made illegal, divorce became difficult and motherhood was acclaimed as women's greatest contribution to society.

Ironically it was during Stalin's rule that some of the policies advocated by Kollontai were partially implemented, not to advance the position of women but in the political and economic interests of the state. Because of the need for women workers in industry and agriculture, the number of places in pre-school nurseries increased dramatically from a quarter of a million in 1929 to nearly five million in 1932 (Dodge 1966: 78). In the marriage legislation of 1944, state benefits were introduced for unmarried mothers. Alimony was restricted to registered marriages only in order to protect soldiers from the responsibility for children they had fathered whilst away from home. State aid for mothers was also introduced to raise the birth rate (Farnsworth 1978: 165).

In the years immediately following the Bolshevik revolution the issue of how Marxist economic theory should be applied in a socialist economy was debated. Some Soviet economists, like Strumilin, argued that capitalist economics should be turned on its head and that all social forms of labour that promoted social welfare should be regarded as productive in a socialist society, whilst labour performed for private satisfaction and enrichment should be deemed unproductive. Because the Soviet economy was, temporarily, unable to devote sufficient resources to the socialisation of domestic labour, he argued that family-based housework was socially necessary and hence should be recognised as productive (Strumilin 1926, cited Heitlinger 1979: 25). Kollontai, on the other hand, opposed this broader definition of 'production' and considered domestic labour to be unproductive because it involved services only and created nothing tangible or lasting. In 1920 she wrote that housework had been reduced to cleaning, cooking, washing and care of clothing and that these tasks, although difficult and exhausting: 'are of no value to the state and the national economy, for they do not create any new values or make any contribution to the prosperity of the country.....Even if a working woman were to live a thousand years, she would still have to begin every day from the beginning. There would always be a new layer of dust to be removed from the mantelpiece, her husband would always come in hungry and her children bring in mud on their shoes' (Kollontai 1977a: 254).

Contrary to Strumilin's arguments, the Soviet system of national accounts and statistics that developed from the 1930s defined productive labour as labour which produced goods or those services related to the production, repair, transportation and distribution of goods (usually referred to as material services). Services which met individual, social and cultural needs were defined as unproductive. Ironically the first socialist society defined wealth as material goods, in the same way that Adam Smith had done in his celebration of capitalism.

The Soviet system of accounts was called the Material Product System. It was actually based on a more restrictive definition of productive labour than the United Nations system of accounts used by capitalist countries, which, in the tradition of Marshall, treats all remunerated (legal) labour as productive. In neither system, of course, was domestic labour considered to be productive (Waring 1989: 327). In the 1990s revisions to the UN system of accounts were under discussion and the fifth Annual Human Development Report for the UN Development Programme recommended that governments revise their national accounts to include that portion of women's unpaid work which was tradable (Brittain 1995).

4.4 THE MARXIST INHERITANCE

Overall Marxism did not sustain the vision of social change of the early socialists in which sex equality was to be an integral part of economic change and the reorganisation of reproduction and production were to be tackled together. It was the potential within Marxism to look beyond monetary transactions and explore the social relationships underpinning economic activity, combined with its failure to acknowledge the role of domestic labour in the reproduction and maintenance of labour power, which encouraged feminists in the 1970s to apply Marxist economic theory to domestic labour. The resulting domestic labour debate is the subject of the next chapter, together with a fuller assessment of the conclusions drawn from that debate about the difficulties involved in trying to integrate Marxist and feminist theory. Here we will focus on assessing aspects of Marxist theory that the domestic labour debate did not explore, specifically its focus on class as the overriding factor in people's identity and interests, its inadequate and contradictory treatment of the family and the way it overplayed the socialisation of housework as the key to sex equality.

A major weakness within Marxism was the exclusive focus on the class dimension of people's identity and interests. This prevented exploration of difference and conflict within classes. This problem was reinforced by the elitist element present within Marxism and most clearly represented in the concept of false-consciousness. If working class people could not be trusted to know their own class interests, conflict within the working class could be dismissed as false consciousness. Marxist theory claimed a definitive knowledge of working class interests. This claim, together with an absence of a democratic culture of debate and disagreement were ultimately bound to be particularly damaging to the inclusion in the socialist project of voices and interests not represented among Marxist leaders. Given the predominance of white, middle class and skilled working class men in these circles, the momentum was lacking for gender and other divisions within the working class to be explored (Gorz 1982: 16).

A major difference of view between Marxist feminists, like Kollontai, and other Marxists was the question of whether the socialisation of domestic labour should be part of the socialist revolution from the start or whether it should be postponed until the necessary economic and political conditions were judged to be in place. No one questioned the assumption that the socialisation of domestic labour was the ultimate goal. There was no exploration of what women and men might actually want as and when choices between domestic and social labour became available. This unquestioning theoretical commitment to the socialisation of domestic labour was based in large part on the assumption that social ownership and collective labour were the goals of socialism and hence that households should cease to be autonomous economic units. The potential for women's liberation through the socialisation of domestic labour was a secondary goal for all but the Marxist feminists.

Marx himself gave little attention to women's interests and concerns. He lived in a milieu where domestic servants were responsible for housework and childcare. In the early 1860s, despite being impoverished, the Marx household employed two domestic servants. Moreover, in the 1860s, when John

Stuart Mill was arguing for women to have the right to earn their own living, Marx and his wife Jenny were opposed to their own daughters pursuing a career (Kapp 1979: 44). The two eldest acted instead as unpaid secretaries for their father. Karl and Jenny Marx's attitudes changed sufficiently for their youngest daughter, Eleanor, to be allowed to work as a private governess, some ten years later. However women's domestic role continued to be perceived as petty and insignificant in relation to the public world of politics and the class struggle, as reflected in Jenny Marx's complaint in her letter to Wilhelm Liebknecht quoted at the start of the chapter.

Insights on the family, domestic labour and gender relations within Marxism derive in large part from Engels whose middle class working life as a Manchester business man provided the financial support necessary for Marx to research and write. However Engels flouted middle class conventions in his personal life, living in turn with two common law wives, both Irish working class women. Engels also admitted the occasional attempt at domestic labour himself, although only when Lizzie Burns was ill and their domestic servant unavailable (Kapp 1979: 185).

Subsequently Marxist feminists, like Kollontai extended Engels' analysis to argue that women's lives should be transformed by ending their dependence on marriage and by the state taking over responsibility for childcare as an integral part of the socialist revolution. These ideas were always peripheral to mainstream Marxism which maintained an ambivalence about the family both in nineteenth century capitalist societies and in the new socialist society in Russia after 1917. The view that it was beneficial, in terms of sex equality, for women to be drawn out of domestic labour into wage labour coexisted with the view that it was preferable from a working class perspective for women to be excluded from wage labour and to maintain their domestic labour role. To reconcile this contradiction women's liberation was envisaged by most as a distant future goal, linked to the socialisation of domestic labour that would be eventually attainable with socialism.

Most Marxists treated production within the household as a pre-capitalist relic, diminishing in significance as capitalism developed and finally disappearing in the socialist society of the future. The prospective elimination of domestic labour was presented as an unambiguously positive development, both in relation to gender equality (which would result from women being drawn out of the home into social production) and to class consciousness (which would develop as all labour became collective, the separation of production from consumption was finally complete and private property disappeared and was replaced by social ownership). The view that all domestic labour should be socialised, although, in practice, never adopted fully by Marxist parties in power, stood in the way of an open-ended exploration of the place of domestic labour in present capitalist or future socialist societies.

The opposition to the family as a productive unit and promotion of the concept of collective labour to the exclusion of all areas of individual and household autonomy is an aspect of Marxist theory criticised by Gorz (1982: 90). He argues that Marxist ideas have been shaped by the tendency within capitalism for all the autonomous capacities of working class people to be destroyed and for work to become useless unless combined with that of a large number of other workers and hence socialised, general abstract labour. This is the current within Marxism, and particularly strong within Leninism, which uncritically adopted capitalist production methods based on specialisation and scientific management as the essential prerequisite for socialism. In opposition to this Gorz argues that socialism would require a restructuring of production and production methods and the creation of a dual economy. This would consist firstly of a socialised production sector in which necessary goods and services were produced subject to rules of economic rationality with maximum efficiency and least expenditure of effort and resources. The other sector of the economy would be a sphere of autonomous production of goods and services outside the market carried out by individuals or in free association with others. The priority of the 'post-industrial' left would be to reduce work-time in the waged, market based sector of the economy and extend opportunities for self-motivated, self-rewarding activity within and outside the household (Gorz 1982: 87–98).

By latching on to the socialisation of domestic labour as the primary strategy for women's liberation, Marxists failed to recognise the need for an interplay between individual and collective support for parenting and other caring work, thus missing the opportunity that a less narrow approach could have given them to win wider support amongst working class women. This weakness provides part of an explanation of women's under-representation in Marxist politics. An important element in the crisis of Marxism in the 1980s and 1990s, was its failure to respond to feminism. On the one hand, the theory of women's liberation which it purported to have was so underdeveloped that it was found wanting when subjected to feminist scrutiny. On the other, in the socialist countries themselves, high participation of women in wage labour and socialisation of some aspects of domestic labour had been accompanied by the intensification of other aspects of domestic labour and the perpetuation of traditional gender divisions in the household. In the next chapter we will look at the attempts of a new generation of Marxist feminists in the 1970s to rework the Marxist theory of domestic labour.

5 The Domestic Labour Debate

> If all housewives were to die at once, and the men were forced to buy everything for use, wages would have to rise immediately. It is by her unpaid labour that the housewife makes it possible for her husband's wages to be kept so low (Mrs Wibaut, 'Working Women and the Suffrage', c.1895, Fleming 1973: 5).

The Women's Liberation Movement of the early 1970s inspired Marxist feminists in Britain to develop a critique of Marx's economic theory. The focus of this critique was Marx's neglect of domestic labour in his analysis of capitalism. However, in other respects, the broad framework of Marx's theory was accepted. The debate which followed came to be known as the domestic labour debate and explored the issue of whether and how Marxist value theory could be adapted to take account of the economic role of domestic labour. This chapter presents a summary of the different arguments and attempts to go beyond other useful surveys (Himmelweit and Mohun 1977, Sokoloff 1980) in disentangling some of the theoretical and terminological differences present but not always explicit in the literature. It assesses the achievements and limitations of the debate on domestic labour and identifies further issues that were to be addressed subsequently when feminists shifted their interest from capitalism to patriarchy (see chapter 6).

The 1970s debate about domestic labour had its origins within the feminist movement of the time. An important forum for the debate in Britain was the London-based Political Economy of Women (PEW) group which brought together participants in the Conference of Socialist Economists (CSE) and other interested feminists and socialists. The PEW group met regularly from 1973 to 1975 and presented papers in 1975 to the CSE Conference and the Women and Socialism Conference. The initial focus of the group was on housework because of the recognition that this was a largely unexplored area of women's productive role in contemporary capitalist societies and that the nature of women's experience of waged work was linked to their domestic labouring role (Conference of Socialist Economists 1976: 1). The conclusions reached in the group's discussions about housework were summarised in a paper written by three of its members (Gardiner, Himmelweit and Mackintosh 1975). Writers did not always fit neatly into distinct theoretical schools and, at the time, the debate was experienced as a fluid and creative process rather than an argument between irreconcilable positions. It is difficult to do full justice to such dynamic and collective intellectual processes in a survey of the literature.

Because, previously, domestic labour had been virtually excluded from Marxist economic analysis, finding a way of theorising the place of domestic labour within the capitalist economy became, for a while in the 1970s, the major concern of Marxist feminist economists. Marxist feminist sociologists, on the other hand, were more interested in exploring how the developing political economy of domestic labour could contribute towards a critique of the way orthodox Marxism had dealt with the issue of women's oppression as a whole. The fact that two different, although interrelated, questions were being asked within the debate was not always explicit. This point was highlighted by Molyneux (1979) when she argued the need for clarity about whether the main concern was to conceptualise the material significance of the domestic sphere and the position of women within it or whether it was a theory of women's subordination that was being sought. The debate was both enriched and made more complex by the fact that participants came to it from different social science disciplines. This chapter explores the debate within political economy on the relationship between domestic labour and capitalism. The next chapter will examine how the issue of gender relations and patriarchy were addressed from feminist sociological and anthropological perspectives.

5.1   THE CONTEXT

Most Marxists writing in the 1960s and 1970s about twentieth century industrial capitalism continued to apply the assump-

tions about domestic labour that had been implicit when
Marx developed his analytical framework one hundred years
previously. Harry Braverman used the concept of the 'universal market' to suggest that all goods and services formerly produced and provided within household units were being
converted by capitalism into commodities to be sold on the
market: 'Thus the population no longer relies upon social organisation in the form of family, friends..., but with few exceptions must go to market and only to market, not only for food,
clothing, and shelter, but also for recreation, amusement, security, for the care of the young, the old, the sick, the handicapped. In time not only the material and service needs but
even the emotional patterns of life are channeled through the
market' (Braverman 1974: 276). The family was deemed to be
changing under the impact of capitalist development from 'a
key institution of social life, production, and consumption'
into a unit of consumption only, 'and that in attenuated form,
since even as a consuming unit the family tends to break up
into component parts that carry on consumption separately'
(Braverman 1974: 277).

The result was a massive expansion of the capitalist service
sector which was drawing increasing numbers of women into
employment to perform jobs they were previously responsible
for within the household. Braverman maintained Marx's
definition of productive and unproductive labour, as discussed
in chapter 5. Work that had been unproductive from a capitalist viewpoint when performed within the home became productive, that is productive of surplus value, when performed
for the market: 'The work of the housewife, though it has the
same material or service effect as that of the chambermaid,
restaurant worker, cleaner, porter, or laundry worker, is
outside the purview of capital; but when she takes one of these
jobs outside the home she becomes a productive worker. Her
labor now enriches capital and thus deserves a place in the
national product' (Braverman 1974: 283).

Some feminists criticised Braverman for not including
housework in his analysis of the deskilling of work in the
twentieth century. They argued that domestic labour had
been transformed by monopoly capitalism from a creative
craft activity to caretaking and machine minding (Baxandall

1976: 6). Braverman's response was that the starting point for analysing what was happening in capitalist society should be the dynamic element (for him the capital accumulation process) not household labour which he characterised as traditional and static. In his view 'the most light will be shed on the totality of problems and issues embraced in the feminist movement, including those of household work, by an analysis that begins, not with the forms of household work that have been practised for thousands of years, but by their weakening and by the dissociation of an increasing number of women from them in the last few decades' (Braverman 1976: 120).

The view that domestic labour was merely a static remnant of pre-capitalist society, that there was little point in studying it and that it was in the process of disappearing anyway, had already been rejected by Marxist feminists. Margaret Benston (1969) had launched an investigation into why women still spent so much of their time on domestic labour, and what relationship this invisible labour had to the economic system as a whole and to women's subordinate position within it. The search for answers to these questions led to the domestic labour debate.

The focus of controversy within the domestic labour debate was the nature of the relationship between domestic labour and capital accumulation. There were two broad approaches to this question. One was to argue that domestic labour subsidised capitalist production through its role in the reproduction of labour power, directly enhancing capitalist profitability. The second approach was to reject the notion of a subsidy but argue instead that domestic labour was essential for the reproduction of labour power in capitalist society.

Within each of these broad approaches there was further debate. For example amongst those participants who argued that domestic labour subsidised capitalist production, there was disagreement about how to conceptualise the notion of a subsidy. Before discussing the different approaches and distinct perspectives within them, it will be helpful to clarify the different ways in which participants in the debate used the terms 'production' and 'reproduction', applying or revising Marx's usage of the concepts.

5.2   PRODUCTION AND REPRODUCTION

Within the domestic labour debate four different definitions of the term 'production' were used, reflecting different conceptualisations, some based on the traditional Marxist usage of 'productive' labour and some based on different conceptualisations, as discussed in chapter 4. Marx himself used the term 'production' in two different ways depending on whether he was discussing societies in general or the capitalist mode of production in particular. Both of these meanings of production were in evidence in the domestic labour debate.

Production (in the general sense) meant the creation of use-values (goods and services), whether sold in the market or consumed directly, regardless of the social and institutional context in which their production took place. On this definition, domestic labour was a form of production because it created goods and services which were consumed directly by family members. This was the approach taken by Benston (1969), Gardiner, Himmelweit and Mackintosh (1975), and Himmelweit and Mohun (1977).

A second approach was to define production as specifically capitalist, namely the creation of commodities or values (goods and services produced within capitalist relations of production and sold through the market). Domestic labour, because it took place outside capitalist relations of production, was not therefore production in this sense and the term 're-production' was therefore sometimes adopted instead. An example of this approach can be found in Humphries and Rubery (1984) who identified domestic labour with the sphere of 'social reproduction'.

Dalla Costa adopted a third usage, abandoning established Marxist conventions by arguing that domestic labour was part of capitalist production and productive of surplus value. Domestic labour was therefore deemed to be the same as wage labour in every respect except the absence of a wage. The controversial demand for wages for housework followed from this perspective (Dalla Costa 1973).

The fourth definition of production within the literature on domestic labour used market relationships to define the boundaries of the production system. Production was deemed to refer to the creation of commodities, (goods and services sold in the market) regardless of whether the relations of production were capitalist or not. Some argued that domestic labour produced the commodity labour power, and therefore should be included as part of the production system, even though it took place outside capitalist relations of production (Seccombe 1974).

The term reproduction was also used in three different ways and sometimes ambiguously. It was used alternately to mean 'social reproduction', 'reproduction of the labour force' or 'human reproduction'. Edholm, Harris and Young (1977) proposed that social reproduction should be used to refer broadly to the reproduction of the ideological and material conditions sustaining a social system. The 'reproduction of the labour force' is a more narrowly defined concept referring to the daily maintenance of workers and future workers together with their education and training. The term 'human reproduction' should be applied specifically to childbearing and lactation. On these definitions 'reproduction of the labour force' is the concept which comes closest to our concept 'domestic labour'. However if it is equated with reproduction of the labour force, domestic labour is reduced to a component of the capitalist production system instead of being integrated into a complex array of different social relationships. Reproduction of labour power is an important but not the only aspect of domestic labour that needs examination.

Unfortunately the term 'reproduction' has not always been used with the precision advocated by Edholm and her colleagues and there has sometimes been ambiguity about which of the three conceptualisations of reproduction is being adopted. Moreover the usage of 'reproduction' has sometimes done more to conceal than reveal domestic labour processes and relations. For example Mackintosh was critical of the way Meillassoux (1975) analysed the relationship between human reproduction and capitalist production without taking domestic labour into account (Mackintosh 1977: 123).

Walby argues that the distinction between production and reproduction is untenable (implicitly adopting the definition of production in Marx's general sense). She also regards the distinction as unhelpful because it tends to perpetuate naturalistic assumptions about necessary links between childbearing, childrearing and other aspects of domestic labour (Walby

1986: 36). However Walby's rejection of 'reproduction' as a
useful concept carries the risk of an economistic interpretation in which the relations of human reproduction become
invisible.

Providing the terms are used in a clearly defined way, both
'production' and 'reproduction' have a role in the analysis of
domestic labour. The key role played by domestic labour in
the reproduction of the labouring population has to be understood if economics is to address issues of gender inequality
(Beneria 1979). These issues will be explored more fully in
chapter 6 which examines the different ways in which the
concept of patriarchy was used by feminists, following on from
the domestic labour debate, to explore the social relationships
of production and reproduction. Let us now turn to an
overview of the different approaches taken to the central question explored by the domestic labour debate, namely the relationship between domestic labour and the process of capital
accumulation.

5.3 DOMESTIC LABOUR SUBSIDISES THE CAPITALIST MODE OF PRODUCTION

The first approach adopted within the domestic labour debate
was to argue that domestic labour played an important role in
maintaining capitalist profitability by keeping down the costs
of reproduction of labour power. Benston had argued that the
support of a family was a hidden tax on the wage earner since
his wage bought the labour power of two people. She suggested that to pay women for their work would imply a massive
redistribution of income away from the capitalist class
(Benston 1969: 23).

Dalla Costa asserted that domestic labour equated with the
reproduction of labour power and that unwaged women were
exploited. She believed that housework created surplus value
and that it was the lack of a wage that concealed their exploitation by the capitalist class: 'the wage commanded a larger
amount of labor than appeared in factory bargaining. Where
women are concerned, their labor appears to be a personal
service outside of capital. The woman seemed only to be suf-
fering from male chauvinism' (Dalla Costa 1973: 26).

Although Dalla Costa first rejected the demand for wages for housework on the grounds that it would 'entrench the condition of institutionalised slavery which is produced with the condition of housework' (Dalla Costa 1973:34), subsequently she argued that wages for housework should be adopted as the main mobilising demand of the women's movement. Wages for housework became a highly controversial demand within the feminist movement (Malos 1980).

Most feminists rejected both the wages for housework demand and the notion that housework should be treated as part of the capitalist production system. Housework needed to be seen as a precondition for capitalist production not an integral component of it: 'The employer is not concerned in the least about the way labor-power is produced and sustained, he is only concerned about its availability and its ability to generate profit' (Davis 1982: 234). Thus, for example, where wage labour is freely available at very low wages, domestic life may be virtually eliminated as for example under Apartheid in South Africa where black workers were forbidden to live in families in the industrial centres.

Harrison (1973b) adopted a different approach from Dalla Costa and one that was closer to Marx's concept of productive labour but still involved a radical reinterpretation of the labour theory of value. My paper presented to the British Sociological Conference in 1974 suggested an approach that was similar to Harrison's (Gardiner 1976a). The argument was that a housewife could not be deemed to produce surplus value but could be said to perform surplus labour if the labour involved in housework exceeded the labour time involved in her own consumption, including the commodities purchased for her out of her husband's wage (Harrison 1973b: 42).

In this approach the value of labour power was redefined as the total labour time necessary for its reproduction. Hence the value of labour power became the necessary labour time involved in housework as well as the abstract labour embodied in commodities consumed. Where there were no commodity substitutes for housework, Harrison defined necessary time as the actual labour time involved in housework. Where commodity substitutes existed and labour productivity was higher in commodity production as compared with domestic labour, actual domestic labour time would be replaced by the abstract

labour time involved in the production of those commodities
to arrive at a measure of socially necessary labour time.

The housewife would be deemed to be performing surplus
labour if the necessary labour time involved in domestic services for her husband exceeded the labour embodied in the
commodities consumed by her that were purchased from his
wage. Although this represented an unequal exchange
between husband and wife it was assumed that housewives'
surplus labour would be appropriated by the capitalist class
through paying male workers a wage that was lower than the
value of their labour power. The possibility that wives consumed less and worked longer hours than husbands, and that
men benefited from women's surplus labour was raised but
not explored. Folbre (1982) and Walby (1986) subsequently
developed similar approaches to explore gender inequality
within the household (see chapter 6).

At the time the major objective was to demonstrate the possibility of capital appropriating housewives' surplus labour as
profit. The mechanism for this was the payment by capital of a
wage that was lower than the value of labour power by the
amount of surplus labour performed by the housewife. The
difference between the wage and the value of labour power
would be likely to diminish if labour productivity rose in those
capitalist sectors producing commodity substitutes for domestic labour (Harrison 1973b: 45).

This approach could accommodate cases where wives
worked for a capitalist employer as well as doing housework.
The effect this would have on the surplus labour women performed and the overall profit accruing to capital would
depend on how much women's hours of work increased, what
happened to the value of labour power for both men and
women, and on the relative productivity levels in the capitalist
and household sectors. Hence whilst domestic labour contributed to profits by keeping down the costs of maintenance
and reproduction of labour power, it would not always be
more profitable for it to be organised in this way. This would
depend on the conditions of capital accumulation and the relative costs of socialising childcare (Gardiner 1976a: 117). It
was theoretically possible for all the economic functions of
housework to be carried out under capitalist relations of production (Harrison 1973b: 51).

A central problem with the above approach, and one that was identified within the domestic labour debate, was the assumption that domestic labour time was comparable with Marx's concept of value or abstract labour time and the associated assumption that the value of labour power could be equated with all the socially necessary labour time involved in its reproduction, not merely that which was embodied in commodities purchased with wages. The consensus that emerged in the Political Economy of Women Group was that the labour theory of value could not be applied in this way to domestic labour (Gardiner, Himmelweit and Mackintosh 1975: 10). Domestic labour was private labour, not subject to capitalist production relations nor to the market forces operating on commodity production. The value of labour power should not be redefined to include domestic labour time but should be limited to the abstract labour time embodied in commodities entering into workers' consumption.

It followed that the value of labour power and the wage paid to workers was premised on other forms of work outside capitalist production relations that provided for the consumption needs of wage labourers, including some work performed in the state sector as well as domestic labour. Hence the contribution domestic labour made to the production of surplus value was that of keeping the value of labour power below the total costs of its reproduction (Gardiner 1975: 54). The mechanism for this was the retention within the family of those aspects of the reproduction and maintenance of labour power which it was not profitable for capitalist production or the state to take over (Gardiner, Himmelweit and Mackintosh 1976: 13–14). The value of labour power of individual workers also depended on the proportion of family members engaged in wage labour at the particular stage in history and hence on the role of women in the wage-labour force. It was therefore possible for women to contribute towards a lowering of the average wage through their wage labour as well as their domestic labour. Hence it was important to link the study of women's domestic and wage labour. To date inadequate capital accumulation or demand for female wage labour and the absence of sufficiently labour-saving technology had prevented the socialisation or transfer of domestic productive activities into capitalist production relations. Future trends in domestic labour would depend on the interplay of the costs of reproduction of labour, the capitalist accumulation process and demand for female wage labour.

5.4 DOMESTIC LABOUR IS NECESSARY FOR THE REPRODUCTION OF LABOUR POWER

For a number of participants in the domestic labour debate, such as Morton (1971), Himmelweit and Mohun (1977) and Seccombe (1974), it was the role of domestic labour in the reproduction of labour power that made it an essential part of the reproduction of the capitalist mode of production rather than any direct link between domestic labour and capitalist profitability.

For Morton the function of the family was the maintenance and reproduction of labour power. The structure of the family, and the role of women as domestic and wage labourers, was determined by the needs of the economic system at any given time for a certain kind of labour power (Morton 1971).

Seccombe argued that domestic labour produced labour power and because labour power was a commodity, domestic labour should be deemed to create value. This value was 'realised as one part of the value labour power achieves as a commodity when it is sold' (Seccombe 1974: 9). However he rejected the view that the housewife performed surplus labour or was exploited. His critics argued that domestic labour was not commodity production and therefore could not be deemed to create value (Gardiner 1975, Coulson 1975, Himmelweit and Mohun 1977).

For Himmelweit and Mohun what was specific about domestic labour was that it was use-value production, not commodity production, and that its ultimate purpose was 'to provide labour-power for sale' (Himmelweit and Mohun 1977: 28). Hence the value of labour power did not include the housewife's labour. The major reason why domestic labour survived was that capitalism required workers to be free individuals selling their labour power on the labour market. They argued that the complete socialisation of domestic labour would require the socialisation of the reproduction of living individuals. This would turn the 'free' labourer into a slave and would be inconsistent with capitalist relations of production (Himmelweit and Mohun 1977: 25). A theory of human reproduction was therefore needed to complement Marx's theory of production relations.

5.5   WHAT CONCLUSIONS WERE DRAWN FROM THE DEBATE?

The domestic labour debate clarified a number of issues which had not been adequately addressed prior to the 1970s. These can be summarised in the following way.

● The household is a unit of production, not just a unit of consumption in industrialised capitalist societies and the economic organisation of those societies is premised on households which produce and consume.
● The standard of living is not based solely on the level of wages and the commodities that wages can purchase. It is a combination of wage goods, domestically produced use-values and public services.
● The historical evolution of the bundle of wage goods which constitute the value of labour power has been dependent on the degree to which domestic labour is available to process or provide substitutes for those goods.
● The Marxist concept of value is an inadequate tool to analyse domestic labour because its products are not exchanged on the market but consumed within the household. Domestic labour is not subject to the same pressures for increased productivity which characterise capitalist production relations (although other pressures towards greater efficiency may be present such as the time constraints where women are engaged in wage labour and domestic labour). Domestic labour cannot therefore be equated with wage labour. The household and the market are analytically distinct.
● The social relations of production in households are different from those of wage labour and need separate investigation. They are linked to the relations of human reproduction to which the attention of some feminists

shifted following on from the domestic labour debate (Mackintosh 1979).

- Transfers of labour and resources take place between the household and the capitalist production sphere and within the household. The complexity of these transfers is not acknowledged in Marx's theory because it equates the costs of reproduction of labour power exclusively with the consumption of wage goods.
- The production and reproduction of people is an essential aspect of an economic system, and needs to be brought within the boundaries of the economics discipline. Domestic labour can be integrated into Marxist economic theory through the concept of the reproduction of the labouring population.

Many of the above issues needed further exploration when the debate effectively finished in the late 1970s. For example the relationship between wage goods and domestic labour was clearly complex and needed historical and empirical investigation. More wage goods did not necessarily imply less domestic labour, even if they included household appliances (see chapter 8). And whether more wage goods meant more or less domestic labour, it was apparent that the value of labour power had become a less determinate and arguably less useful concept. It followed that returning to the classical political economy concept of the costs of reproduction of the labouring population might be a more fruitful approach (Picchio 1992), as discussed in chapter 2.

Having established the inadequacy of the Marxist conceptual framework for analysing the reproduction of labour power and the overall standard of living, the domestic labour debate provided an impetus for feminist and sociological research on the distribution of costs and benefits involved in household provisioning between men and women (see chapters 6 and 7). Subsequent research, primarily within a sociological framework, largely avoided the issue of quantifying costs and benefits in value terms. The focus shifted to social not economic inequality in response to the finding that domestic labour inputs were not measurable according to Marxist conventions of measurement. The concept of economic inequality depended on methods of quantifying costs and benefits. The domestic labour debate established the limited usefulness of the Marxist conceptual framework in this respect. It left some feminists dissatisfied with the apparent conclusion that the domestic sphere was a site of oppression for women, not of exploitation. 'The verdict was logical within the terms set, but that logic was difficult to grasp and seemed irrelevant for women to whom it was already obvious that their free work was materially benefiting both husbands and capitalists' (Scott 1984: 143). The debate left unresolved the issue of how the poverty that is linked to responsibility for domestic labour should be tackled. The failure of the domestic labour debate to offer a framework for tackling issues of concern to feminists and the limited nature of the terms of the debate led many of the participants in the debate to conclude that there was little mileage in taking the debate further. Within a few years the creative energy that had been generated got dissipated. The next section discusses the limits of the debate, the criticisms of it made at the time and some of the contextual reasons why participants in the debate turned their energies to other issues.

5.6   THE LIMITS OF THE DEBATE

In retrospect it may appear that the domestic labour debate provided a more significant stimulus to feminist research from the criticisms it generated than from the analytical frameworks it explored. At the time it was much easier to identify the limits of the debate than its achievements. The list of criticisms made at the time is a long one. Not all the criticisms could be or were applied with equal force to all contributions to the debate. The focus here is on the major limits identified at the time within the domestic labour literature as a whole rather than the specific weaknesses of particular contributions.

- The debate ignored gender relations and neither addressed the issue of why it was women who carried out the bulk of domestic labour nor explored the possibility that men as well as, or instead of, capitalists might be the beneficiaries (Delphy 1977 and Hartmann 1979b).
- It tried to fit the debate about housework into a Marxist

conceptual framework and excluded most women themselves because of its esoteric and academic nature. It was a
debate within Marxism not a debate within feminism
(Kaluzynska 1980).

● It used an abstract ahistorical framework (the mode of
production) to analyse an issue that needed historical and
empirical investigation (Molyneux 1979: 20).

● It accepted a functionalist perspective, assuming that domestic labour survived because it served a function for
capitalism. It merged the notions of cause and effect and
paid insufficient attention to the possibility of a contradictory relationship between capitalism and the household
(Humphries 1977 and Molyneux 1979: 20).

● It was reductionist and economistic, in the sense of attempting to investigate social phenomena through economic categories alone, ignoring ideology, politics and
sexuality (Barrett 1980: 24, Humphries and Rubery 1984).

● It talked about domestic labour as if it was a universal category, failing to address the different significance it might
have in different societies and cultures, for example with
different degrees of development of markets (Mackintosh
1979).

● It gave insufficient attention to the way the combination of
domestic and wage labour, rather than domestic labour
alone, shaped women's experience of capitalism (Coulson
1975: 60); some critics suggested an alternative more orthodox Marxist perspective of housewives acting as a
flexible reserve of labour for the capitalist mode of production and, as such, disguising the high levels of unemployment typical of advanced capitalism (Molyneux 1979:
26).

● It focused on housework rather than childcare and on
the maintenance of the adult male labourer, not on generational reproduction. For example Molyneux (1979:
26) argued that women's domestic labour was beneficial
to capitalist states primarily because it provided a childcare service at minimal cost. (The point that caring for
elderly and disabled household members was omitted
from the analysis would also have been a valid criticism
although this issue does not seem to have been raised at
the time.)

- It looked only at the production of use-values (goods and services in the home) and ignored the production of people themselves, namely human reproduction (Himmelweit and Mohun 1977, Mackintosh 1981).

Some might conclude from this list of criticisms that enough has already been written about this debate. The scale of the criticisms certainly contributed to the debate ending and to participants moving off in new and different research directions. At the time it was difficult to make definitive concluding statements about the debate or to assess its achievements. In retrospect it can be seen as an important process of exploration which brought some of the weaknesses in the theoretical underpinnings of Marxism and feminism into the open. Most of the criticisms of the debate were valid but the degree of interest generated by the debate confirmed its contribution to the developing women's studies research agenda. Its significance is evidenced by the number of references to it in the international literature on women's work.

One reason why the energy that had been generated by the debate got dissipated so quickly was that it was an ambitious project, launched from a weak, unresourced and marginalised base of Marxist feminist intellectuals who came together and collaborated briefly and creatively. One of the most interesting aspects of the domestic labour debate as a moment in the history of feminist theory was that feminist economists came together to look at the implications of feminism for economic theory, specifically Marxist economic theory, in collaboration with feminist intellectuals from other academic disciplines. It was an ambitious project fraught with difficulty. First, the exclusive concern with Marxism, meant that the debate was on the fringes of economics as a discipline, where Marxism, always in a marginal position, from the mid-seventies onwards was becoming a less and less significant force. Feminist Marxists were in a doubly marginalised position because of the history of neglect of gender relations within the Marxist tradition. Feminist economists elsewhere, notably the USA, engaged more directly with mainstream economics. Although they were still invariably struggling at the fringes of the discipline, they had greater success in establishing a base for their work.

5.7   WHAT DID THE DEBATE ACHIEVE?

Twenty years on the significance of the domestic labour debate appears clearer. It was one of the rare attempts by feminists to develop a critique of economic theory. It identified the neglect of domestic labour within economics as central to the discipline's marginalisation of women. It was specifically focused on a problem within Marxist theory which had not been systematically addressed before, namely the neglect of women's specific relationship to capitalist production and the associated neglect of household economic activity in industrialised societies. The fact that the major oppositional strand within economics as a discipline, namely Marxism, had so little to say about domestic labour, reinforced the difficulty of getting feminist concerns on to the research agenda. In retrospect, the focus on Marxism as a medium for inserting a feminist discourse into the economics discipline, appears over-optimistic, but Marxism offered important insights which still have relevance to this project. Theoretical feminism still draws on the Marxist inheritance and was strengthened by the debate about domestic labour. Much of the conceptual framework of feminist theory is based on reworked Marxist concepts: patriarchy, the social relations of production and reproduction. In the 1970s, it appeared more logical than twenty years later to attempt to stretch Marxist value theory in new ways.

The domestic labour debate represented a significant part of the process of Marxists coming to terms with the problems and limits of Marxism. This in turn was part of the developing crisis within Marxism and the left and of the weakening of the radical political economy tradition within the UK. The development of a feminist political economy will be an important element in the renewal of those radical traditions. There is now a strong link between feminism and radicalism in intellectual work. The growing conservatism in evidence in economics research and teaching in Britain in the last two decades of the twentieth century is partly explained by the absence of a feminist current within it. It is not surprising, in the circumstances that it was within other social science fields in Britain sociology and social policy in particular, that feminists opened up some space in which to pursue their research agenda in the 1980s. The next chapter explores the debate about gender and patriarchy which followed the 1970s debate about domestic labour and capitalism.

6 The Patriarchy Debate

> ...the categories of marxist analysis, 'class', 'reserve army of labor', 'wage-laborer', do not explain why particular people fill particular places. They give no clues about why *women* are subordinate to *men* inside and outside the family and why it is not the other way around. *Marxist categories...are sex-blind* (Hartmann 1979b: 8).

One of the main criticisms of the domestic labour debate was its failure to address the question of why domestic labour was women's work. It neither explored why the gender division of labour was so persistent nor men's relationship to domestic labour. Some feminists in the 1970s and 1980s sought to develop an alternative analysis of domestic labour and gender relations which retained some Marxist terminology but re-worked into a new feminist analytical framework. For example there were various attempts to apply 'exploitation' to men's appropriation of female domestic labour and to develop an analysis of patriarchy to complement Marxist analysis of capitalism. Much of the feminist debate that took place from the 1970s around these issues was concerned with exploring whether and how the concept of patriarchy could be usefully applied. This chapter offers a critical review of the various applications by feminists of the concept of patriarchy to the gender division of domestic labour and gender inequality in general and concludes with a discussion of the value and limits of patriarchy as an analytical concept.

6.1 THE EVOLUTION OF PATRIARCHY AS A POLITICAL CONCEPT

The etymological derivation of patriarchy is 'rule by the father'. In seventeenth century England patriarchalism was a dominant political philosophy which credited fathers with natural authority over their wives and sons, and the king, as father of his people, with absolute authority over his subjects

(Laslett 1949). From the time of the Reformation onwards both Church and State had supported the growth of paternal power, and male heads of households were perceived increasingly as society's moral guardians in place of priests. Seventeenth and eighteenth century liberal philosophy set out to replace the notion of the 'natural authority' of patriarchs with a model of free, equal and rational individuals. However, some ambivalence remained about women's place in the new egalitarian philosophy (Coole 1988: 71). This ambivalence was reflected in classical political economy, as discussed in - chapter 2.

Marx and Engels adopted the 'rule of fathers' concept but gave it a new economic, not just political, dimension. They identified a patriarchal mode of production as the dominant economic system over a particular phase of pre-capitalist history when families/households were property owning and producing units. Ownership of property and direction of the production process was vested in male/paternal heads of household. Households produced goods for their own consumption and for sale. The bulk of society's production was organised in this way. The subordination of women and children to male authority followed logically from men's ownership and control of property and production, although widows could escape their subordinate position by assuming the role of head of the household economy. Women as wives had a twofold economic value because of their labour power and their reproductive capacity. Husbands had a dual material interest in controlling their wives' sexuality and fertility. On the one hand large numbers of children were needed to ensure that enough would survive into adulthood to constitute and in turn reproduce the family labour force. On the other hand, men wished to ensure that they were themselves the father of the heirs to their property.

As industrial capitalism developed, this mode of production was undermined as the dominant mode within society and, in *The Communist Manifesto*, they described how: 'modern industry has converted the little workshop of the patriarchal master into the great factory of the industrial capitalist' (Marx and Engels 1967: 87). Nonetheless family/household commodity production relations survived alongside the dominant capitalist relations and continued to reproduce a petty bourgeoisie of self-employed and small businesses. Marx and Engels assumed that households in this class were characterised by patriarchal gender relations as were the capitalist property owning households in the middle and upper middle classes (Engels 1972). Hence within traditional Marxism, patriarchy was an economic and historically specific concept.

In the 1970s radical feminists like Millett (1971) began to use patriarchy in a much more general way to refer to men's power over women, rather than the rule of the father. Within radical feminist theory, patriarchy was no longer confined to analysing power relations within the family or at an interpersonal level but began to be applied to the relations between men and women throughout all of society's institutions. Subsequently feminists debated whether patriarchy as a concept could provide analytical and not just descriptive insights. For patriarchy to explain rather than merely describe gender inequality the specific social relationships and processes of patriarchy needed to be identified. For some feminists like Delphy (1977) and Hartmann (1979a and 1979b) these were economic (see section 6.3). For Mitchell (1975) they were psycho-cultural. For others like Mackintosh (1977) and Folbre (1983), patriarchy was grounded in the social relationships of human reproduction and childrearing (see section 6.4). Others argued that patriarchy was based on women's biological reproductive role (Firestone 1970) or men's capacity to rape (Brownmiller 1975). Some of these approaches, especially the psycho-cultural and biological tended towards an ahistorical concept of patriarchy which failed to account for the significant variations in men's power over women in different contexts and times (Beechey 1979 and Rowbotham 1982). Others, like Walby (1990), offered a framework of different patriarchal structures operating in different configurations, which enabled them to explore historical variation in gender relations.

Sections 6.2 to 6.6 of the chapter explore feminist analyses of the gender division of domestic labour, in terms of patriarchy and patriarchal relations. Most feminist writers who participated in this debate were interested in exploring the relationship of the gender division of labour to women's oppression in society as a whole. The patriarchy debate therefore had a broader agenda and a broader social science base than

he domestic labour debate. The focus was increasingly on the-
rising women's oppression in general rather than domestic
ıbour specifically. Most of the feminist writing on patriarchy
nd domestic labour was done in the 1970s and early 1980s.
.ater studies of patriarchy and work focused on gender rela-
ons in employment. For example Walby (1986) argued that
he labour market, not the household was the key site for pa-
riarchal relations in contemporary Britain (see section 6.3).
Vith the growing interest in ideology and discourse within the
ocial sciences, feminist interest also shifted away from econ-
mics to sociology and anthropology.

.2   FEMINIST PERSPECTIVES ON PATRIARCHY AND
)OMESTIC LABOUR

.lthough feminists, following on from Millett (1971) often
sed patriarchy to denote male power in general, it was also
sed in more specific ways that are particularly relevant to
ender relations in the household and more closely aligned
⊃ its historical origins as a concept. Feminist writing on pa-
riarchy and domestic labour can be divided into four broad
trands. The first strand, discussed in section 6.3, uses a
road definition of the patriarchal family, equating it with a
ousehold which consists of male breadwinner and depen-
ent wife and children. This is presented by some feminist
riters as the typical family structure in contemporary
Vestern capitalism, encompassing different classes, occupa-
onal groups and unemployed people and underpinning
hat is perceived to be a common male interest in ensuring
hat women remain available to service them in the house-
old. Some writers, for example Delphy (1977), identified
narriage as the key institutional mechanism through which
atriarchy is perpetuated. Others, for example Hartmann
1979a and b) and Walby (1986), developed a broader
efinition of patriarchy encompassing social relations
etween men in the public sphere which are deemed to
naintain male control of female labour in the private
phere. As women gain greater access to employment and
ther measures of social equality, male authority within the
amily unit declines and gender segregation of jobs becomes

the primary means for perpetuating women's economic dependence in the patriarchal family. The material underpinnings of gender inequality are perceived to be located less and less within the household and more and more in the labour market. Human reproduction and childrearing are not considered to be important explanatory factors.

The second approach, discussed in section 6.4, is to argue that patriarchy is most appropriately reserved for situations in which society is organised under identifiable patriarchs, and not weakened to include more socially diffused systems of male dominance (Mackintosh 1981: 7). Whilst there is a need to explore the relationship between the form and degree of women's subordination and the development of the forces and relations of production, Engels and other Marxists are criticised for their economic reductionism and overemphasis on the role of private property in the subjugation of women. Patriarchal societies are characterised as those in which physical violence and ideology combine with economic mechanisms to produce a systematic subordination of women (Young and Harris 1978: 51). Such societies are more likely to be found at particular levels of development of the productive forces, for example societies consisting of peasant households dominated by the oldest male. The social relations of human reproduction are as important as the social relations of production in shaping the gender division of labour. An essential ingredient of patriarchy is the control by men of women's sexuality and fertility. This definition of patriarchy underlies the work of Mackintosh (1981) and Folbre (1983). The third strand of the debate, which offers a global and ecological perspective on patriarchy is illustrated in the writing of Mies (1986) and will be discussed in section 6.5.

The fourth strand in the debate represents the most important critique of patriarchy theory, that by black women. They argued that white feminists' use of patriarchy failed to address the diversity of women's experience and the specific experiences of black women and men. Black feminists developed an analytical framework for exploring the ways in which race, ethnicity and culture are enmeshed with class and gender. African-American feminist analysis of patriarchy and domestic labour will be explored, in particular, as the most influential contribution to black feminist theory in this area, illustrated by the writing of Hooks (1982 and 1984) and Collins (1990) (see section 6.6).

The following discussion of feminist writing on patriarchy and domestic labour is not intended to be a comprehensive account, but rather an attempt to highlight the most important and influential ideas that framed the debate. The writers whose contributions are discussed have been selected to illustrate the different strands of argument. An examination of the literature cited would guide the reader to the work of many other feminists who have made important contributions to the debate.

6.3   PATRIARCHY, MARRIAGE AND THE LABOUR MARKET

6.3.1   Delphy

Christine Delphy's (1977, 1984 and 1992) theory of marriage and gender inequality uses the concept of a domestic mode of production in which husbands appropriate their wives' domestic labour. For Delphy the essential difference between the domestic mode of production and the capitalist mode of production is the fact that those who are exploited are not paid but maintained (Delphy 1984: 18). Unequal sharing of goods within the household unit is disguised because it is not mediated by money.

Delphy's family-based household is a household organised around a married couple and children, with or without other relatives. She argues that this family is the norm in contemporary Western societies and that most of the households that do not fit this norm consist of people who are in transition from t or towards it. She describes the family as a patriarchal institution in which the male head of household is responsible for maintaining the other dependent members and in turn appropriates their labour. A distinction is drawn between household work and family work. Household work refers to all work done within family household units by any person. Family work refers to that work which is done by dependent members or the household head. Family work is unremunerated, in the sense of being provided as a service for others, as well as being unpaid in monetary terms. Domestic exploitation is based upon work being both unpaid and unremunerated. The household work done by household heads or single people for themselves is not considered to be unremunerated because they own the product of this labour and benefit directly from it, either in terms of extra consumption or in terms of reduced expenditure. However family work (work done by dependent members of the household) is unremunerated because it is done for the household head. All family work constitutes a form of exploitation because the term exploitation is interpreted to apply to any unequal transaction in which the things produced by the labour of one person are consumed by someone else or converted into that other person's property. Any service performed for the head of household is assumed by definition to be an unequal transaction.

There are a number of problems with Delphy's analysis. It is based on the assertion that husbands/fathers universally appropriate all the household work done by their wives and other dependent members of their households. The main thrust of the argument is that the breadwinner, defined economically, legally and ideologically, owns, controls and directs the labour of family members and the products of their labour. Therefore, by definition, all family work is done for him. There are three types of products of this family labour. The first is his labour power which is obviously owned by him. The second are products which are sold in the operation of a family business which is vested in him. The third are children, described as 'his' in the sense that they bear his name. The husband/father also derives benefit from family labour in the sense that he would have to do the work himself if his wife did not do it (Delphy 1992: 125).

It is assumed that 'exploitation' takes place but no attempt is made to compare the amount of work done by wives with the consumption standards they enjoy. On the contrary, emphasis is given to the lack of an exchange relation between husband and wife and the impossibility of measuring equivalence. Although the wives of high income men are likely to receive a higher level of maintenance and do less family work than the wives of men on low incomes, exploitation follows automatically from the fact of women servicing men as part o the marriage contract, regardless of how much they receive from them in material terms. Delphy makes an implicit assumption that wives always contribute more to husbands' consumption than husbands contribute to wives' consumption. For example she argues that exploitation is demonstrated most sharply where wives have well paid full-time employment and still do the bulk of childcare and domestic work or pay someone else to do it (Delphy 1992: 117). She does not consider the scenario where women have high material consumption but do relatively little domestic labour. She also assumes that husbands direct women's labour and decide what family income should be spent on, ignoring the variations in decision making identified in different types of households (Pahl 1989). Delphy is only interested in what she perceives all women to have in common not in differences between classes and races.

6.3.2 Hartmann

Heidi Hartmann (1979a and b and 1981) emphasises a network of patriarchal social structures as opposed to the emphasis placed by Delphy on marriage as the key institution of male power. Patriarchy does not rest solely on childrearing in the family but on the whole array of social structures that enable men to control women's labour. Nonetheless men's control over women's labour power within the household remains an essential ingredient of patriarchy for Hartmann. This control is achieved by excluding women from access to economic resources (in capitalist societies, jobs paying adequate wages for independent living) and by restricting women's sexuality. The crucial underpinnings of patriarchy in contemporary industrial society are: heterosexual marriage, female childrearing and housework, women's economic dependence on men (enforced by arrangements in the labour market) and a whole array of social institutions based on social relations among men (such as churches, schools, trade unions, clubs).

Hence Hartmann's concept of patriarchy encompasses the social relations between men operating in the public sphere which sustain solidarity among men and hence enable them to dominate women in both public and private spheres. Whilst men of different classes and races have different places in the patriarchal hierarchy, they are united in their shared dominance over their women and they depend on each other to maintain that domination. Hence housework and childcare remain women's work because men have the power to control women's labour. Men's motivation for controlling women's labour power is based on the personal and sexual services they receive, on avoiding having to do housework and childcare and on the sense of power that comes with it.

Marxism is criticised for failing to acknowledge the benefits men derive from these arrangements. Capitalism and patriarchy are seen to be two distinct but generally mutually supportive sets of social relations. In the nineteenth century capitalism was forced to adjust to the interests of patriarchy with the exclusion of women from wage labour and the development of the family wage. But this accommodation suited capitalists at the time because they were concerned to ensure the reproduction of healthy future workers. In contemporary industrial capitalism a new accommodation between patriarchy and capitalism in which married women are wage earners and domestic labourers is sustained through wage differentials and job segregation which perpetuate women's economic dependence on men (Hartmann 1979a: 19 and 1979b: 208). Men continue to benefit both from higher wages and from the domestic division of labour.

Hartmann developed a perceptive and influential feminist critique of traditional Marxism and the domestic labour debate. However her analysis of domestic labour has a number of weaknesses. Like the domestic labour debate and Delphy's analysis, it is implicitly functionalist in offering an explanation based on the benefits of domestic labour for men and capitalism. It underplays the tensions that are likely to arise between patriarchal and capitalist interests in the attempt to control female labour power (Walby 1986) and the possible contradictions that may arise for men in maintaining the patriarchal family unit (Folbre 1983). Although recognising hierarchical divisions between men it does not take account of black women's very different experience of family and work (Collins 1990). Like other feminist theories already discussed it offers a top-down analysis of power relations in which women are merely passive victims.

6.3.3 Walby

Sylvia Walby (1986 and 1990) adopted much of Hartmann's approach but used the concept of the patriarchal mode of production as well as developing the dual concept of public and private patriarchy. Initially she defined patriarchy as 'a system of interrelated social structures through which men exploit women' (Walby 1986: 51). An essential social structure within this system is the patriarchal mode of production within which housewives or domestic labourers are defined as the producing class and husbands the exploiting class. The labour process within this mode of production is the generational and day to day production of labour power. Walby used the term exploitation in preference to Hartmann's usage of 'men's control of women's labour power' (Walby 1986: 43) and argued that it was the mode of exploitation which constituted the central difference between patriarchy and capitalism. Patriarchy was defined as a system through which men exploited women whilst capitalism was a system in which capital exploited wage labourers. She adapted the Marxist definition of exploitation, suggesting that men's exploitation of women in the patriarchal mode of production was based on the producer's lack of ownership of the means of production (the exhausted husband who is the object of her labour) and the product of her labour (his replenished labour power). He sells his labour power to the employer who exploits him by paying him a wage less than the value of the goods he has produced. He in turn exploits his wife by giving her a smaller portion of his wage for herself than he retains to spend on himself. Moreover it is assumed that the wife typically works longer hours than the husband and that the wife is performing surplus labour which the husband expropriates. The wife's surplus labour is equated with the extra wage income the husband receives compared with that which is allocated to the wife for her own consumption. He is able to exploit her because he has control over the wage which he has received for the labour power which she produced (Walby 1986: 53). Walby does not suggest attempting to quantify and compare levels of consumption and labour time nor does she address in her definition of patriarchal exploitation, the consumption of children or wives' contribution to the wage income of their families. Walby's discussion of women's domestic labour as surplus labour appropriated by their husbands bears some similarity to Harrison's model in the domestic labour debate, as discussed in chapter 5. The major problem with this model of how domestic and wage labour can be quantified in a comparable way is not addressed.

Walby's analysis is similar to Harrison's in another way, namely her patriarchal mode of production is always in articulation with another mode of production, for example capitalism, which is dominant and whose laws of motion give rise to changes or continuity in the patriarchal mode. The patriarchal mode of production does not have any autonomous laws of development and is therefore similar to the concept of a client mode of production (Harrison 1973). For example the expansion of capitalist production into such commodities as clothing and food production and the extension of public utilities like running water, gas and electricity have reduced the time spent on domestic labour (Walby 1990: 83). At the same time women continue to work within the patriarchal mode of production because of the unfavourable terms on which they are able to sell their labour power in the capitalist mode of production. Because patriarchal relations are personalised relations between individuals, the forces of production remain relatively backward and technologically inefficient. Larger scale cooperation and socialisation of the labour process are ruled out and tasks have to be duplicated within each household (Walby 1986: 54). It is partly the tension and conflict of interest between capitalism and patriarchy, as two competing systems of exploitation, which brings about change in the forms of patriarchal relations. It is also the impact of feminism and struggles by women against patriarchy.

In her more recent writing, although Walby still refers to men's exploitation of women taking place in the patriarchal mode of production, patriarchy itself is defined more broadly as a system of social structures and practices in which men dominate, oppress and exploit women (Walby 1990: 20). Exploitation is a more general concept and public patriarchy is assumed to be more significant relative to private patriarchy in contemporary industrial capitalist societies like Britain. Whilst individual men still exploit their wives within the patriarchal mode of production, women spend less and less of their time within privatised patriarchal production relations and more time under capitalist production relations which are 'patriarchal in a different way' (Walby 1990: 83). Moreover patriarchal relations in employment through which women are segregated into low paid jobs are the main means by which the patriarchal mode of production is sustained. The 'exploitation' of women within public patriarchy means that they are disadvantaged in all public institutions. The expropriation of women is done collectively rather than by individual patriarchs. The main example of public patriarchy that is relevant to a discussion of domestic labour concerns childrearing. Women's ability to dissolve marriage weakens husbands' control over their wives' domestic labour power. However although women can free themselves from an oppressive marriage they retain responsibility for childcare after the marriage is dissolved. Although women in female headed households escape the duties of serving their husbands, they also lose access to the income marriage might have brought. Walby suggests that women without men usually live in poverty. Hence while losing their own individual patriarch they retain the work, responsibilities and costs of childcare and remain subordinate to wider patriarchal structures (Walby 1990: 197). She suggests variations between ethnic groups in the forms of patriarchy with Afro-Caribbeans experiencing a predominantly public form of patriarchy (high female participation in paid work and high rates of female headed families), Muslim Asians a predominantly private form (lowest rates of paid work, male-headed families) and whites somewhere between the two but moving more closely to the Afro-Caribbean model (Walby 1990: 181).

Walby's analysis represents a refinement of Hartmann's dual systems theory. She identifies the potential for tension between capitalism and patriarchy which is largely absent from Hartmann's analysis and takes into account both the different experience of white and black women and the active role played by women themselves in bringing about change in patriarchal relations. Her work represents an ambitious search for a theory of patriarchy that is capable of encompassing major historical changes in women's position and large differences in the experiences of women of different races. However, patriarchal 'exploitation' is asserted but not defined in a way that can be tested. The maintenance of patriarchy in contemporary Britain is deemed to be sustained by a shift from 'private' to 'public' patriarchy but there is no clear analytical definition of public patriarchy. An omission in the theoretical approaches of all the writers discussed in this section is that, in focusing on gender divisions in production, they have relatively little to say about human reproduction. This issue is taken up in the next section.

6.4   PATRIARCHY AND THE SOCIAL RELATIONS OF HUMAN REPRODUCTION

6.4.1   Mackintosh

For Maureen Mackintosh (1977, 1979 and 1981) the defining feature of patriarchy was 'the control of women, especially of their sexuality and fertility, by men' (Mackintosh 1977: 122). Hence patriarchy was grounded in the social relationships of human reproduction and any attempt to analyse the gender division of labour which did not take these relationships into account would provide an inadequate account.

Mackintosh developed a feminist critique of both structural-functional and Marxist theories of gender inequality. Structural-functional social scientists, like Levi-Strauss, argued that the universal existence of a gender division of labour (the allocation of certain tasks predominantly or exclusively in relation to gender including wage work and non-wage work) could be explained by the need to maintain a reciprocal state of dependency between the sexes. For feminists however it is apparent that gender divisions of labour create, not reciprocal, but asymmetrical relations of dependency between the sexes and perpetuate men's control of women in a number of different ways. With the exception of the physical process of childbearing, there is no reason other than gender inequality for gender to be an organising principle of the social division of labour. A society where men and women were equal would be one where the arbitrary fact of sexual difference did not mark out the possibilities and limitations of economic activity for the individual (Mackintosh 1981: 4). Marx and Engels were wrong to assume that women's status varied directly with the extent to which they were engaged in social production. In some societies it is precisely the extent of women's responsibility for production that limits their political participation (for example where women bear the major responsibility for cultivation alongside fetching water, wood, childbirth, lactation, childcare and food preparation). Where women are the main producers, men's economic dependence upon them is often masked by ideological mechanisms which exaggerate the economic importance of men's tasks relative to women's and by political mechanisms which limit women's control of economic resources. An understanding of ideology, culture and political institutions is necessary to complement analysis of economic activity.

Mackintosh concluded that whatever form taken by the gender division of labour, men commonly had greater access to social resources, greater physical mobility, lesser responsibilities for self-maintenance and for care of the young and the old and less confined sexuality. That aspect of the gender division of labour which consisted of the care of children and provision of a range of domestic services for adults, referred to by some as 'reproductive work' (Beneria 1979), was a central element of the asymmetrical relations between the sexes (Mackintosh 1981: 9).

6.4.2 Folbre

Nancy Folbre (1982, 1983 and 1994) reintroduced into the discussion of patriarchy the original 'rule of the father' dimension. She emphasised the link between patriarchal control over adult children and patriarchal control over women. Where fathers were able to derive positive economic benefits from their children they had an incentive to maintain control over their wives' labour power and to see that it was devoted in large part to childbearing and childrearing (Folbre 1983: 270). She identified the key motivations underlying patriarchal control of women as men's interest in high rates of fertility, where this was of economic benefit to them, and their desire to minimise the costs to themselves of having children. Capitalism undermines patriarchal control of adult children and reduces the benefits to parents of children relative to the costs of having them, hence the historical decline in fertility rates associated with capitalist development. Patriarchy is therefore weakened as it is in men's interest for their wives to bring wage income into the household economy rather than children. Patriarchal control of women survives in truncated form in the sense that men have an interest in ensuring that they shift as much as possible of the cost of children and child-rearing on to women.

However for Folbre, patriarchy is only part of the explanation for women assuming the major responsibility for children. Men's desire to benefit from women's domestic labour does not provide a full explanation for it. Children and therefore the next generation and society as a whole also benefit (Ferguson and Folbre 1981: 319). In industrial societies it is society as a whole that has an interest in children as the most important human resource, not individual patriarchs. The concern that pervades industrial capitalist societies that women might reject their traditional childrearing responsibilities is not merely the product of patriarchy. It has emerged from the failure of society to generate new social arrangements and patterns of responsibility for childrearing. The question of what these new social arrangements might be relates to broader questions of the resourcing of childcare as well as to the division of labour in individual households (Folbre 1983: 279). Children may benefit as much or more from domestic labour than men but it would be unhelpful and inappropriate to describe the unequal exchanges between parents and children as 'exploitation' (Folbre 1982: 328).

However exploitation in the household is possible and Folbre (1982) suggests a way of adapting the labour theory of value and the concept of socially necessary labour and applying these to domestic labour. She justifies this by arguing unlike Walby, that economic rationality does operate on the choices made within households about how time is allocated. This acts as a force for efficiency in household labour which is comparable to the pressures of competition in capitalist production. It is therefore possible in theory to quantify both the socially necessary labour hours worked by individuals in wage labour and/or non-wage labour and the value of the product of waged and unwaged labour which they consume (or the value of their labour power according to Folbre's redefinition of value). The difference between labour hours worked and labour hours consumed is described as a form of surplus value (Folbre 1982: 322). This model gives rise to a number of possible outcomes in terms of relationships of exploitation. If the husband only is exploited as a wage worker outside the home and there is equal exchange within the household unit, only the husband is exploited. Alternatively the husband may recoup the surplus value appropriated by the capitalist through unequal exchange within the family and hence other family members are exploited instead of him. A third possibility is that the burden of exploitation is shared equally. Having argued that household labour is socially necessary labour and therefore commensurable with wage labour, Folbre concludes that it is possible to test the hypothesis that unequal exchange takes place within the family using the data available from household surveys and time budget studies on relative hours worked and relative quantities consumed.

The increased cost of children is an important but neglected aspect of economic development which Folbre has identified. This increased cost of children has been borne disproportionately by women within the confines of the household who, in most countries, have lacked the political, economic and cultural power to secure adequate support from fathers and society as a whole: 'Both the expansion of markets and the enlargement of state participation in the economy empowered women and youth just enough to destabilise the patriarchal organisation of social reproduction, but not enough to generate a non-patriarchal system that might fairly and efficiently meet the needs of children and other dependants' (Folbre 1994: 248).

In Folbre's writing, patriarchy emerges as a useful analytical concept which is grounded in historical and economic development. She clarifies the link between patriarchy and the social relations of human reproduction and acknowledges that women may play an active role in decisions about household labour and fertility. She provides a framework for empirical investigation of different possible gender relations within households which is worthy of further development. Her attempt to apply the concept of exploitation to domestic labour is more questionable. She does define exploitation more rigorously than some other feminist writers discussed in this chapter and sets out to test it empirically. However the analysis rests on the

problematic neoclassical economic assumption that households allocate their time rationally and that this ensures an
efficient allocation of time to domestic labour on a par with
the forces of competition in the market.

Nonetheless Folbre's historically grounded theory of patriarchy, which takes account of changes and variations in men's
motives and abilities to control women, of childrearing as a
labour process and of the distribution of the costs of rearing
the next generation in capitalist society, provides a helpful
framework for further development. The third strand of feminist theory that will be considered is one that combines global
and ecological perspectives.

6.5   PATRIARCHY AND GLOBAL CAPITALISM

Maria Mies (1986) sees capitalist patriarchy as a global system
in which women experience triple exploitation: by men (economically and as human beings) by capital as housewives and by
capital as wage workers. She defines exploitation, rather
loosely, as taking place where someone is 'living at the
expense of someone else' (Mies 1986: 36) and where the production process is controlled not by the direct producers but
by those who appropriate its products (Mies 1986: 71).

Mies' central argument is that the production of life and the
labour which produces use-values for the satisfaction of
human needs (subsistence production) is a precondition for
all other productive labour. The exploitation of non-wage
labourers (housewives, colonies and peasants) makes wage
labour and capitalist accumulation possible. This argument in
relation to colonies and peasants is in the tradition of Rosa
Luxemburg's argument about imperialism as a source of
capital accumulation, referred to in chapter 4. Mies charts the
development and spread of 'housewifization' across classes in
Europe and the USA in the context of colonial and imperialist
expansion of 'capitalist patriarchy'. Housewifization refers to
the transformation of women into housewives, first in the
middle class and, subsequently, in the working class. In the
eighteenth century housewives emerged in the European merchant capitalist class, linked with the development of the
luxury consumption that came with colonial trade (Mies 1986:

02). In nineteenth century Europe, working class women became housewives in order to ensure enough workers and soldiers for capital and the state and because male workers sought to exclude women from employment. By the end of the nineteenth century mass housewifization was also driven by capitalism's need for women as agents of consumption.

Here there are contradictory explanations offered but not explored and all are highly functionalist in approach. On the one hand the work of housewives was assumed to reduce the costs of reproducing labour power. On the other it was needed to create new markets for consumption goods (Mies 1986: 06). At the same time working class men also had an interest in having women as housewives because it enabled them to monopolise available wage work and control the money income of the family. Proletarian 'housewifization' in industrial capitalist countries would not have been possible without colonial exploitation. Hence Western male working class living standards were premised on the exploitation of external colonies as well as their wives' domestic labour.

Mies rejects Marx's distinction between necessary labour and leisure. For Marx self-realisation and human happiness could only be achieved outside the sphere of necessity, hence scientific and technological advances that enabled production to be automated and the working week reduced were necessary for humans to be able to devote themselves to self-fulfilling activities. Mies considers that most women would not share this perspective since, as mothers, they experience labour that is both burdensome and a source of self-fulfilment and who, unlike Marx are aware that much necessary labour, associated with the production of life, could not and should not be eliminated. Mies suggests an alternative feminist concept of labour focusing on the production of life as the goal of work and not the production of material wealth and argues that shortening daily or life-time labour time should not be the feminist objective. A vision of society in which labour time was reduced to a minimum and nearly all time was leisure time would not be an attractive vision for Mies (Mies 1986: 217).

Mies offers interesting insights here into the nature of work and the different ways it may be perceived by men and women. However the conclusion she draws that self-fulfilment through work is dependent on consumption and production being brought together is less compelling. She argues for economic autarky in which a community of people produce for their own needs within a specific region, emphasising in particular self-sufficiency in food and a transformation of the gender division of labour. She asserts, without explaining how it will happen, that men will have to share responsibility for the immediate production of life, childcare, housework, the care of the sick, elderly and 'relationship work' (Mies 1986: 222).

Mies stimulates many ideas and has attempted the challenging task of linking together analysis of gender, the international economy and ecological perspectives. She places the production of life, including the labour of giving birth to a child, centre stage as a human purposive activity. However Mies' conclusions and suggested strategies are disappointing. She does not distinguish between domestic labour which is highly burdensome and could be eliminated by the application of science and technology and domestic labour which is self-fulfilling and not subject to mechanisation. She romanticises use-value production and underestimates the benefits people and, especially women, derive from access to goods and services produced for the market. She provides no evidence to support her suggestion that economic autarky (with its associated shift of population from industry to agriculture) and women's liberation are compatible.

6.6   BLACK FEMINIST THEORY

A major critique of feminist patriarchy theory was initiated by black women who rejected the generalised concepts of 'men' and 'women' and highlighted the ways that white feminists use of universal concepts excluded the experience of black women and men (Carby 1982, Amos and Parmar 1984). White feminists had not taken sufficient account of the way in which, the experience of racism was often a more powerful and pervasive experience for black women in racist white societies than the experience of sexism. Hence the common interest, which black women and men shared, in resisting racism was as important, if not more important, than the divisive experience of sexism and patriarchal relations. Equally, the divisions between black and white women were often seen to be more significant than divisions between black women and men. For example, in Western European societies, at least some white women are in a dominant position, economically and culturally, relative to black men as well as black women.

In relation to domestic labour, household structure and gender relations, there are major differences in experience across races and ethnic groups. Many of the generalisations made by white feminists are inaccurate representations of black women's experience. There is also a diversity within black women's experience. The following discussion cannot do justice to this diversity since it draws primarily on African-American women's perspectives on race and patriarchy. These perspectives are offered as an important case study of how race and culture affect our understanding of gender and economics.

African-American and African-Caribbean women's experience is shaped by the history of slavery and colonialism in which black men were systematically denied positions in the white male hierarchy (Carby 1982: 215). For these black women, paid work has always been a necessary adjunct to motherhood since black men were denied access to a family wage. Full-time motherhood and housewifery never predominated in these communities and the opportunities available to white women to dedicate themselves to caring for their families were interpreted as a privilege to which many black women aspired:

> historically, black women have identified work in the context of family as humanizing labor, work that affirms their identity as women, as human beings showing love and care, the very gestures of humanity white supremacist ideology claimed black people were incapable of expressing. In contrast to labor done in a caring environment inside the home, labor outside the home was most often seen as stressful, degrading, and dehumanizing (Hooks 1984: 133–4).

Whilst privileged and powerful classes and groups have a number of social structures and institutions on which to rely, the household may be the primary support system available for the powerless and most oppressed groups (Hooks 1984: 37). Hence the white feminist interpretation of unpaid domestic labour as exploitation by men, fails to recognise the way in which black women have often seen it as resistance to oppression (Collins 1990: 44). The identification of the family as the central site of women's oppression in contemporary society in 1970s feminist theory was not helpful for black women seeking to analyse their own experience of oppression:

> We would not wish to deny that the family can be a source of oppression for us but we also wish to examine how the black family has functioned as a prime source of resistance to oppression. We need to recognize that during slavery, periods of colonialism and under the present authoritarian state, the black family has been a site of political and cultural resistance to racism (Carby 1982: 214).

Black feminists also questioned the way traditional feminist accounts oversimplified gender relations as top-down relations of domination and submission in which unwilling victims were forced to bend to the will of more powerful superiors and no account was taken of the acquiescence or resistance of the victim (Collins 1990: 227). This understanding is now more generally recognised in feminist accounts of women's experience of gender divisions. It is also accepted that certain social relationships can be experienced quite differently by different groups of women, with different histories and perspectives. Ironically black women have sometimes demonstrated a stronger desire for patriarchal arrangements than black men. Hooks (1982) highlights a tendency present among African-American women to aspire to construct the patriarchal family relations they witnessed in the white community: 'Much of the tension in black marriages and other male-female relationships was caused by black females' pressuring men to assume the breadwinner, head-of-the-household role. Often black men were not as upwardly mobile as black women wanted them to be' (Hooks 1982: 92).

However the patriarchal aspirations of men have been a strong cultural force in black movements. Anti-racist movements led by black men have often expressed this aspiration: 'The black male quest for recognition of his "manhood" in American society is rooted in his internalization of the myth that simply by having been born male, he has an inherent right to power and privilege' (Hooks 1982: 100).

Patriarchal aspirations can be understood in the context of the particular history of racism and gender construction. This is illustrated by the discredited black matriarchy myth in which black women were presented as rejecting their femininity by working outside the home. White male scholars perceived the independence, determination and initiative of black women as an attack on the masculinity of black men (Hooks 1982: 75).

A final important strand within the black feminist literature which is pertinent to our theme is the history of black women's employment in paid domestic work especially in contexts of formalised race segregation. In the USA whilst white men were able to exclude black men from well-paid jobs, 'white women were eager to surrender household chores to black female servants' (Hooks 1982: 91). In 1910 when over a half of all black women were in paid employment, a third of them were private domestic workers (Davis 1982: 237). By 1930 the proportion had risen to three fifths. A wider range of jobs opened up to black women during the Second World War but one third of those who were employed were still in domestic jobs in 1960. It was only the subsequent massive expansion of clerical employment that significantly dented black women's dependence on domestic service employment in the USA. Similar opening up of employment in South Africa in the post-apartheid era is likely to lead to a diminution in black women's dependence on domestic service there. Private domestic service was not a major source of employment for black women in Britain during the twentieth century, although a disproportionate number of African-Caribbean women found themselves restricted to cleaning and domestic work in the corporate and public sectors of the economy. The experience of black women's historical segregation in paid domestic work has informed critical perspectives on both the socialisation of domestic labour, as discussed in chapter 4, and on wages for housework, as discussed in chapter 5.

5.7   THE TWO WAVES OF FEMINISM

Post-1960s feminism differed from the feminism of the nineteenth and early twentieth centuries in the emphasis it placed firstly on male domination (as opposed to female subordination) and on the gender division of labour. Prior to the 1960s, the gender division of labour was perceived across the political spectrum to be natural. Even most of the champions of women's rights, whether Marxists or liberals, believed that it was natural and desirable for women to take responsibility for housework and childcare, either themselves or by delegating to servants, and that women were therefore, if employed, more likely to be suited to certain types of work than others. Earlier feminists, whilst accepting as given the gender division of labour, were opposed to the patriarchal context in which they perceived domestic labour to take place. For liberal thinkers like Mill, legal reform was required to give women equal rights within marriage and equal rights to education and employment. For Marxists it was the private aspect of domestic labour that was problematic, not the fact that it was done by women. These notions were based on assumptions about a natural link between childbearing, housework and childcare. Because the household was normally constituted as the unit for human reproduction, the more significant and time consuming human reproductive activities were, the more logical it seemed for women to undertake other domestic labour.

Human reproductive activities can be defined as those in which a clear biological division of labour exists between the sexes, a sexual as opposed to gender division of labour. Although grounded in biological difference, human reproductive activities vary in different historical and social contexts. Examples of this variability would be access to contraception, the duration of lactation, infant mortality rates, the degree of medical and professional intervention in childbirth, the number and spacing of births. Historical and social changes in human reproduction have disrupted what used to be perceived as a natural link between the gender division and the sexual division of labour. The ability to conceptualise the gender division of labour is itself a product of these historical changes.

Women in contemporary industrial societies generally have greater control of their fertility and sexuality than has been possible in other types of society. There have been important gains by feminist and labour movements in terms of rights to contraception, abortion, health care, sex education and divorce, and a diminution in the power of religious organisations to resist these changes. Children in industrial capitalist societies are no longer an economic asset but rather a drain on household resources, which intensifies the more households rely on both parents' earnings. Although the proportion of women bearing at least one child rose in the twentieth century, the average duration of time spent in pregnancy, childbirth and lactation was considerably less by the 1970s than it was during the first wave of feminism in the nineteenth and early twentieth century.

In industrial capitalist societies, women's capacity to earn is commonly valued more highly than their reproductive capacity. Mothering is often evaluated in terms of opportunity cost. A major impetus for second wave feminism was the opportunity for women to have children with fewer constraints than those imposed on women in previous generations by their human reproductive role. As what once appeared to be natural constraints have receded, men's resistance to gender equality became increasingly apparent. This may explain why conceptualising patriarchy was so important for feminists when, historically, patriarchal relationships were actually being undermined.

6.8   CONCLUSION

Patriarchy emerged as an important and widely used term among feminists in the 1970s. Its greatest value was in making visible the existence of the material social relationships and institutional underpinnings of men's power over women. It was used to extend understanding of gender inequality beyond a liberal feminist emphasis on the ideology of sexism. It was also important as a political concept, a 'struggle concept' conveying the totality and systemic nature of the oppressive and exploitative relations affecting women (Mies 1986: 37).

In the course of the 1980s, in response to black women's critique and the growing influence of post-structuralism and post-modernism (Barrett and Phillips 1992), attention shifted away from attempts to find overall explanations for women's oppression towards more localised empirically grounded research which looked at gender relations in clearly defined groups. The attention of socialist feminists shifted away from a general analysis of the relationships between capitalism and patriarchy, production and reproduction, class and sex oppression. The focus shifted to specific instances of gender domination and its interrelationship with class and race. Patriarchal relations, rather than patriarchy appeared a more appropriate concept, implying variation not universality (Smart 1983). Overarching structural explanations of inequality in terms of patriarchy and capitalism gave way to a more diffused concept of patriarchal power embedded in all social interactions. There continues to be a tension within feminism between the recognition of diversity and the aspiration to identify the common experiences among women on which contemporary feminism is based. It is understandable that feminists should have tried in the ways discussed in this chapter to develop a theory of patriarchal exploitation. The domestic labour debate established the limited usefulness of the Marxist conceptual framework as applied to domestic labour. However it left feminists dissatisfied with the conclusion that the domestic sphere was a site of oppression for women not of exploitation.

Nonetheless a careful consideration of all the different feminist attempts to apply exploitation to gender relations leads to the conclusion that the concept is neither necessary nor particularly helpful from an analytical standpoint. In many cases it has been applied very vaguely with no attempt to ground it empirically. The one attempt that has been made to define it more rigorously and in a way that can be verified empirically, has rested on the problematic neoclassical economic assumption that households allocate their time rationally and that this ensures an efficient allocation of time to domestic labour on a par with the forces of competition in the market. If specifying and measuring exploitation is so difficult we should ask ourselves whether it is really necessary or helpful to do so. We do not need the concept exploitation in order to demonstrate gender inequality or the fact that men benefit materially and economically from women's domestic labour. It is more helpful to concentrate on collecting and analysing empirically more straightforward data such as time use, income and consumption patterns. Another reason for rejecting exploitation as a useful concept for analysing domestic labour is the way it diverts attention away from what has become the central component of domestic labour in industrial capitalist societies, namely the care of dependent children and adults. The centrality of childcare to domestic labour in industrial societies is discussed in chapter 9.

Feminists have used the concept patriarchy in several different ways that have been discussed in this chapter. Sometimes it refers to the arrangements through which men control women's sexuality and fertility and to the organisation of human reproduction. Sometimes it refers to more diffuse social relationships between men which contribute to women's economic subordination. Sometimes it survives as a cultural aspiration amongst men, and even women, to whom racism or class have denied a stake in economic development.

For the concept patriarchy to be analytically useful it needs to be grounded in the social relationships of human reproduction and restricted to contexts in which individual patriarchs can be identified. Patriarchy derives from particular household social relationships which characterise particular historical periods, or classes, or races or societies and which are sustained by forces internal and external to the household. The essential elements of patriarchy are present where husbands/fathers are heads of household, wives/mothers are economically and legally dependent on the head of household, children are an economic resource and husbands control their wives' sexuality and fertility. In periods of patriarchal stability all these elements are present and these relationships are sustained because all the different parties involved have an interest in sustaining them, not just men. Women have an interest in marriage because it provides them with an economically supported and socially acceptable context in which to carry out what is perceived to be their natural reproductive role. The more children constitute an economic resource, the more highly valued motherhood is likely to be. This is not to deny that in highly patriarchal societies there is resistance among women to their subordinate status and persecution of women who attempt resistance. The wider society (church, state) also has an interest in sustaining patriarchy because it provides a framework for intergenerational and parental mutual aid which limits the incidence of poverty and dependence on social structures external to households and families.

Where patriarchy is used to refer to more socially diffused power relationships outside the household and becomes detached from its link with human reproduction, it loses its analytical force and is reduced to a description of male dominance rather than an explanation. This is not to deny the historical connections that may have existed between, for example gender segregation in the labour market and patriarchal household forms. Nor is it to minimise the importance of male bonding and solidarity across social institutions other than households. Rather it is to say that gender relations are constituted by a shifting matrix of elements including race, class, sexuality, fertility and care of dependants, all of which operate with degrees of autonomy and linkage. Patriarchy offers a historically grounded rather than universal explanation of male dominance. It is as unhelpful for feminists to use patriarchy as a universal explanation for gender inequality as it is for men to maintain it as a universal aspiration. To tease out the linkages between domestic labour and gender inequality in Britain in the last decades of the twentieth century requires a closer examination of the changing nature of domestic labour and shifting patterns of employment. The next chapter focuses on this task.

7 Domestic Labour, Employment and Gender Relations

> Typical male paid work patterns – full-time continuous employment across the life-cycle – impose an external constraint on families' time budgets; women provide the flexibility. Although most women define their decision to work part-time as 'voluntary', the decision is based on the household division of labour (OECD 1994: 90).

This chapter is concerned with the ways domestic labour interacts with women's employment and with the socio-economic and gendered context of women's work choices. Although there are different interpretations of the extent to which women's employment has increased in the UK in the post Second World War period and the previous 100 years (Hakim 1993), there is no dispute about the rise in women's labour force participation since the 1950s. The typical married couple household has been transformed from one that has a male breadwinner and female housewife to one that has husband and wife both in employment, although there has also been an increase in the proportion of unemployed couples (Barclay 1995: 23). This chapter discusses recent research on trends in domestic labour and the interrelationships between patterns of women's employment and the gender division of domestic labour, mainly with reference to heterosexual couple households.

7.1 TRENDS IN DOMESTIC LABOUR

Trends in domestic labour and gender divisions have been difficult to track. Not only are there problems of measurement and interpretation of data for domestic labour/household production (Goldschmidt-Clermont 1982). There is also a shortage of comparable data for different historical periods. Time budget studies, based on respondent diaries, are the method that has proved most effective (Gershuny and Robinson 1988) and these have been used as a basis for drawing some general conclusions about trends in domestic labour time within particular industrialised countries and for the group of industrialised countries as a whole.

In the UK, prior to the 1980s, the only time use studies available for longitudinal analysis were those carried out by Mass Observation and the BBC Audience Research Department. Analysing the results of these time budget studies for housewives (including part-time employed as well as non-employed women), Gershuny found that time spent on domestic labour had increased from 47.5 hours per week in 1937 to 52 hours per week in 1961 (1985: 150) in spite of the widespread diffusion of household utilities and appliances in that period (see table 7.1).

Gershuny's explanation for the increase in time spent on domestic labour during that period was the virtual disappearance of domestic servants in middle class households. Whilst servants were almost universal in the middle class households surveyed in 1937, they were very rare in the 1961 sample (Gershuny 1985: 151). (The small number of middle class

Table 7.1   Time spent by housewives on domestic work (in hours per week), UK, 1937–61

	all housewives (non-employed and part-time employed women)	working class housewives
	hours per week	
1937	47.5	66.0
1961	52.0	52.0

Source: Gershuny 1985: 150
Data are derived from time use diaries collected by Mass Observation in 1937 and a national sample time budget diary survey carried out by the BBC Audience Research Department in 1961.

housewives without domestic servants in 1937 actually spent rather more time on domestic labour than working class women.) Whilst middle class housewives increased the time they spent on domestic labour, there was a decline in time spent on domestic labour by working class housewives from 66 to 52 hours. Gershuny suggested that this decline in domestic labour for working class housewives reflected the diffusion of domestic technology and increasing participation in part-time employment (though the data for non-employed housewives also showed a declining trend). By 1961 the difference in the amount of time being spent by working class and middle class housewives on domestic labour had virtually disappeared with both groups spending about 52 hours per week (7.4 hours per average day).

Thereafter there appeared to be little distinction to be drawn in the patterns of overall time spent by women in different social classes but there were clear differences between non-employed, part-time employed and full-time employed women. Thomas & Zmroczek (1985), based their study on the viewer/listener availability surveys of the BBC, from which Gershuny and Thomas (1980) had constructed comparable data sets. They found that between 1961 and 1975 women generally reduced the time they spent on domestic labour from an average of about 37 hours per week to about 32 (see table 7.2). The average time spent by men on domestic labour was a lot less and also declined slightly from about 10 hours per week to just over 9 hours during the same period, although this decline was accounted for entirely by a reduction in time spent gardening. If gardening is excluded men's domestic labour time actually rose from 7 hours per week to 8 hours with increased time spent on shopping, domestic travel and odd jobs (Thomas & Zmroczek 1985: 113). There were significant reductions in the time spent by women part-time workers and non-employed women on domestic labour (from 43 to 35 hours and from 53 to 44 hours respectively). However the domestic labour time of full-time employed women remained constant at about 18 hours. Thomas and Zmroczek concluded that women in full-time jobs had reduced their domestic labour time to a level below which it was unlikely to fall without a significant increase in the contribution of other household members (1985: 112).

Table 7.2   Time spent on domestic work* (in hours per week), GB, 1961–1975 by sex and employment status

	All women	Full-time employed women	Part-time employed women	Non-employed women	All men	Full-time employed men	Non-employed men
1961	36.8	17.7	42.6	53.4	9.9	8.3	26.4
1975	31.5	17.6	35.4	44.3	9.3	7.7	21.7

Source: Thomas & Zmroczek (1985: 113)

* Domestic work here includes childcare, shopping, domestic travel, odd jobs, gardening, knitting and sewing as well as routine domestic work.

Data are derived from BBC Audience Research Department national time use sample surveys of individuals from which Gershuny and Thomas (1980) had constructed comparable data sets.

More recently an ESRC-funded national time budget sample survey (Gershuny et al. 1986) produced data for 1983/4 which was comparable with the earlier BBC research data. In the period from the mid-seventies to the mid-eighties, women reduced and men increased the time they spent on routine domestic work (see table 7.3). These data have been interpreted as marking the beginnings of a more egalitarian shift in the gender division of domestic labour (Gershuny et al. 1994) following on from women's increased participation in employment. There is clear evidence that men were participating to a greater extent from the mid-seventies in domestic labour, including the traditionally female areas. Men in full-time employment for example increased the time they spent by an average of half an hour a day, from less than 8 hours a week to 11 hours, with most of the increased time spent on routine domestic work, shopping and travel (see table 7.3).

However the reduced domestic burden on women which might have been expected with men's increased participation did not materialise. As Wajcman (1991: 93) points out, the reduction in the time women spent on routine domestic work was offset by increased time spent on childcare and shopping. The time spent by women on domestic labour overall remained static between the mid-seventies and mid-eighties (for women in full-time employment at nearly 21 hours a week) or actually rose (for women in part-time employment from 33 to 37 hours and for non-employed women from 43 to 45 hours a week) during this period. The data in table 7.3 suggest that men's slightly increased role in routine domestic work enabled women to reduce the time they spent on this component of domestic labour but that, for women with children, this was offset by spending more time on childcare. Moreover men's increased involvement in shopping did not reduce women's involvement, partly because of the trend for more shopping to be done by couples together. For those in full-time employment, the average time spent by men of 11 hours a week on domestic labour remained at only about half that of the 21 hours average for women.

It is therefore not surprising to find that employed women have less time for leisure activities than employed men, and women who are employed full-time have the least amount of free time. For example in 1992/93 female full-time employ-

Table 7.3   Time spent on different categories of domestic work* (in hours per week), UK, 1961, 1974/5 and 1983/4 by sex and employment status

	Women, Full-time Employed	Women, Part-time Employed	Women, Non-employed	Men, Full-time Employed
Routine Domestic Work				
1961	15.5	29.4	35.9	1.5
1974/5	15.2	24.2	29.2	1.5
1983/4	13.7	23.2	26.4	2.8
Shopping/Travel				
1961	2.7	4.8	6.3	0.8
1974/5	3.5	5.6	7.0	2.0
1983/4	4.3	7.5	8.3	3.3
Childcare				
1961	0.5	2.2	4.6	0.5
1974/5	0.7	1.6	4.2	0.6
1983/4	1.2	4.0	6.8	1.3
Odd Jobs				
1961	1.5	1.5	2.0	2.8
1974/5	1.2	1.4	2.1	3.4
1983/4	1.5	2.3	3.4	3.6
Total domestic labour				
1961	20.2	37.9	48.8	5.8
1974/5	20.5	32.8	42.5	7.5
1983/4	20.7	37.0	44.8	11.0

Source: Gershuny and Jones (1987: 24)
* Domestic work here excludes gardening as the data were not comparable. Data are derived from national time use surveys of individuals carried out in 1961 and 1974/5 by the BBC Audience Research Department and the national ESRC time-budget sample in 1983/4 (see Gershuny et al. 1986).

ees, although spending about 5 hours less per week on employment and travel to work than male full-time employees had about 14 hours less free time per week than their male counterparts, because of the extra time they spent on domestic labour (see table 7.4). Full-time male employees spen

about 26 hours per week on 'essential activities' (routine domestic work, shopping, childcare and personal hygiene) whilst
female full-time employees spent 47 hours per week on these
activities (more than the time they spent on employment).
Female part-time employees had more free time than female
full-time employees (9 hours more per week), but less free
time than male full-time employees (5 hours less per week).
Although full-time housewives had more free time than male
full-time employees, there is an interesting similarity between
the amounts of time spent on 'essential activities' by housewives in 1993 (68 hours per week) and the amounts of time
spent on domestic work by working class housewives in 1937
(66 hours per week) (see table 7.1).

To summarise, in the two decades between the early 1960s
and 1980s in Britain, women who were in part-time employment or not in employment reduced the time they spent on
domestic labour but there was no reduction overall for women
in full-time jobs. Whilst all groups of women reduced the time

Table 7.4   Time use in hours per week by employment status and sex, GB, 1992/93

Minutes per day spent on:	Full-time male employees	Full-time female employees	Part-time female employees	Full-time housewives
Employment and travel to and from work	47.1	42.2	20.8	0.4
Essential cooking, shopping and housework	13.0	25.6	32.6	38.2
Essential child-care, other shopping and personal hygiene	13.2	20.0	25.2	29.4
Free time	45.7	31.4	40.6	51.1

Source: The Henley Centre for Forecasting cited Central Statistical Office
1994a: 130

they spent on routine domestic work, this was more than offset
in the case of women in full-time employment by the greater
amount of time spent on shopping and childcare. For non-
employed women and those in part-time employment, labour
saving gains between 1961 and 1974 were partially offset by increased domestic demands on their time during the next
decade up to the mid-1980s. Paradoxically this was the period
when men increased the time they spent on domestic labour
most significantly by about half an hour per day. Men's increased involvement in domestic labour during this period
appears to have been in response to increased demands on
the household unit rather than any overall substitution of
male for female domestic labour.

Chapter 8 will discuss the extent to which households were
able during this period to substitute market goods and services for domestic labour. In Britain, market substitution for
domestic labour was limited and increased married female
employment primarily served two other functions. For many
households, especially during periods of recession, it facilitated the maintenance of living standards in the context of in-
secure and lower male earnings. For other households, and in
the boom years, married women's employment increased material standards of consumption, supporting growth in consumer expenditure, especially on manufactured goods. On
balance, for couples aged 24–55, rising female labour force
participation in the 1980s slowed the growth of income inequality because female earnings were less polarised than
male earnings (Barclay 1995: 22). The share of family income
contributed by female partners rose most where male partners
were on low incomes. For the population as a whole there was
an increased polarisation of income between the relatively
'work rich' couple households of working age (particularly
those without children) and the 'work poor' groups like single
pensioner and lone parent households, dependent on state
benefits pegged in real terms (Gregg and Wadsworth 1994).

Most of the reduction in time spent by women on domestic
labour from the early 1960s to the 1980s can be accounted for
by the declining proportion of women engaged in full-time
housework. There was remarkably little reduction in the time
spent by women on domestic labour once allowance is made
for the increased proportion of women in employment

Within each employment category women reduced and men increased the time they spent on routine domestic work during this period and overall there was a reduction in routine domestic work, supported by improvements in household technology, which will be discussed in chapter 8. However women continued to carry out the bulk of routine domestic work and even women in full-time employment did about 11 hours a week more of this type of domestic labour than men in full-time employment. Both men and women also spent increasing amounts of time on childcare, shopping and associated travel. Men (in full-time employment) increased their participation in domestic labour overall from 6 to 11 hours a week. However women in full-time employment still spent 21 hours a week in the early 1980s, nearly double the time spent by men.

The above discussion is based entirely on data drawn from samples of individual men and women, taking account of different employment categories for women. It gives an overview of trends over time but only limited insight into the gender division of labour in specific households. Sections 7.2 to 7.4 will relate this discussion to evidence available on the different types of heterosexual couple household in terms of women's employment status. Variations in time spent on domestic labour by men and women are related to female employment status in these households. The next three sections explore the interrelationship between female employment status and the domestic gender division of labour in households where partners are married or cohabiting. Evidence on the domestic division of labour is discussed in the different cases where female partners are in full-time and part-time employment and where they are not employed.

7.2   WOMEN IN FULL-TIME EMPLOYMENT

It is well established that women who are in full-time employment spend less time on domestic labour than non-employed and part-time employed women. In the mid-eighties domestic labour time varied between 45 hours a week for non-employed women and 21 hours for full-time employed women (see table 7.3). The Henley Centre for Forecasting estimated that in

1992/3 women who were not employed spent 22 hours more per week on essential domestic activities than full-time female employees (see table 7.4). There is a trade-off for women between domestic labour and paid employment, irrespective of the presence of dependent children. This is hardly surprising since there are only so many hours in a day and if women are absent from the home for reasons of employment for more than 40 hours per week, they will obviously spend less time on domestic labour. But how is this to be interpreted? Do they use their wages to purchase goods, services and technology that replace or reduce domestic labour? Do partners take a greater share of the domestic labour? Do they carry out tasks more quickly and efficiently? Do they accept lower or different standards of household and family care? Is there less to do just because their absence means that demands that would otherwise arise are not made, a kind of reverse Parkinson's Law? All these possibilities have something to contribute to explaining why full-time employed women spend less time on domestic labour. However it is also the case that getting employment can actually raise standards of domestic labour. A woman in her fifties, who had worked at home full-time for twenty years and then got an office job, made the following comment in Luxton's study of three generations: 'I used to work around the house in old slacks and I had to wash my clothes maybe once a week. Now I rinse out my nylons every night and I wash my blouses and underthings at least twice each week and sometimes more' (Luxton 1980: 183).

Full-time employment does increase the likelihood that partners will take a greater share of domestic labour. Martin and Roberts (1984: 101) found that wives and husbands were most likely to share domestic labour equally if the wife had a full-time job. Childcare was more likely to be shared than housework and was considered to be shared equally by 67 per cent of the wives in full-time employment and 41 per cent of non-employed wives (see table 7.5). Housework was considered to be shared equally by 44 per cent of wives in full-time employment and by only 17 per cent of non-employed wives. The researchers were of the opinion that these results understated the proportion of domestic work done by women since many appeared to interpret 'sharing equally' as meaning only that tasks were shared when husband and wife were both at home even if she was doing additional work when he was not at home. This point however does not invalidate the clear relationship that is demonstrated between women's employment status and the gender division of domestic labour. However, in 1980 when the survey was carried out, a majority of full-time employed women (54 per cent) considered that they did most or all the housework and 29 per cent thought that they did most or all the childcare.

This link between the degree of sharing of domestic tasks and the employment status of women is also demonstrated for the late 1980s to early 1990s by the *British Social Attitudes* report (Social and Community Planning Research 1992: 101). The 1991 survey found that in households where both the man and woman worked full-time, responsibility for general domestic duties was shared equally in 24 per cent of households. Equal sharing was reported in only 13 per cent and 6 per cent respectively of households where the man worked and the woman worked part-time or was not employed. The *British Social Attitudes* report also supports Martin and Robert's other conclusion that the people they interviewed had overstated the degree of sharing by husbands of domestic work. Two thirds of the women in couple households who were in full-time employment were still mainly responsible in 1991 for general domestic duties (see table 7.6). This continuing double burden is the main reason why women who are in full-time employment have less leisure time than any other group. Marsh (1991: 68) also found full-time women employees reporting higher levels of fatigue than males or part-time females.

One group of women full-time employees who are likely to suffer most from work overload are those who return to full-time jobs after maternity leave. Brannen and Moss found that among couples who had recently had a child and who both worked full-time, women did well over half the domestic work. The women also spent over 20 hours a week longer in sole charge of their child than the men (Brannen and Moss 1991: 161).

The fact that full-time employment by no means guarantees equal sharing of domestic labour between partners suggests that other factors are also important. Relative incomes of spouses also appear to influence the domestic division of labour and women's overall lower earnings will tend to work

Table 7.5   Women's views about how housework and childcare is shared with husbands by wife's employment status, GB, 1980

All married women*			
	Full-time employed	Part-time employed	Not employed	All
Views about housework	%	%	%	%
Wife does all or most	54	77	81	73
Shared half and half	44	23	17	26
Husband does all or most	2	0	2	1
Married women with children under 16*			
Views about child care	%	%	%	%
Wife does all or most	29	44	59	49
Shared half and half	67	55	41	50
Husband does all or most	4	1	0	1

* Excludes women with disabled husbands and cases where most of the housework/childcare is done by someone else.
Source: Martin and Roberts 1984: 101–2

against husbands taking an equal share. Ross (1987) in her US study found an inverse relationship between husbands' participation in the domestic division of labour and the husband/wife earnings differential. She also found that black husbands were more likely than white husbands to share

Table 7.6   *Responsibility for general domestic duties in couple households 1991 (1987 figures in brackets) by woman's employment status*

| | Respondents living in households where man is employed and woman is: | | |
	full-time employed	part-time employed	not employed
Who is responsible for general domestic duties?	%	%	%
Mainly woman	67 (72)	83 (88)	89 (91)
Shared equally Who looks after sick children?	24 (22)	13 (7)	6 (5)
Mainly man	3	2	–
Mainly woman	44	51	80
Shared equally	52	48	20
Who organises household money and bills?			
Mainly man	27	29	40
Mainly woman	44	41	36
Shared equally	28	30	23

Source: Social and Community Planning Research 1988: 184 and 1992: 101 and 104

housework and that more educated husbands made a larger contribution to domestic labour (although women's educational background had no effect on the domestic division of labour). The combination of male unemployment and female full-time employment is one that is particularly conducive to a more flexible and egalitarian division of domestic labour (Wheelock 1990: 111 and Morris 1993: 48).

Men's attitudes about who should be responsible for domestic tasks also correlates more closely with the division of labour in their own household than is the case for women. Newell (1993), in her study of male and female full-time employees in two major UK companies, found that the men had a much more traditional and gendered view of the domestic division of labour, while women were more likely to believe in the equal sharing of all tasks. Moreover there was a close relationship for the men between their vision of how tasks should be divided and how they were actually divided. For women there was no such general relationship. The reality was more traditional and gendered than they believed should be the case.

The more egalitarian division of labour which is demonstrated in some households where women have full-time employment, may come about after a lengthy process of negotiation and adaptation. Gershuny's analysis of the use of time and work histories of a sample of couples in 1987 found that the longer wives had been in full-time employment, the more likely it was for husbands to take a greater or equal share of household work (Gershuny 1992: 90). Where wives had been in full-time employment for less than 21 months, husbands' share of total work time (paid and domestic) averaged 46 per cent. Only when women had been in full-time employment for over five years did men's contribution rise to 50 per cent. This led Gershuny to conclude that there was a process of 'lagged adaptation' in men's participation in domestic work following on from their wives returning to full-time employment.

Bonney and Reinach found that in couple households where the woman was in full-time employment there was more likely to be discussion about, and change over time, in the division of domestic labour. Whereas in two thirds of the households where the woman was not employed or in part-time employment, respondents reported that they 'did what seemed natural at first, without change' (Bonney and Reinach 1993: 623).

Although attitudes are generally more egalitarian in couple households where the wife is in full-time employment, even in these households men have a more traditional view of the gender division of labour than women. The British Social Attitudes Survey found 72 per cent of women and 58 per cent of men in these households disagreed with the statement: 'a husband's job is to earn the money; a wife's job is to look after home and family (see table 7.7).

Bonney and Reinach found that women in full-time employment were the group least satisfied with leisure time (33 per cent dissatisfied compared with 19 per cent dissatisfied among non-employed and part-time employed women). It appears that there is little interest among men in trading money for more time to spend with their families. Marsh found that 16 per cent of full-time female employees, but only 8 per cent of men, would seek a job with shorter hours for less pay if they moved to another job (Marsh 1991: 75). Conversely 19 per cent of men and only 10 per cent of full-time women would seek a job with longer hours for more pay.

To summarise, full-time employment for women increases the chance of an egalitarian domestic division of labour but at the cost of reducing the time they have available for leisure as compared with men and with women who are not employed or employed part-time. Moving from a traditional gendered division of domestic labour to a more egalitarian one may not be achieved for several years after women return to full-time employment, following a break in employment or a period of

Table 7.7   *Male and female attitudes to the gender division of labour in couple households by woman's employment status 1991*

Man is employed and woman is:	% disagreeing or strongly disagreeing to statement: 'A husband's job is to earn the money; a wife's job is to look after home and family'	
	Men	Women
employed full-time	58	72
employed part-time	49	45
not employed	33	40

Source: Social and Community Planning Research 1992: 99

part-time employment, and may require protracted negotiation and renegotiation initiated and sustained by women
themselves. Perhaps it is not surprising in these circumstances
that many women opt instead for part-time employment and
the more traditional gender division of domestic labour which
comes with it.

7.3   WOMEN IN PART-TIME EMPLOYMENT

The last thirty years have seen dramatic shifts in social attitudes to women's employment. The bar that operated on
married women's employment in many occupations in the in-
terwar period did not finally disappear until the 1960s. During
that decade, most women as well as men believed that only
single women and childless married women should have paid
jobs (Hunt, 1968a: 188, 1968b: 289). But by 1980 only
30 per cent of married women agreed with the statement that
'Women can't combine a career and children' and 53 per cent
disagreed with it (Martin and Roberts 1984: 175). By 1991 all
but 6 per cent of men and women believed that women with
children should be in paid employment after their children
start school. However, part-time employment was the preferred option for mothers of school-aged children for 63 per
cent of the population (Social and Community Planning
Research 1992: 100). As many as 33 per cent also thought that
women should work part-time when they have a pre-school
child (although 52 per cent still considered these women
should not do any paid work). The actual patterns of employment among women with dependent children are discussed in
more detail in chapter 9 (see table 9.1).

Women with dependent children are usually considered to
be the typical part-time employee. In 1992 40 per cent of
part-time workers were in this category. Married women with
dependent children were more likely to work part-time (40
per cent of this group) than lone mothers of whom only 24
per cent were employed part-time in 1991/3 (OPCS 1995:
65). However women without dependent children represented a slightly higher proportion (45 per cent of part-time
workers) and the remaining 15 per cent were men (see table
7.8).

Two thirds of people, when asked why they worked part-time in 1990, stated that they did not want a full-time job (Watson and Fothergill 1993: 216). People preferred part-time employment for a number of different reasons, 31 per cent of part-time workers choosing to do so in order to spend more time with their children and 14 per cent saying that they would like to work full-time but it would be too difficult for them because of domestic commitments. It is clear that while most women who work part-time make a positive choice to do so, others feel constrained to accept it as the only realistic option. Women's work strategies are not preconceived blue-prints but responses to the opportunities and resources that are available to them (McCrone 1994: 89).

In the early 1990s there was a rise in the proportion of part-time workers stating the reason for part-time employment was that they could not find a full-time job, from 6 per cent in 1990 to 14 per cent in 1993/4 (Labour Force Survey esti-mates). This shift reflected the impact of the recession, struc-

Table 7.8   Part-time employment by sex and for women by age of youngest dependent child, GB, 1992

	% of part-time employees
Men	14.6
Women	85.4
of whom youngest dependent child is aged:	
0–4	15.6
5–10	14.7
11–15	9.8
women with no children under 16	45.4
Total	100

Source: Watson and Fothergill 1993: 214

tural changes in the demand side of the labour market and a rise in the proportion of men in part-time jobs, who were more likely than women to be seeking full-time employment. Amongst male part-time employees 33 per cent stated that they could not find a full-time job compared to 16 per cent of females without dependent children who were part-time employees and 7 per cent of females with dependent children. A rising proportion of part-time workers were also students (36 per cent of males and 15 per cent of females without children) (Sly 1994: 405).

Women part-time workers have a variety of reasons for working part-time and motivations often change over time. In Watson and Fothergill's sample the largest group were voluntary part-timers who had initially chosen to work part-time because of childcare or other domestic responsibilities although most of these acknowledged 'that "if things were different" they might work full-time, but given their circumstances they did not want to' (Watson and Fothergill 1993: 216). More detailed reasons mentioned were: the view of the women that childcare is the mother's primary responsibility, especially in the early years; not wanting children to be 'latchkey kids'; the problem of school holidays; as children grow up other care responsibilities taking over; husbands and sons wanting dinner on the table when they come home from work; and husbands wanting their wives at home.

Part-time jobs are generally low paid and low skilled, particularly in Britain (Organisation for Economic Cooperation and Development 1994: 83) as indicated by the fact that average hourly earnings of female part-time employees are only 74 per cent of those of full-time female employees (Department of Employment 1993: A9.7 and F178.3). It is therefore somewhat surprising to find that part-time employees report higher levels of job satisfaction than full-time employees (Watson and Fothergill 1993: 220). It appears that for part-time employees job satisfaction may be derived as much from the way the job dovetails so conveniently with their domestic labour commitments as from the intrinsic qualities of jobs that are part-time. Marsh found that women in part-time employment expressed much higher levels of satisfaction with the time they had both for their families and for their own leisure, as compared with male and female full-time employees (1991: 68). It should be noted however that women who work part-time still have less free time on average than men who are employed full-time (see table 7.4).

Gallie and White (1994: 100) also found a higher level of job satisfaction among permanent part-time workers than any other category of workers and that hours of work was the point on which they stood out as most satisfied. However they also demonstrated greater levels of satisfaction with supervisory arrangements, job security, the ability of management, even with their pay, than permanent full-time workers. Given the evidence that they had less discretion and lower rates of pay than full-timers, these results suggest that high levels of job satisfaction for part-timers are linked in part to lower levels of expectation about certain aspects of employment (Gallie and White 1994: 102). The only issue on which permanent part-timers were relatively dissatisfied was promotion prospects.

Although part-time women employees spend over twenty hours per week on average on paid work, the gender division of domestic labour in their households remains very similar to that in households where the woman is not employed (Social and Community Planning Research 1992: 103). Perhaps this is not surprising as the commonest pattern for couples' working hours is for the woman's shorter hours to be contained completely within those of the man. Marsh (1991: 71) found that 48 per cent of women employed part-time started paid work each day after their partners and finished before them.

However evidence from the *British Social Attitudes* survey suggests that there are two domestic tasks where the gender division of labour is similar for households with part-time and full-time women workers. In both cases men take a similar and much greater role in looking after sick children (see table 7.6). Also women are most likely to organise household money and bills. Other research indicates a rather more complex pattern of household management and control of finances linked to both levels of household income and proportion of household income contributed by wives. The higher the household income the more likely it is for the husband to control finances and the higher the proportion of income contributed by the wife, or the lower the household income, the greater the wife's control of finances (Pahl 1989: 109).

Apart from the specific areas just discussed, it does not appear that any major changes occur in men's participation in domestic labour as a result of their partners switching from full-time housework to part-time employment. This is less surprising when account is taken of the fact that women's part-time earnings will normally be very low in comparison with those of men. Average hourly earnings of part-time female employees were only 59 per cent of average male hourly earnings in 1993 (Department of Employment 1993: A8.11 and F178.3). Their jobs will normally offer little hope of future promotion or earnings enhancement and are more likely to reflect downward than upward occupational mobility (Gallie and White 1994: 91). In this context the expansion of part-time female employment has brought only minor changes to the traditional male breadwinner/female housewife model of gender divisions.

Morris found that households with an unemployed male partner and part-time employed female partner had the most rigidly segregated gender division of domestic labour. Men who feel their gender identity has been challenged by unemployment may be able to resist any further challenge to this identity because their partners' part-time employment continues to accommodate traditional female domestic responsibilities. Part of the explanation may also be that the combination of male unemployment and female part-time employment is expected to be a temporary one because of the financial disincentive to women working for low earnings in benefit-dependent households. If the assumption is that the man will shortly find employment again there will be less pressure for traditional domestic arrangements to be altered (Morris 1993: 49).

However, in the 1990s there were some signs that men whose wives worked part-time were beginning to recognise the need to increase their participation in domestic labour. Warde and Hetherington (1993) found in their survey of couple households in Greater Manchester that the husbands of part-time workers were the most likely to state that they did less than their fair share of routine domestic tasks. Of these men 47 per cent said they did less than they should, compared to

33 per cent of men in general. It can also be seen from table
7.6 that the proportion of men sharing responsibility for
general domestic duties with their wives rose in these households from 7 per cent in 1987 to 13 per cent in 1991 (Social
and Community Planning Research 1988 and 1992). Horrell,
Rubery and Burchell (1994a: 119) found that male partners of
women in part-time employment were more likely to be involved in looking after children after school than was the case
where female partners were in full-time employment. This is
probably explained by the higher incidence of shift or stag-
gered working patterns where women have part-time jobs.
Among women, part-time employees are more likely to work
evenings and weekends than full-time employees (Horrell et
al. 1994a: 108). These working patterns make it more likely
that husbands will take responsibility for meals and childcare
in their wives' absence.

7.4   FULL-TIME HOUSEWORKERS

Although the proportion of women in this group has declined
to only 17 per cent of women in the 16-59 age range (Sly 1993:
484), most married women and many non-married women
still experience a period of full-time housework at some stage
in their working lives. Lone mothers formed a growing proportion of full-time houseworkers in the last three decades of
the twentieth century. Not surprisingly non-employed married
women spend more time on domestic labour than other
married women and their households demonstrate the most
traditional form of gender division of domestic labour.
Although, on average, non-employed women have more time
for leisure than employed women (see table 7.4), there is a
large variation in experience within the group. Those women
who care for sick or disabled elderly relatives (Nissel and
Bonnerjea 1982) or who have children under school age can
be on call for up to 24 hours a day and therefore experience
the heaviest workloads of all. On the other hand there are still
significant numbers of full-time houseworkers who do not
have major childcare responsibilities. The ESRC Social
Change and Economic Life Initiative survey found that only
about a half of full-time houseworkers mentioned responsibili-

ties for young children as the reason for not looking for paid work (Bonney and Reinach 1993: 617).

Bonney and Reinach found that most of their Aberdeen sample of full-time houseworkers whose youngest child was under five spent at least 84 hours a week on dependent care (1993: 619). These women were asked to compare full-time housework with previous paid employment. They reported an increased variety of tasks as houseworkers but increased tiredness and social isolation and reductions in the level of skills employed.

In Piachaud's 1984 study of households with young children, mothers whose youngest child was under two spent an average of 51 hours a week on a range of childcare tasks whilst their husbands spent 6 hours on average. Mothers with youngest child aged between two and four spent 39 hours (husbands 5 hours) (Piachaud 1984: 16). These figures understate the total time spent on domestic labour since they exclude domestic work which would still need to be done in the absence of young children. Not all these women were full-time houseworkers (two fifths had paid, mostly part-time employment) and so the time spent by the full-time houseworkers was probably higher than the averages given. Of the mothers who had no paid employment, 71 per cent said that they had no break of at least an hour during the week when they were completely free from responsibility for children. (The women who had a job fared slightly better, 52 per cent saying that they did not get a break from childcare, apart from their paid work.) Of the women who were not employed, 89 per cent said that their current workload was greater than their previous full-time job (Piachaud 1984: 17). It was in households with a non-employed wife that Warde and Hetherington (1993) found the greatest disparity between men's and women's perceptions of the fairness of the domestic division of labour. In these households 75 per cent of women felt that they did more than their fair share (compared with 60 per cent of women in full-time employment). However 69 per cent of men in these households thought they did a fair share (compared with 59 per cent of all men).

The pressures experienced by women with full-time responsibilities for domestic childcare are explored in greater detail in chapter 9. There was a sharp decline in the proportion of married women with young children who were outside the labour force in Britain in the 1980s. In 1977/79 only 27 per cent of married women with children under five were in employment (5 per cent full-time and 22 per cent part-time). By 1990/92 the proportion in employment had risen to 44 per cent (13 per cent full-time and 31 per cent part-time) (OPCS 1994a: 116). There are striking differences here between different occupational groups (see table 9.1 and chapter 9 for further discussion).

On the other hand unemployment and benefit dependency have propelled a significant minority of married women and a much higher proportion of lone parents out of the labour market and into full-time housework. Full-time domestic labour was transformed in the course of the twentieth century from a symbol of middle class and upwardly mobile working class status to represent increasingly a state of social and economic exclusion, within which the means-tested social security system trapped unemployed women and lone mothers.

7.5 STRUCTURAL CONSTRAINTS AND INDIVIDUAL CHOICE

It is clear from the evidence discussed in this chapter that women living in households with men face structural constraints which men do not. Women in full-time employment attain greater domestic equality and economic bargaining power but have less leisure than men and other groups of women. Where women work part-time, a more traditional domestic division of labour is likely. Women in part-time jobs are likely to experience higher levels of job satisfaction but lower levels of pay, downward occupational mobility and poor promotion prospects. Full-time houseworkers are a heterogeneous and diminishing group. Some have very demanding care responsibilities which prevent them from seeking employment. Others may be in this position because their husbands' unemployment and benefit position acts as a disincentive to them to find or keep a job. In all these instances the domestic division of labour is likely to take the most traditional form.

Human capital theory supports the view that women who work part-time have lower levels of labour market commitment than full-time workers (see chapter 4). According to this view, women can choose to achieve either a family-centred lifestyle in which labour market commitment takes second place, opting for part-time work and traditional gender divisions, or a career on the male model of full-time continuous employment. A recent example of this approach can be found in Hakim (1991). Hakim rightly emphasises the need to draw a distinction between full-time and part-time employment when assessing the extent of secular change in women's labour force participation. She argues that the increase in female labour force participation in twentieth century Britain has been exaggerated because of a failure to take account of the expansion of part-time relative to full-time female employment (Hakim 1993). Hakim suggests an explanatory hypothesis for the paradox that women report higher levels of job satisfaction than men in spite of their continuing concentration in the lowest paid and least skilled jobs. The hypothesis is based on dividing the female population into two distinct groups with different sets of priorities with regard to work and home commitments, namely 'grateful slaves' and 'self-made women' (Hakim 1991). This argument risks oversimplifying the complex interconnections between structural constraints and opportunities, on the one hand, and individual values and preferences on the other. Neoclassical economics, in asserting the primacy of labour market supply and individual choice, over labour market demand and employer and state strategies, fails to capture these complex interconnections. Here a more balanced perspective is suggested that takes account of the interaction of individual choice and structural constraints, and of supply and demand forces.

Socialist feminist and Marxist analyses of the labour market have been rightly criticised for identifying only structural, demobilising and oppressive class and gender constraints and underplaying the scope for individual choice, action and agency. On the other hand neoclassical economics goes to the opposite extreme of positing social explanations based entirely on trade between rational individuals. The challenge for social scientists is to develop a more sophisticated theoretical framework in which there is scope for interaction between individual preferences and socio-economic constraints and opportunities.

Values, attitudes and aspirations are not mechanistically imposed upon individuals by their position in the socio-economic structure. Individuals make choices which do have an impact on their future lives. Longitudinal research in the USA, cited by Hakim (1991: 111), demonstrates that young women who had definite career plans were much more likely to be in paid employment 15 years later than those who had no career plans or were less certain about their future intentions. However the extent of individual choice available for women varies historically, between different societies and between different cultures within societies. In societies typified by patriarchal structures, as discussed in chapter 6, individual choice will be highly constrained. With the decline in patriarchal household structures in industrialised countries like Britain, many women have gained greater degrees of choice about their lives. Those women who have greater freedom of choice because of education and earning power are most likely to reject traditional attitudes to gender roles whilst those subject to the greatest structural constraints are most likely to accept these attitudes.

Younger and more highly educated people have more egalitarian values in general and within particular ethnic groups (Bhopal 1993). The *British Social Attitudes* report found greater agreement between men and women under 45 about gender roles, with youngest people having the most progressive attitudes (see table 7.9). The greatest disparity in attitudes was found to be in the 45-54 years age group where 53 per cent of women but only 30 per cent of men rejected the traditional male breadwinner/female housewife model. This is the generation of women who were aged 24-33 in 1970 and whose shifting experience and attitudes gave rise to and were shaped by the feminist movement at that time.

Whilst women make choices about work on the basis of their own attitudes and values, these choices are made in social and gendered contexts. Whilst attitudes affect choices made, experience is important in shaping attitudes. Attitudes on how best to combine having children with employment have been found to be closely linked to women's own prior experience. Women who experienced a particular type of relationship with the labour market at a previous stage are likely to support that type of economic behaviour. For example, women who had worked

Table 7.9   Male and female attitudes to the gender division of labour
by age group 1991

% disagreeing or strongly disagreeing to statement: 'A husband's
job is to earn the money; a wife's job is to look after home and family'

Age group:	Men	Women
18–34	65	68
35–44	54	54
45–54	30	53
55–59	29	31
60 or older	13	19

Source: Social and Community Planning Research 1992: 98

part-time when their children were at school were likely to
favour this arrangement (Alwin et al. 1992: 25). The different
behaviour of different groups of women is due to the interaction of attitudes and experience, choice and socialisation, the
culture they live in, the options and bargaining power they
have. Devine's (1994) research on women scientists and en-
gineers demonstrates that, although individual choice was a
significant factor in these women's entry into 'gender atypical'
technical professions, preferences and plans were made in the
particular social contexts of middle-class family backgrounds,
academically oriented schools and fathers' involvement in
science and engineering professions. Educational and occupational choices were not based on a rational economistic decision-making process but on a combination of vaguely defined
plans, partial knowledge of options, likes and dislikes and
chance factors (Devine 1994: 95).

   Where women prioritise domestic over paid work commitments, husbands' preferences are often an important
influence (Martin and Roberts 1984: 107). This being the
case, to what extent can women who defer to men and allow
their attitudes to influence their own behaviour still be considered to be exercising choice? Hakim, following the New Home
Economics which was discussed in chapter 3, argues that

women know their husbands' attitudes before they marry and therefore exert their own free will through their choice of marriage partner (Hakim 1991: 110). Whilst this may be true, the attitudes of potential male partners are known to be consistently more traditional than women's, as well as strongly related to age and educational background. Women's choice of male partner attitudes is clearly circumscribed and socially constructed.

Whilst the values and attitudes of different groups of women need to be differentiated, a simple dualism between career-centred and home-centred women is not a helpful way forward. Hakim recognises that there may be no sharp boundary between the two groups of women and that many women will switch between the two sets of attitudes in the course of their working lives. But there is a more fundamental problem with the dualistic distinction between 'grateful slaves' and 'self-made women', namely that it posits the choice for women as that between traditional masculine and traditional feminine aspirations. It assumes that there is only one way for society to organise and support the reproduction and care of people. If there was a political commitment to explore options for care at a social level, as discussed in chapter 10, there would begin to be a much greater range of choice for individual women and men and for households.

Women increasingly have a choice about whether or not to have children. More women are now exercising the choice not to have children because of the conflict between work aspirations and childcare commitments (Grant 1995). Career aspirations exert a negative influence on young women's childbearing plans (Hakim 1991:112). Other care responsibilities, as for example caring for a sick or disabled parent or relative, are less likely to be so actively chosen, in spite of the fact that they fall disproportionately on women. For women who decide to have children, unlike men, there are complex choices that have to be made between the various options discussed in this chapter. It is not just a question of choice between work and family. There are other choices made between career, skills, earnings and equality of household relations on the one hand and time for self and family on the other. If cheap alternatives to domestic care arrangements are not available, the only women carers who can choose to make a commitment to full-time work are the minority who have access to earnings sufficient to employ a substitute carer.

It is also important to avoid a dualistic treatment of employment in which part-time work is used as a proxy for low work commitment. Hakim (1991: 114) argues that where, as in Britain, there is the option of part-time peripheral work, the distinction between full-time and part-time workers may act as a proxy differentiating those women with a work commitment similar to that of men from those with little commitment to paid work and a preference for the homemaker role. Yet if commitment to jobs is measured by length of time with current employer, part-time employees appear to be no less committed to their jobs than full-time employees. Marsh investigated the length of time respondents to the *Hours of Work Survey* had spent with their current employer and found very little difference between the distributions for full-time and part-time female employees (Marsh 1991: 57).

In other studies work commitment has been assessed by asking respondents: 'If without having to work you had what you would regard as a reasonable living income, would you still prefer to have a paid job?' Hakim herself recognises that a significant shift in women's attitudes to work, particularly those of women in part-time employment, appears to have taken place in Britain during the late 1980s, according to *British Social Attitudes* reports. Up to the mid-eighties the proportion of male employees saying they would still prefer a paid job if they did not need to work for financial reasons, was higher (74 per cent) than that for female employees (66 per cent) and that for full-time female employees was higher (71 per cent) than for part-time female employees (56 per cent) (Hakim 1992: 142). By 1989 female part-time employees were only slightly less likely (74 per cent) than female full-time employees (77 per cent) to say that they would still prefer a paid job. Moreover by 1989 male full-time employees were marginally less likely (72 per cent) than female part-time employees to say that they would still prefer a paid job if they did not need to work for financial reasons. This evidence suggests that it is questionable to portray women part-time workers as less committed to the labour market, merely because they work shorter hours. It is interesting in this context to note that male part-time employees emerge from the same research as the most positive group of all, 80 per cent of them stating that they would still want a paid job if they did not need to work for financial reasons. The only basis left for arguing that women have less commitment to the labour market is the continuing differential between male and female labour force participation rates (86 per cent and 71 per cent respectively of the working age population in 1993). However this difference reflects not so much a difference in commitment but the different earning capacities of women and men and the continuing assumption that women, not men, will stay at home to look after children and that women can choose not to do paid work in a way that men cannot.

Moreover part-time employment is not a homogeneous form of peripheral or secondary employment (Gallie and White 1994). It covers a wide set of contractual arrangements from very short hours and casualised contracts to career break schemes which are integrated into internal labour markets. It is also the case that there are two very different types of labour market and childcare policy contexts in which female part-time employment is high. One is the UK model of part-time work being predominantly low paid, outside internal labour market ladders, concentrated in sexually segregated women's occupations and having the policy context of very low levels of childcare provision. The other is the Scandinavian model of part-time work acting as a transitional stage within professional careers and other areas of skilled work, being available for men as well as women (even if men rarely choose this option), and having as a context high levels of childcare provision. In this type of labour market context, although employers still seek a low paid flexible labour force, they may turn increasingly to young people of both sexes to provide this rather than to women with dependent children (OECD 1994: 93). This type of part-time employment pattern is most likely in a context of recognition by employers that they need to retain and develop their female employees and of state support for women to be fully integrated into the labour market.

Movement from full-time to part-time employment and vice versa is common in Sweden (although only for women with stable employment contracts). In the UK it appears that women, once they have been employed part-time, do not often move back into full-time employment (Marsh 1991: 27). The reasons for this are complex. Many women genuinely prefer the greater flexibility and leisure opportunities which come with part-time jobs. Alternatively they may just accept that they are out of the running for full-time jobs and perceived by employers as insufficiently experienced or motivated. Watson and Fothergill found that, for a majority of the part-time workers they interviewed, the advantages of part-time work outweighed the disadvantages and this is why they had continued to work part-time even when the original reasons for doing so were no longer relevant. However it is not clear whether these respondents were comparing part-time work primarily with no paid employment or with full-time work. The view that part-time work represented 'the best of both worlds' was mainly expressed by older people and those who were financially better off whilst younger people and single parents were less positive (Watson and Fothergill 1993: 220).

Whilst women should not be treated merely as passive victims of patriarchal or capitalist relations, to replace a structural analysis with one which is primarily based on individual choice is not the way forward. It is true that part-time work is most common in the less skilled occupational groups and least prevalent in professional and managerial grades. Among women from an unskilled manual background 55 per cent were in part-time employment in 1990-92 and only 8 per cent were in full-time jobs (whilst 6 per cent were unemployed and 31 per cent economically inactive) (see Office of Population Censuses and Surveys 1994a: 116). Among women in the professional and managerial group only 16 per cent were in part-time and 67 per cent were in full-time jobs. (The corresponding proportions unemployed and economically inactive were 3 per cent and 14 per cent.) It is however unhelpful to suggest that the main cause of this disparity is the higher commitment of professional and managerial women to the labour market and their lower commitment to domestic responsibilities as compared with unskilled women.

Different patterns of female employment in different countries are the result of the interaction between labour supply factors, the level and structure of demand for labour, and state economic and social policies. Britain is not unique in experiencing several significant shifts in labour supply: a long term rising trend in female labour force participation supported by changing social attitudes and aspirations of women, an increase in the supply of well qualified women, an increased dependency of households on two earners, an increase in women's financial independence, increased instability and diversity of households. The level and structure of demand for labour is also affected by long term and international changes in the structure of employment which have favoured the expansion of service industries and occupations relative to those in manufacturing and production industries. However patterns of labour demand show significant variations between different countries which are linked to different national institutional and policy contexts.

Applebaum and Schettkat's (1991) comparative research on the USA and West Germany demonstrates that in the period 1979-87, although employment growth was concentrated in service industries in both countries, a much higher proportion of jobs created in the US were casual part-time jobs as compared with West Germany. Education, health and social welfare services took a significantly larger share of new jobs in West Germany than in the USA. Conversely catering, hotels and the retail trade provided a larger share of employment growth in the USA than in West Germany (Applebaum and Schettkat 1991: 147). These differences reflect differences in state policy. The 1980s Reagan administration stimulated a consumer boom based on tax cuts, increased military spending and expansion of low wage and low productivity employment. Matzner and Streeck (1991: 6) characterise the USA in the 1980s as one in which employment growth was achieved by means of an internationally uncompetitive 'servant' economy. In contrast West Germany and other north European economies maintained commitments in the 1980s to strong social security systems, high wage standards and higher levels of investment and productivity growth. For example in West Germany shorter working hours for full-time workers were negotiated by unions and employers down from 40 hours to between 37 and 39 hours (Applebaum and Schettkat 1991: 50).

In Britain a number of government policies in the 1980s contributed to the specific pattern of growth of female employment. In the early 1980s monetarist policies, combined with a lack of commitment to the maintenance of the production sector, exacerbated the decline of manufacturing output and employment. Subsequently it was the private services sector, heavily reliant on female and part-time labour, that saw the greatest expansion in the consumer credit-led boom of the late 1980s (Humphries and Rubery 1992: 252). The government's strategy for employment expansion was closer to the US policy of encouraging low wage employment than to that of its north European competitors who remained committed to high wage, high value added growth. Hence the British government set about dismantling national labour standards and agreements, introducing subcontracting and compulsory competitive tendering in the public sector, weakening wages councils and encouraging localised company bargaining and performance related pay. Humphries and Rubery (1992) argue that the interaction of long-term shifts in supply and demand and the short-term policy context of the 1980s produced a particular polarisation within the expanding female labour force. The growing numbers of well qualified women benefited from the expansion of managerial and professional jobs. Over half of the total increase in jobs for women between 1983 and 1990 were in these categories (Humphries and Rubery 1992: 245). Women in full-time employment actually improved their earnings relative to men in the boom years of the second half of the 1980s. On the other hand the pay of women in part-time employment declined during the 1980s relative to male and female full-time earnings, reflecting the concentration of new part-time jobs in low paid sectors.

Shifting patterns of labour supply should be analysed in terms of the different sets of structural constraints and degrees of choice facing women in different social classes and with different types of educational experience. An approach which puts primary emphasis on individual choice as the explanatory factor is unhelpful to women whether they are in part-time or full-time employment because it merely legitimises available employment opportunities. It fails to illuminate the limited nature of the choices open to most women. It deflects attention away from attempts to convert part-time work from a low paid, dead end for women into a bridge to further training and development. It forces women in full

ime jobs to continue to keep their domestic commitments
hidden and perpetuates the anxieties and guilt so clearly
documented by Coward (1992) that drive some women out of
employment altogether.

An overemphasis on individual choice also deflects attention away from the particularly strong shift in labour demand
towards part-time jobs for women that took place in Britain
from the late 70s to the late 80s. Apart from the Netherlands,
the UK had the largest substitution of part-time for full-time
female employment in the OECD countries in that period.
Between 1979 and 1986 there was a 3 per cent growth in
female employment in the UK, consisting of a rise of 7 per
cent in part-time employment and a decline of 4 per cent in
full-time employment (OECD 1994: 78). Demand conditions
in the labour market were a major influence on the changing
patterns of female employment in the economy as a whole,
complemented by growing numbers of women with children
who were seeking part-time jobs (Sly 1994) and an increase in
the supply of female labour with educational qualifications.
Although female full-time employment grew faster than
female part-time employment in the boom years of the late
1980s this pattern was again reversed in the recession of the
1990s. The proportion of the female working age population
in full-time employment was 36 per cent in 1993, the same as
it had been in 1979, and down from its peak of 38 per cent in
the 1989/90 boom years (Sly 1993: 484). During the same
period the proportion of women in part-time employment
rose from 22 per cent to 29 per cent. However women did take
a larger share of full-time employment, as compared with
men. In 1993 32 per cent of those in full-time employment
were women as compared with 28 per cent in 1993. Likewise
men took an increased share of part-time employment
(3 per cent in 1979 and 14 per cent in 1993).

Given the important role of the political economic context
and the resulting pattern of labour demand in shaping opportunities for part-time and full-time employment it would be
unwise to conclude that most women will necessarily continue
to be satisfied with part-time jobs on a permanent basis, at
least the type of part-time jobs currently available in Britain. In
this context, Hewitt (1993) risks overplaying the benefits of
part-time work in general for women and exaggerates the

extent to which the growth of part-time employment is the result of 'a consumer attitude towards production time itself' (Hewitt 1993: 168). She gives insufficient attention to the lack of control over hours worked which often characterises part-time employment. A significant number of women part-time employees would like to be able to work longer hours. Marsh (1991: 75) found that 23 per cent of part-time women employees would prefer longer hours and more pay than they had. Growing numbers of part-time employees also took more than one part-time job in the 1990s. Amongst Hewitt's interviewees the older women in part-time jobs were the most dissatisfied: 'their children had grown up and needed them less, but their work did not compensate. They found it hard to get the hours they wanted...but also the responsibility which they deserved' (Hewitt 1993: 80). In the light of these experiences it is hardly surprising that as many as 34 per cent of employed women with dependent children under five were opting for full-time employment in the early 1990s (Sly 1993: 486).

Full-time employment for women is more likely than part-time employment to act as a catalyst for change in gender relations both in the workplace and in the household. However sometimes the catalyst is more like a slow fuse which fails to ignite before women give up the fight exhausted. Most women with young children prefer part-time to full-time employment and probably even more would do so if it did not mean a loss of career prospects. The experience of Sweden demonstrates that where parental leave and reductions in working hours are offered women readily take these opportunities. The fact that men are less willing to do so is not a reason for rejecting these policies. Men have shown themselves to be much slower than women to accept changes in gender relations and patterns of working time. In spite of all the obstacles facing them, women are competing with men in the labour market with increasing success. Men are spending more time on domestic labour than before, prompted by reductions in their own working hours and women's increased employment. However the time women spend on domestic labour as a whole did not decrease in the decade prior to the mid-1980s as increased time spent on childcare and shopping more than offset reductions in time spent on routine domestic work. There is little evidence yet of any greater willingness on the part of men to choose shorter working hours to spend more time on childcare. Women for the foreseeable future will be forced to balance their own priorities, to negotiate with partners if they have them, and to make the adjustments that labour market conditions impose upon them. The next chapter looks at why rising incomes have not significantly reduced the time spent on domestic labour or its gendered nature.

8 Domestic Technology and Market Substitution

Housework provides the material basis for the rest of domestic work and for the social relations of the house-hold....Technical changes and the resulting re- organization of labour have reduced housework time and have allowed the housewife to be more responsive to the social relations of the household' (Luxton M. 1980: 159).

As discussed in chapter 3, the neoclassical New Home Economics analysis of labour supply identified the substitution of market production for household production as the dominant influence bringing about a rise in married women's labour force participation rates in the 1950s and 1960s. Post-industrial theorists from the 1970s also argued that, in mature industrial societies, consumer demand would shift from manufactured goods to services, and marketed services would replace the personal services provided within the household. This chapter explores in greater detail evidence on the extent to which market goods and services were substituted for domestic labour in Britain in the latter decades of the twentieth century. It also examines the relationship between technology and labour in the household context. Although commonly assumed to have facilitated the expansion of women's employment in industrial capitalist economies in the twentieth century, domestic technology does not necessarily reduce time spent on domestic labour. Feminists have argued that domestic technology may even be associated with reinforcing the traditional gender division of labour. The chapter relates the evidence offered in chapter 7 on changes in domestic labour to debates about technology.

8.1 DOMESTIC LABOUR AND THE POST-INDUSTRIAL DEBATE

There are different perspectives on the extent to which marketed services replace domestic labour. Post-industrial theorists assumed that rising incomes would lead to an increased demand for marketed or state provided services, some of which would take the place of services traditionally provided within the household. However critics of post-industrialism argued that the rising cost of wage labour, combined with the limited impact of new technology on personal services, continued to make the demand for manufactured goods more buoyant than that for services. Moreover growth in consumer expenditure on manufactured goods might be associated with a growth in self-servicing and therefore more, not less, domestic labour. The provision of state services was also reduced as governments shifted spending from care-giving services to income support for the unemployed, placing yet more pressure on households to service themselves.

One strand within twentieth century political economy was critical of economic growth from the perspective that increased material standards of consumption are premised on an increasing scarcity of time (Harrod 1958, Linder 1970, Hirsch 1976, Burns 1977). Purchased consumer goods are recognised as intermediate products requiring inputs of household labour to convert them into final consumer products (Hirsch 1976: 28). Processing purchased goods requires time to be spent on maintenance, administration and consumption itself (Linder 1970: 14). Higher incomes are associated with less time for leisure and culture, not more, as most proponents of economic growth assumed (Linder 1970: 94).

This pessimistic perspective on economic growth was countered by post-industrial theorists like Bell (1973 and 1980) who envisaged the expansion of the market-based service sector as a primary or major component of economic growth. Bell argued that consumers would spend an increasing proportion of their rising incomes on personal services instead of goods, hence purchasing the time of others as a substitute for their own. He envisaged in the 'post-industrial era' an expansion specifically of human services, such as education and health, and of professional services like research and information activities (Allen 1988: 105). Whilst agreeing that a restructuring of employment away from manufacturing and production industries and towards services was apparent in mature industrial societies, critics of Bell's thesis questioned the conclusions he had drawn about shifts in consumer demand. Personal service, by its very nature was unreceptive to mechanisation and technical innovation and therefore much less subject to the productivity growth that was typical in the production of goods (Hirsch 1976: 27). As incomes rose with productivity growth in manufacturing, the relative cost of personal services increased, limiting most people's ability to purchase the time of others as a substitute for their own (Gershuny 1978). Contrary to Bell's predictions, rising incomes were associated with continuing buoyancy of demand for goods and the expansion of self-servicing on the part of houscholds. In fact consumers were switching expenditure from services to goods, not goods to services, particularly in areas like transport and entertainment (Gershuny 1983: 76).

Galbraith (1973) was alone in focusing on the gender dimension of these changes in patterns of consumption. Personal service, he argued is uniquely vulnerable to industrial development and the search for surrogates for paid domestic servants led men to one of their greatest, if least celebrated, economic achievements: the 'conversion of women into a crypto-servant class', available not just to the upper and middle class male who in pre-industrial times would have been able to afford servants, but 'democratically, to almost the entire present male population' (Galbraith 1973: 79). Galbraith argued that the modern economic edifice of ever-expanding material consumption rested on the foundations of women's servant role. Without this, consumption would be limited by the time required to manage it, 'to select, transport, prepare, repair, maintain, clean, service, store, protect' purchased consumer goods (Galbraith 1973: 79). Household appliances might alleviate but would not eliminate the burdens placed on women in their servant role.

More recently Silver (1987) argued that, contrary to Gershuny's notion of the 'self-service economy', the increase in women's employment, particularly full-time employment, combined with an absence of any significant rise in men's contribution to domestic labour, has led to shifts in consumer expenditure towards services. She distinguishes between services which require the presence of the consumer, 'time-expensive' services (leisure services, health and education) and those where the service provider replaces the consumer, 'time-conserving' services (such as childcare). Her argument is that, in the USA at least, from the 1950s through to the early 1980s, there was a large rise in the demand for time-conserving services like childcare (both marketed and state-funded) and restaurants/fast food outlets (Silver 1987: 35).

There is less evidence in Britain for any significant shift in overall consumer expenditure towards time-conserving services. The nature of the economy is such that more people who seek access to the labour and time of others to free their own time obtain it from unpaid sources. A high and growing proportion of part-time female employment as evidenced in the UK (unlike the USA) is consistent with relatively low levels of consumer demand for services which offer substitutes for women's domestic labour. Women who are in part-time jobs continue to meet most of their own households' service requirements, both because they have more time and because they receive levels of pay that are inadequate to afford to purchase services (employing workers on comparable wage rates to themselves).

In the UK expenditure on services overall declined as a proportion of total consumer expenditure from the early 1950s to the beginning of the 1980s, in line with Gershuny's analysis of washing machines replacing laundries and television replacing cinema (Wells 1989: 41). In the 1980s the share of services in consumer expenditure rose steadily but only reaching its 1952 level again by the end of the decade. During these four decades the share of manufactured goods had nearly doubled as a proportion of consumer expenditure.

The more recent growth in consumer demand for services in the 1980s in the UK does not appear to reflect to any great extent a shift in service provision from the household to the market. The only buoyant service area where substitution of this kind may be present is catering (meals and accommodation) which represents 17 per cent of the increase in expenditure on services between 1979 and 1987 (Wells 1989: 41). On the other hand the most important item in the growth of service expenditure in the 1980s was the boom in foreign holidays. There was a growing need for childcare services to support increased employment among mothers of young children and there was some expansion, particularly of private childcare services in the 1980s (especially childminding and nurseries), linked to the especially rapid growth of employment amongst women with young children in professional and managerial occupations. However overall levels of spending remained very low and the vast majority of mothers continued to rely on unpaid, informal and very low paid sources of labour (OPCS 1994b). (See chapter 9 for further discussion of the pattern of childcare services in Britain.)

It is to be expected that affluent and middle class households are more likely to purchase services as a substitute for their own time and labour than other classes and income groups and this finding is supported by Warde's study of households in the North West (Warde 1990: 511). But even among the relatively affluent households in his research, there is little evidence of expenditure on services to replace the traditional female areas of domestic labour. Expenditure on services for these households was concentrated in the typical male areas of home maintenance and improvement and car maintenance. Routine housework was nearly universally carried out by household members with the single exception of cleaning windows (Warde 1990: 504). In 1993 less than 1 per cent of average household expenditure went on 'domestic help' (compared with 3 per cent on house repairs and maintenance) and, even in the top 10 per cent of households, less than 2 per cent of expenditure was on domestic help (CSO 1994b). On the other hand, within the narrower band of dual career households (where both partners are in full-time professional or managerial employment) there is evidence of higher levels of spending on domestic childcare and cleaning. Gregson and Lowe (1994) found that about a third of these households employed paid domestic workers. These households remain a very small, if rising, proportion of married couple households.

In Britain relatively few women were able in the last three decades of the twentieth century to make significant use of marketed services as a substitute for their own domestic labour. The growth of catering services in the 1980s is probably the most significant example where some substitution took place. Meals consumed at work may be the prime example in Britain of domestic labour time saving through the substitution of market goods and services (Horrell 1994: 219). In 1993 nearly 4% of household spending was on meals bought outside the home (CSO 1994b). Purchased meals are more likely to be weekday lunches or to replace entertaining at home and special occasion family meals rather than to be substitutes for routine evening and weekend home cooking, at least in multi-person households. DeVault (1991) documented the complex interpersonal, mental and emotional processes involved in 'feeding the family'. The family is 'a setting in which wives and mothers learn to attend to quite particular needs, and others learn to expect such attention' (DeVault 1991: 90). Personal service of this kind, involving as it does attention to individual and idiosyncratic tastes, cannot be provided on a mass scale by a market in which businesses depend for profitability on some degree of standardised production.

Where households have the financial resources to afford it, household work traditionally performed by men, like home improvement, appears more likely to be replaced by marketed services than those areas that are typically female. One reason why a substitution of marketed services for household labour may be more likely to occur in traditional male areas of work could be that these areas of household work tend to be more detached from the care and interpersonal work aspects of domestic labour. Men's domestic labour has tended to be more involved with physical tasks which remove them from interpersonal contact (DIY, car maintenance) whereas women's domestic labour has come to focus more and more predominantly on care and on managing interpersonal relations within the household. Another reason could be that higher earnings provide men with greater incentive and bargaining power to purchase substitutes for their own domestic labour.

The links between the work women do in the home and the types of jobs which have been created for women in the last fifty years in the labour market have sometimes been oversimplified in discussions about the growth of female employment. There is an implicit and sometimes explicit assumption within both neoclassical economics and radical political economy that women have been drawn out of the household economy into wage labour or state employment to perform the tasks they once performed in the home. The increased proportion of female employment in part-time service industry employment in industrial economies, if considered superficially, appears to support this conclusion. However the purposes and nature of most of the work done by women in the labour market are, in the main, very different from the domestic labour done traditionally and contemporarily by women. There are areas of overlap and examples where work can be seen to move backwards and forwards between the market or the state and the household such as caring work with young children and with elderly, sick and disabled people. Employed women also can find themselves performing personal service roles for their male colleagues and managers, especially in areas like clerical work. But overall the massive growth of female service employment has had remarkably little impact on the scale of women's service work within their own households. It is apparent that analyses which attempt to equate, or compare too simplistically, the two areas of women's work lead to misleading conclusions. The next section looks at the contradictory evidence and argument surrounding the impact of technology on domestic labour.

8.2   DOMESTIC LABOUR AND TECHNOLOGY

Prior to the 1970s social scientists showed little interest in the question of what impact developments in household technology had on the amount and nature of domestic labour. New household appliances were assumed to have played a crucial role in enabling women to participate more fully in the labour market. However in 1974 Vanek published the results of US research that suggested that, during a period of major changes in household technology (from the 1920s to the 1960s), although employed women had reduced the time they spent on domestic labour, the time spent by full-time housewives had actually increased. Not only did these women spend more time in the 1960s on shopping and childcare but they also spent more time on laundry, an area of domestic labour which had been particularly affected by technological change (diffusion of hot and cold running water, automatic washing machines, detergents, synthetic non-iron fabrics).

Much subsequent research in the 1970s and 1980s confirmed the view that the effect of modern domestic technologies on women's domestic labour time was negligible compared with the effects of family size and women's employment (Bereano, Bose and Arnold 1985: 175). Feminist writers went further to emphasise ways in which traditional gender relations shaped the development and use of domestic technology and could be further strengthened by it (Cowan 1974 and 1983, Wajcman 1991).

Technological change affects domestic labour in a number of different ways which can be distinguished as follows (Hartmann 1974, Thomas and Zmroczek 1975): first there is the development of *utilities* or infrastructural provision, namely water, gas, electricity, sewerage; second there are new *appliances*, the machines, utensils and tools used in the domestic labour process; third are developments in *materials*, the purchased goods that are inputs in the domestic labour process like convenience foods, detergents and fabrics; finally there are new types of *services* both commercial and public, which interconnect with or replace domestic labour (launderettes, catering, teleshopping, armchair banking.)

Most of the literature on domestic technology has focused on the impact of appliances. It is, however, acknowledged that the development of utilities probably had a greater impact on domestic labour than other types of technological change (Ravetz 1965: 257 and Bereano, Bose and Arnold 1985: 172). In 1917 running water saved between one and a half and two hours a day of a housewife's time (Rowe 1917). In Britain the basic domestic technology infrastructure was in place for most of the population by 1939 (although electricity supply did not become standardised until after its nationalisation in the postwar period). In the post Second World War years, the most important changes in domestic technology came from the diffusion and development of household appliances.

There are two possible interpretations of the paradox that 'labour-saving' household appliances do not necessarily reduce the overall time spent on domestic labour (Cowan 1983). The first interpretation is that within the labour processes into which appliances are introduced, there are countervailing pressures to increase domestic labour time (for example as domestic labour becomes more productive, standards rise). The second interpretation is that the labour saved within particular labour processes by the introduction of household appliances is counterbalanced by increases in time spent on other domestic labour processes (for example time spent on routine housework declines whilst time spent on childcare and shopping increases).

Let us examine first the case where household appliances reduce labour time per unit of output within particular labour processes but not necessarily the total labour time allocated to those processes.

8.2.1 Homes, households and standards

Gershuny offered one explanation for the 'domestic labour paradox', the empirical observation that: 'labour saving devices' appeared to increase the amount of domestic labour, at least in the early years of their diffusion (Gershuny 1983: 146). He argued that there are two parallel processes interacting to determine whether domestic technological innovation leads households to spend more or less time on domestic work. On the one hand, as technological innovations make household labour more productive in certain areas of production, for example washing clothes, it is rational for households to increase total production in those areas, that is to wash more clothes. However just as economists assume a diminishing marginal utility of extra income, there will be a diminishing marginal utility of extra clean clothes. Hence demand for the particular household service rises but at a diminishing rate. On the other hand, there is a 'product cycle' with each technological innovation in which initially the market for the product (washing machines) grows as fast or faster than the industry's capacity to supply the product and there is little pressure on manufacturers to improve product performance. Eventually the expansion of production capacity overtakes the more slowly growing market and competition between producers with respect to price and product performance intensifies. This encourages new technological innovations and improvements in the productivity of appliances such as the development of the automatic washing machine. Gershuny concluded that the interaction of the processes of consumer demand and product innovation and design offered an explanation for the expansion and subsequent contraction of domestic labour during the preceding fifty year period.

In addition to the countervailing economic forces identified by Gershuny, other contextual factors are likely to have influenced the relationship between changes in technology and the pattern of domestic labour. These factors include the nature of housing development, the marketing strategies of household appliance sellers, the aspirations of different groups of women themselves, birth rates and family size. More domestic technology is often associated with larger and more complex homes to be cared for (Robinson et al. 1972: 125). It is significant in this respect that the first wave of diffusion of domestic appliances in working class homes in Britain in the 1950s and 60s coincided with a period in which many households acquired for the first time their own self-contained dwelling units. When Hannah Gavron conducted her survey of housewives in London in 1960, 71 per cent of the working class wives she interviewed lived in rooms and most of these were in houses that were divided up and rented to several families (Gavron 1968: 59). Most of these families had no bathroom and nearly half had to share a toilet with other households. Poor housing dominated the lives of most working class women and most longed for a house or flat of their own. It is understandable in this context that for most people rising standards of living should have a higher priority than reducing workloads and that household appliances would be seen as supporting the higher standards women aspired to.

This expectation was undoubtedly reinforced by the marketing strategies of companies selling appliances which emphasised the issue of standards rather than the possibility of an easier life for women. For example electric appliances were promoted as enabling the committed housewife to achieve 'Spring Cleanliness Every Day' (Byers 1981: 11). Enthusiasts for scientific management in the home had always emphasised the potential for mechanisation to increase the standard of housework, not save women time (Frederick 1920). For most it was not clear what was the point of saving time for the housewife other than to give them more time to study domestic science (Arnold and Burr 1985: 159). Only a few early feminists like Charlotte Perkins Gilman had perceived the liberating potential of domestic technology and advocated the industrialisation of housework (see chapter 4). Feminists have generally emphasised the social irrationality and limits to productivity that can be attained through household technology because of its individualised small scale application (Wajcman 1991). There is a class and race dynamic in historical debates about the socialisation of housework. Working class and black women, because of their experience as domestic servants of doing other people's housework, have been generally less attracted to the notion of collectivisation, aspiring instead to improved private homes and the opportunity to do their own housework, feed and care for their own families. For middle class feminists, on the other hand, the collectivisation of housework, childcare and catering offered an attractive alternative in the late nineteenth and early twentieth centuries, in a context in which availability of domestic servants was declining (Hayden 1982).

Household appliances were seen to offer an important new market for mass production engineering industries in the post Second World War period. In addition domestic technology was perceived as a means of alleviating the burdens of motherhood, in a context in which women were being encouraged to have more children. In fact, it was concern about the falling birth-rate that was the main context in which the labour saving potential of domestic technology was discussed at that time. A large amount of evidence was submitted to the Royal Commission on Population (1949) from women's organisations arguing that women were having fewer children because it was the only way they could ease the burden of domestic labour. 'In a period when nearly every section of workers was enjoying improved conditions through Trade Union and Parliamentary action, those who were engaged in the biggest single occupation in the country – that of working housewife and mother – began to buy a little leisure with the tin-opener and birth control' (Royal Commission on Population 1949: 147).

Political and Economic Planning highlighted the link between household appliances and population policy:

> The duties of the housewife become more arduous as her family increases, and it has been suggested that one of the reasons for the falling birth rate is that mothers increasingly appreciate leisure and social activity. If this is so, then it should be possible to compensate to some extent for the extra work normally imposed by children, by installing more

mechanical appliances. In any case, it would seem that if measures are successfully taken to increase the birth rate, this may well lead to a greater demand for household appliances, particularly for those, for example water-heating appliances, which assist in the care of children (Political and Economic Planning 1945: 20)

Women were marrying and becoming mothers in ever increasing numbers in the post Second World War period. By 1961, 87 per cent of women aged 30-44 years were married as compared with 72 per cent of women in that age group who were married in 1921 (Gardiner 1976b: 63). Moreover 73 per cent of women who married in the late 1950s had two or more children as compared with only 60 per cent of women who married in the early 1920s. Rising marriage and birth rates from the late 1940s through to the mid-1960s accompanied the first wave of diffusion of household appliances, providing other pressures counteracting their labour saving potential within particular labour processes like laundry, cooking and cleaning. Not surprisingly it was among young childless married women (who, prior to the Second World War, had been excluded from employment by the marriage bar in many occupations) and older women with few childcare responsibilities that employment rates increased most in the 1950s and 60s.

Hence it is likely that any increased domestic labour productivity resulting from the first wave of diffusion of household appliances to a mass market in the UK, was largely offset by improved standards of housing and rising birth and marriage rates. The scale of domestic labour processes expanded to offset the increased productivity made possible by the new capital equipment. Whilst middle class women were substituting their own labour for that of paid domestic servants, working class women were seeking and securing self-contained, larger dwellings and higher living standards. Earlier and higher rates of marriage and fertility brought greater domestic responsibilities to more women through to the mid-1960s. Let us now turn to the second interpretation of the limited labour-saving impact of household appliances which emphasises the changing nature of domestic labour.

8.2.2   The restructuring of domestic labour

An explanation of the domestic technology paradox which
focuses on the changing nature of the domestic labour
process appears of particular relevance for the period from
the 1960s through to the 1980s in Britain. During this period,
reductions in time spent on certain domestic tasks, associated
with further diffusion and improvements in domestic technology, were offset by comparable increases in time spent on
those domestic tasks for which technology was a less significant
factor. Time budget research demonstrated that women and
men in the UK increased the time they spent on both shopping and childcare between 1961 and 1984 when the overall
time spent on routine domestic work declined (Gershuny and
Robinson 1988: 548 and see chapter 7 for further discussion).

There are various reasons why shopping time expanded
during this period to fill some of the time saved on routine
domestic work. Changes in the location of housing and the
concentration of food retailing in large out of town supermarkets increased the time spent travelling to shop. The shift to
mass production and distribution of food transformed what
DeVault refers to as the 'provisioning' process. When shoppers
engage with the major supermarkets: 'They must deal with the
superfluity of products and information about them, and with
the essentially antagonistic marketing techniques designed to
disrupt their routines and induce them to buy new products.
In this context, the screening and sorting that shoppers do is a
specific kind of skilled practice' (DeVault 1991: 70). Moreover
consumers spent less and less of their income (proportionately) on food and more on manufactured goods (see section
8.1). As a result shopping became a more differentiated and
less routine activity and one that involved research and information gathering and large investments of time and money. It
was increasingly a shared activity involving negotiated decisions in couple households. Shopping is also an activity in
which the consumerist culture of the 1980s and new shopping
precincts encouraged a blurring of the boundaries between
leisure and domestic labour.

The reasons for the expansion of time spent on childcare
are more complex. Comparing studies of household time use
with patterns of women's employment reveals an apparent

paradox. Time use studies have generally not identified child-care as a particularly important component of domestic labour except for the occasional study which focused on households with young pre-school children, for example Piachaud (1984). Yet responsibility for young children, including those aged 5–11 who are at school, is still one of the most significant variables influencing women's participation rates and hours in the labour market (see chapter 9). Hence there is an apparent contradiction between the evidence that responsibility for children is one of the most important influences on the amount of time women spend at home and the general invisibility of childcare in most time use studies of domestic labour. This paradox suggests that childcare activities may be particularly difficult to measure and that the methodology adopted in time budget studies may not be appropriate for identifying those processes which are central to childcare. Time budget studies tend to focus on physical tasks and therefore have greater difficulty identifying the less tangible work of planning and maintaining the social relationships of the household which goes on alongside physical tasks. Time studies 'miss most of the planning and coordination involved in household work, as well as the constant juggling and strategizing behind the physical tasks' (Devault 1991: 56). People are asked to list the things they are doing at different points in the day and consequently it is the physical tasks that are likely to be recorded even when an important part of what they are doing is planning, supporting, supervising and communicating with children. Also caring for older children involves less physical and more mental work than caring for babies and young children and is therefore even harder to track. The most skilled aspects of domestic labour are often the least visible, which reinforces the low social valuation of domestic labour. Physical domestic tasks provide an infrastructure for the maintenance of social relations, sometimes a battleground within which those social relations are undermined. In one person households, domestic labour is about servicing personal consumption and maintaining the physical environment. In multi-person households, care of people and the maintenance of social relationships are, increasingly the central aspect of domestic labour and yet much of this work is not visible or even perceived as work by those who do it.

Where a parent is at home for reasons of childcare, many of the physical tasks carried out alongside childcare may only be necessary and rational activities because childcare prevents them from working outside the home. Baking, tidying and cleaning may be subsidiary activities carried out because the primary childcare activity creates mess and time at home to do other things. Yet the time budget methodology may result in the physical tasks being recorded as primary and the childcare as secondary.

As domestic technology has reduced the time that needs to be spent on physical tasks, and routine domestic work has consequently declined in significance, the interpersonal work that is a central feature of women's domestic labour has become more visible. Where children are present a responsible adult needs to be on call, even if not directly tending to their needs. This aspect of women's domestic role was much less visible when the tasks involved in routine housework filled all the time they had available. As that ceases to be the case childcare becomes a more visible and prominent part of the domestic labour process. Meanwhile the emotional and educational aspects of parenting have assumed ever greater importance relative to the provision of physical care, placing additional pressures on women to focus on their childcare responsibilities (Coward 1992). The implications of these changes will be discussed more fully in chapter 9.

Although domestic technology, for those who can afford it, has reduced the physical tasks and drudgery associated in the past with domestic labour, it has by no means eliminated these. Although men increased their share of routine domestic work in the 1970s and 1980s (see chapter 7), there is some evidence that women retain responsibility for the most labour intensive jobs and those which have been least affected by domestic technology. For example Gregson and Lowe (1994: 83) found that in dual career households, wives were more likely to be responsible for the most labour intensive domestic tasks, cleaning (especially surfaces and bathrooms) and ironing, even where husbands shared responsibility for more gender neutral tasks like cooking and washing up. This was the context in which a decision to employ a cleaner was often taken.

The presence of people generates mess and dirt which has to be noticed and dealt with. Cleaning is the aspect of routine domestic labour which has remained the least amenable to technological change. The most significant household technological developments and applications in the 1980s and 1990s were related to telecommunications and computerisation and the concept of the 'smart house' or 'intelligent home'. Self-cleaning does not, unfortunately, come with computerisation. Haddon, editor of 'The Intelligent Home' uncovered a wide disparity between what consumers desire from home automation and what it has to offer. The major areas of development for the 'smart house' have been energy management and conservation, security, education, entertainment, shopping and financial services. Yet top of the list of things that people would like home automation to do for them was the removal of dust and dirt (Hardyment 1990).

This is not a new dream. In 1896 Maria Gay Humphries wrote 'A busy woman is accustomed to say that her idea of the house of the future is one that can be cleaned down with a hose' (cited Hardyment 1990: 8). The technological development that is most relevant to this aspiration is the central vacuum cleaning system (CVS), first invented in the early 1900s and marketed in the late twentieth century in the developed world as a product which makes vacuuming easier and more hygienic. A Finnish study (Smeds 1994) found that the main reason given by owners of a CVS for their purchase was hygiene and the elimination of microdust from the indoor atmosphere. The CVS, which was four times the cost of an ordinary vacuum cleaner, was particularly popular with households who suffered from dust allergy or asthma. However only a few households reported that the CVS had reduced allergic symptoms to a great extent. Simply owning a CVS does not make a difference; it still requires considerable time to be spent for it to be effective. 'A device that keeps the home dustless without human intervention is still no more than a dream' (Smeds 1994: 37). Whilst households with CVS reported some increase in men's participation in vacuuming following on from the purchase, this response was most likely in households where the economic and educational status of the woman was high relative to the man. It is the social relationships within the household which shape the use of technology. Whether ownership of a particular household appliance leads to greater gender equality in the domestic labour process will depend on how gender relations are constructed and renegotiated (Ormrod 1994: 43).

8.3 CONCLUSION

Women's increased access as consumers to markets for goods and services has not led to the kind of straightforward substitution of market for household production that the neoclassical economic framework assumes. In Britain it facilitated increasing material standards of consumption, based on a sustained growth in consumer expenditure, especially on manufactured goods. In spite of the large increase in women's employment in service industries there was only limited scope for marketed services to replace women's domestic labour, in Britain, where part-time employment was high and wage rates low among those women with the greatest domestic responsibilities.

Most of the growth in production for the final consumer in industrial capitalist economies in the twentieth century involved goods and services that were never produced in the domestic economy rather than the substitutes for household production which were more typical in the early stages of industrialisation, such as textiles. Children's and women's clothing is probably the major area of growth in consumer demand in the period after 1950, where manufactured goods clearly substituted for domestic labour. Increased consumer expenditure on material goods increase the demands placed on domestic labour in terms of certain activities like shopping, maintaining and cleaning, especially if accompanied by improved standards of housing. The objective of reducing the time women spend on domestic labour has never been a primary concern of those who develop, produce and sell household appliances and women's need to find ways of reducing the demands on their time continues to have little impact on the most recent developments in domestic technology.

On the other hand feminists and socialists have tended to underestimate the transformative potential of domestic technology and to overestimate the likely benefits of collective solutions to domestic problems. Capitalism and the market economy have made possible some alleviation of the burden of domestic labour. Developments in domestic technology, especially infrastructural innovations like running water, heating and lighting, but also some household appliances such as washing machines, vacuum cleaners and dishwashers are important because they facilitate, to some extent, an erosion of the traditional gender division of domestic labour.

However, on its own technology has a limited effect. It can alter the way physical tasks are performed and reduce the labour required to perform those tasks but it cannot replace people in respect of mental, emotional and interpersonal work. As many of the physical tasks of domestic labour have been eliminated or reduced by technical developments, the less visible but most skilled aspects of domestic labour have assumed a growing importance, especially in larger households and those with children or dependent adult members. Social scientists have had difficulty tracking these changes because much of the research methodology has focused on recording the performance of physical tasks.

Research is now beginning to focus on the interpersonal aspects of domestic labour and to uncover some of its important and unique features. It is becoming clear that, just as increased expenditure on manufactured goods does not necessarily reduce domestic labour time, there are strict limits to the extent to which marketed services are likely to expand to replace domestic labour. An important limit is that households are built on and maintained by highly personalised service work which cannot be replaced by the market or the state. Whilst the physical aspects of service work can be performed in any of these sectors, interpersonal aspects require individualised attention to individual needs and wants.

This interpersonal work is central to domestic labour and to the construction and maintenance of households and families. For men to take a more equal share of domestic labour, it is not enough to share the physical tasks. They need to recognise, value and learn how to do the interpersonal work as well. This change has barely begun to happen but will be an essential part of the development of the social relations of households which will make it possible for the full potential benefits of household technology to be realised. Domestic technology facilitates an erosion of the traditional gender division of labour because it makes it easier for adults to service themselves. This potential has been insufficiently recognised in feminist literature. For this potential to be realised, technology has to be harnessed in particular ways in the context of changing social relationships. Changes in technology on their own do not transform and sometimes can freeze social relationships, as in instances where technology makes it possible for women to combine employment with domestic labour rather than getting men to take a greater share. The use of technology in households depends on the social relationships within them (Cockburn and Ormrod 1993).

Nonetheless domestic technology makes adult self-servicing more possible. Instead of washing taking a whole day it can be done in the evening after work and dried in time for the next day. Heating a house, shopping and preparing food no longer require one person in every household to be permanently home based. Domestic technology increases the viability of single employed person households and households where all adult members are in employment. However the full-time worker who is also a parent continues to need someone to look after his/her children. Childcare makes rigid demands that technology can only alleviate to a limited extent. This is at the heart of feminist scepticism about the benefits of domestic technology. But the feminist argument has also been linked with a general radical anti-consumerism which does not always correspond with popular attitudes among women. Feminists have underplayed the way domestic technology has supported changes in the labour market which have eroded women's dependency as wives. The traditional male breadwinner/female domestic labourer model of marriage was an understandable aspiration in the pre-modern era of domestic technology which really required the presence of somebody in the home in every household.

The core and unique aspects of domestic labour which are those concerned with interpersonal care and the management and maintenance of the social relations of the household have become more visible as domestic technology has reduced the physical aspects of domestic labour. As long as women continue to take prime responsibility for the interpersonal work of the household neither technology nor the market will significantly transform the gender division of labour. Since it is women's relationship to childcare which is central to this interpersonal work the next chapter explores the shifting relationship between domestic labour and children.

9 Children and Childcare

Childcare is the key task determining the future of household production (Reid 1934: 364).

It was argued in the last chapter that childcare is an increasingly central component of domestic labour in industrial societies. It is thus essential to understand gender divisions in parenting for any broader economic analysis of the divisions of labour in households and in society. The presence of dependent children reinforces the traditional gender division of domestic labour (Newell 1993) and the presence, age and number of children are significant factors influencing how much time women spend on domestic labour, employment and leisure activities. On the other hand children appear to have no significant effect on men's allocation of time (Walker and Woods 1976 and Horrell 1994: 214). It is argued here that the number and ages of children will affect, not just the time spent on childcare, but also the scale and complexity of other types of domestic labour. As was discussed in chapter 8, for people who are tied to the home by the presence of young children, the substitution of market goods and services for domestic labour is more problematic than envisaged in neoclassical economic accounts. The labour and responsibilities associated with mothering have a deep impact on women's economic lives, both during the years that their children are dependent and subsequently (Joshi 1987).

This chapter looks first at why children and childcare are under-represented in the British socio-economic research agenda and then examines household-based childcare as a labour process and the changing nature of that labour process. The effects of parenthood on women's employment patterns are then discussed, taking account of social class divisions and demographic shifts in the last twenty years in Britain. The chapter concludes with an exploration of the pattern of childcare provision in relation to changes in women's employment and a discussion of potential parental

demand for alternative childcare arrangements. Chapter 10
will discuss childcare policy issues and options.

9.1 CHILDREN AND THE SOCIAL SCIENCE AGENDA

There was relatively little socio-economic research in Britain on
the childcare component of domestic labour in the last three
decades of the twentieth century. Caring for dependent adults
and disabled children rightly received greater attention from
the early 1980s (Finch and Groves 1983, Baldwin 1985, Parker
1985, Lewis 1988, Ungerson 1990) but, during that period
there was little research on domestic caring for healthy able-
bodied children. Domestic childcare often appears as a taken
for granted but unknown domain. For example the explanation offered for the increased time spent by women and men
on childcare between the 1970s and 1980s, as discussed in
chapter 8, was that it was a largely 'recreational' activity and
hence associated with increased leisure time (Gershuny and
Jones 1987: 36). Whilst it is impossible in the household to
draw the clear boundaries between work and leisure that are
part of the culture of the market economy, it is also clear that if
leisure means free time for self, childcare should not be
equated with leisure. Activities that are recreational in certain
contexts, may cease to be so in the presence of children
because of the way supervision of behaviour, management of
social relations and, in the case of young children, the frequent
intrusion of physical care, can overshadow other aspects of the
experience. Lone mothers are less likely to eat meals with their
children because managing the children's meal is hard work
and incompatible with enjoying their own (Devault 1991: 54).

The early 1980s saw the beginnings of a significant feminist
research agenda on children, childcare and parenting (Fonda
and Moss 1980, Backett 1982, Boulton 1983, Riley 1983,
Yeandle 1984, Sharpe 1984, New and David 1985). More recently there were important research contributions from a
social psychology perspective (Walkerdine and Lucey 1989
and Coward 1992) as well as policy debate stimulated especially by the Equal Opportunities Commission and the
European Commission Childcare Network (EOC 1986 and
1990, ECCN 1990, Cohen 1988 and 1990). However, overall,

British feminism was more successful at probing gender relations and divisions other than those associated with the organisation of parenting (Freely 1995). This is partly due to the
internal dynamics of feminism itself but the extent of neglect
in Britain must also be linked to the way the feminist research
agenda has been shaped by the broader political and economic context. The feminist movement of the 1970s and 1980s
was pulled in two opposing directions. On the one hand there
was the need to assert that women had an identity apart from
children, and an entitlement to lives without children. Most
feminists were rightly critical both of naturalism, which attributes social relationships to biological factors, and of essential-
ism, which attributes to women, as a sex, qualities that are
specifically appropriate for mothering.

On the other hand feminists also wanted to improve
women's lives and therefore to recognise the pressing needs of
mothers. They committed themselves actively to improving
conditions for mothers such as the campaign to retain
mothers' right to child benefit, the campaign for married
women's financial and legal independence, campaigns for
lone mothers and many local nursery and under-fives campaigns. As Riley (1983: 151) pointed out there is a long-
standing tension within feminism 'between refusing to elevate
maternity into some engulfing feminine principle, and demanding that the needs of mothers be met.' There have also
been tensions between the woman-centred approach which
stresses the creative and positive qualities associated with
mothering and caring labour (Gilligan 1982 and Ruddick
1989) and the recognition that idealising motherhood ignores
the competitive and individualistic social environment in
which mothering in contemporary Britain takes place
(Coward 1992). Moreover the strategies and demands generated by women's experience of mothering proved the most
contentious of any feminist strategies. The unfortunately
phrased 1970 Women's Liberation Movement demand for 24
hour nurseries created the impression that feminists sought
separation from children not flexibility of provision.
Firestone's radical feminist stance that women's liberation required an end to childbearing was equally extreme and unpopular as was the demand for wages for housework to enable
mothers to receive a wage at home (Borchorst 1990: 175).

Feminists have been particularly critical of the highly pervasive 'dual role' approach which dominated social science research on women from the 1950s to the 1970s and which rested on an implicit naturalist/essentialist perspective. *Women's Two Roles: Work and Home* (Myrdal and Klein 1956), although it appeared radical at the time for advocating married women's right to work, was influential in the development of a post-war political consensus which supported increased labour force participation for married women whilst maintaining their primary responsibility as parents. However feminists in the 1970s and 1980s found it easier to reject this perspective than to replace it with one that takes account of responsibility for childcare. Feminist academics with children, like other full-time professional women, have been under pressure to remain silent about their experience as parents in the knowledge that this is unlikely to enhance their credibility at work. It is hardly surprising that so few of them have opted to focus their research efforts in this area. Research on women's experience in my own workplace revealed a conscious avoidance on the part of academic women to talk about their children (Gardiner and O'Rourke 1996). Male colleagues with young children were perceived to be much more likely to take their children into work with them than were the women.

Feminist research has also been shaped by the policy context in which it takes place. Graham (1991) for example noted how feminist research on care in Britain in the 1980s had been largely focused on the domestic labour associated with care of elderly, sick and disabled adults and children and not with caring for able-bodied children although there were a small number of exceptions to this (Land 1978, Graham 1985 and Joshi 1987). The British official definition of 'carer', adopted also in the academic literature, actually excludes people involved in caring for healthy able-bodied children. This contrasts with the Scandinavian countries where 'care' is used to encompass the work involved in looking after all dependants including children (Ungerson 1990: 9). This difference is explained by the very different policy contexts in which the various types of care are organised in Britain as compared with Scandinavia. Specifically the definition of state childcare within British social policy has been highly restricted, focusing by the 1980s more or less entirely on cases where parents are deemed not to be adequately caring for their children or whose care responsibilities have been removed from them. Children 'in care' are those that have become the responsibility of the state because of parental 'failure'.

British feminists have adopted much of the policy makers' concept of caring in the context of the development of community care policies in the 1980s (Graham 1991: 64). Care is defined as caring for a dependent person by that person's family, friends or neighbours such that the person is able to remain in their own home rather than in state provided residential accommodation. Care in Britain has never been accepted as a universal entitlement but rather interpreted as something provided in response to an assessment of need. In the Scandinavian countries there has been political support for the notion that society has an obligation to ensure that care is available for individuals of all ages who need it. Hence the concept of care has developed in articulation with statutory social policy. Where the state assumes responsibility for childcare across the board, as in Sweden and Denmark, the definition of household care has been broader.

9.2   CHILDCARE AS A LABOUR PROCESS

Two feminist analyses of caring from outside Britain are particularly helpful in unravelling the nature of childcare as a complex labour process involving physical, mental and interpersonal elements. Waerness (1984) argues that caring can apply to three different types of relationship between carer and cared for. First there are personal service relationships which involve an unequal relationship between carer and cared for and where the person cared for could, physically, provide the services for him or herself, but social and cultural expectations, economic and political power or physical force enable the cared for to command someone else's labour. This is the classic patriarchal service relationship operating as between father/husband and daughter/wife. Second there are care-giving relationships where the people cared for are unable to provide services for themselves, in a given environment, because they have a disability, are ill, or too young and therefore dependent on a care-giver to provide services for them. Third there are spontaneous care relationships where care is offered on a reciprocal basis in emergency or crisis situations without incurring expectations of continuity.

Childcare is clearly a form of care-giving work because of children's dependence on adults to provide services which they are too young to provide for themselves. As children grow older they learn to service themselves. The process of reaching adulthood, from this perspective, is one in which, in theory, young women and men assume responsibility for self-servicing, for reciprocal care, for care-giving to others, as well as for earning a living, and parents relinquish their care-giving and economic support role. However, in practice, this is a transition to adulthood which approximates more closely to young women's experience than to men's, where earning a living is commonly given greater priority than self-care and care of others. In patriarchal households this gendering of the maturing process takes a particularly sharp form.

Tronto (1993: 106) also provides a useful framework for analysing care in the context of caring for dependent adults. She identifies four elements or stages within caring, namely awareness, responsibility, action and responsiveness. Awareness involves the recognition that care is necessary and the identification of need. The next stage is the assumption of responsibility for identified need and determining how to respond to it. Action is about actually meeting care needs. Responsiveness refers to the sensitivity of the carer to the care-receiver.

I would suggest expanding this framework to encompass other elements which are essential aspects of childcare as a specific labour process. Awareness is the first stage involving the definition and perception of children's needs and wants. This is followed by responsibility for ensuring that, and deciding how, needs are met. With young children there is also an absolute requirement for someone to be present to attend to children's needs as they arise. Action involves carrying out the physical, mental and interpersonal tasks required to meet those needs. Management of social relations is about dealing with and being responsive to the interpersonal relations among children and between children and adults within and outside the household. Finally there is learning from the experience of childcare, which is one of constant change in needs and interpersonal relations and reviewing childcare strategies.

Perceived in this way it becomes obvious that childcare activities are enmeshed with other aspects of domestic labour where children are present. Devault's research on *Feeding the Family* brings this out very clearly, showing how meal preparation and management, in the domestic context, is essentially about the management of social relationships. Whilst class, culture and household composition will differentiate how the elements of childcare are perceived and addressed, all these elements of the process need to be carried out if children are to be adequately cared for.

If domestic childcare is viewed as a labour process it becomes apparent that many of the tasks, skills and personal qualities involved in it are fairly high level ones, normally associated with professional and managerial occupations. This is illustrated by a small study of 'home managers' which sought to identify the managerial skills developed by mothers in the home and to compare these with the skills required of paid managers (Howard 1986). Married and some lone parents were interviewed, drawn from two Scottish community centre women's groups and a housewives register group. Although this was not a random sample of full-time mothers, the research demonstrated that, for this group, most of the personal qualities, communication, interpersonal, financial, intellectual and supervisory skills required of managers were in evidence, although the women themselves had not perceived themselves as having managerial skills.

It is also apparent, in contemporary Britain, that women who become mothers and need to develop these skills in the context of domestic responsibility for children, do so with minimal formal support and training, largely on their own and on a trial and error basis. Parenthood and childrearing are seen as skills based on 'maternal instinct' or learned through direct experience in one's own family (Backett 1983: 13). Being responsible, on your own for significant amounts of time, for a young baby and possibly an additional young child or children is one of the most challenging forms of on the job training and skill acquisition that anyone ever experiences. The skills acquired include planning and organisational skills, flexibility and coping with unpredictability, resourcefulness, combined often with a very low budget, ability to cope single-handed with unremitting pressure, ability to carry out several tasks at once, ability to stay calm and relaxed with no personal or private space. The fact that so many women go through this process does not make it any less remarkable. Women somehow get through this period of their lives and emerge with enormous energy which is then often frustrated if the skilled and responsible jobs they could be taking on are not available or accessible to them. The work experience they have gained and the skills they have acquired during the time they have had out of the labour market are neither recognised nor valued. On the contrary their skills and work experience are normally perceived as depreciating during their absence from the labour market.

9.3 THE CHANGING NATURE OF DOMESTIC CHILDCARE

> When you give your child a bath, bathe him in language
> (Bullock 1974 cited Walkerdine and Lucey 1989: 180).

The ideas and practices of mothering are not universal and timeless but developed in specific historical and political conditions. The pattern common in Britain in the twentieth century for mothers to have continuous and exclusive responsibility for pre-school children is, historically and culturally, very unusual (Boulton 1983: 199). In nearly all non-industrial societies mothers combine childcare with important other economic responsibilities and share responsibility for children with other people. It is culturally rare both for people to specialise in domestic childcare and for domestic childcare to be the responsibility of isolated individuals.

Boulton interviewed fifty married women from different social classes with between two and four children, at least one of whom was under five, living in outer London suburbs and not in full-time employment. Two thirds said that motherhood gave them a sense of purpose, but half found childcare a predominantly frustrating and irritating experience. These women felt overburdened by their boundless obligations to children, found pre-school children difficult and demanding and disruptive of otherwise enjoyable activities and experienced anxiety and guilt as a consequence of the conflict between their responsibilities as mothers and housewives (Boulton 1983: 205).

The concept of the sensitive mother as the prerequisite for the child's intellectual and emotional development became increasingly influential in Britain in the second half of the twentieth century. Such a notion requires that, for women with children, domestic labour is focused around children not housework and that household tasks become pedagogic tasks. Domestic labour began to merge with supporting children's cognitive development. Walkerdine found that housework had gone underground in middle class homes, transformed by women into pedagogic or fun activities. Working class women maintained more of a distinction between housework and play and were more likely to resist their children's demands on the grounds of having to get tasks done because of other pressures on their time. However Boulton found that nearly all mothers, working class as well as middle class coped with the conflict between childcare and housework by giving priority to childcare (Boulton 1983: 85). Tension was experienced about the effect of childcare demands on housework standards, especially among working class women who tended to identify more with the housewife role, had fewer household appliances and less space. The social expectation that mothers should devote themselves to their children's emotional and intellectual development induces guilt and resentment in mothers from professional occupational backgrounds (Coward 1992: 79). Most find they lack the time or energy to do the stimulating and creative things with their children that mothers are expected to do and many admit to finding even cooking and cleaning preferable. 'At least you can think while you are doing it' (Coward 1992: 79). They find their own identities and interests disappearing when they focus on children's activities and play.

Parenting has continued to be a highly gendered activity across social classes although the reasons for that are complex. Yeandle (1984: 141) found that about two thirds of the married employed mothers she interviewed reported husbands' involvement in childcare. In all but a few cases the husband's involvement in childcare was related to the fact of

the wife's employment. Husband's willingness to care for children was frequently the key factor enabling respondents to
take a paid job, especially where the job was part-time. Whilst
in some cases husbands took on some of the labour of childcare, in a majority of cases the husband's involvement was
merely to be present and on hand if needed, indicating a
minimal engagement with most of the elements of childcare
as defined earlier in the chapter. In Backett's sample of
middle class couples with two young children where the wife
had stayed at home to care for the children, men's involvement in childcare was perceived to be highly circumscribed.
Husbands were perceived to fall into three categories
(Backett, 1982: 78). Some were described as competent,
willing to do things and able to cope if the need arose. Others
were competent but lacked awareness of what needed to be
done. A third group were described as incompetent in terms
of childcare.

The strongest degree of involvement on the part of husbands was typically the willingness and ability to substitute for
the mother when the need arose. Male 'involvement' of this
kind was contrasted with female 'overall everyday responsibility' (Backett 1982: 187). Whereas wives had a 'diffuse, overall
responsibility for childrearing and housework' husbands
tended to have much more specific and well defined spheres
of involvement in the total domestic division of labour
(Backett 1982: 188). Fathers' involvement in domestic childcare tended to take one of three forms. They might focus entirely on an activity which was with or for children. They might
be carrying out a task in which children were involved.
Alternatively they might be carrying out a task separate from
children.

Mothers on the other hand were expected to be constantly
available to children and willing to have any activity inter-
rupted or to be carrying out several tasks at once. Coward
found that both mothers in employment and full-time
mothers felt pressurised by the demands of childcare and the
difficulty of ever finding time for themselves. Both found it
hard to preserve their own identity in the face of ever-
expanding demands of children, declining public provision
and the philosophy of totally altruistic childcare. For mothers,
responsibility for childcare had a way of invading conscious-

ness at all times. Men were more able to detach themselves from this full-time sense of responsibility. In this context one reason why women seek employment, particularly part-time employment, is that it gives them: 'time of your own, time to think, time to have a cup of coffee, time to use your mind rather than be constantly attending to the minds of others. In this bizarre situation work is seen as an escape from the insistent and draining demands of the home.' (Coward 1992: 86)

Men's increased involvement in childcare seems to have been prompted more by their wives' employment than by a commitment to greater sharing of parental responsibilities or to developing direct relationships with their children. This latter type of paternal involvement is evident much less than support for mothers' parenting (Backett 1982: 209). Men perceive themselves as a back-up for their wives and often resist an active engagement in parenting as a learning process for themselves. An exaggerated version of this approach is captured in a father's comment: 'if I'm asked I'll stand on my head but by and large I don't recognise the things which have to be done' (Backett 1982: 80).

Men are found to 'opt in' to childcare whilst women have to 'opt out'. However women as well as men are active in defining the respective roles of parents in childcare. It is clear that women have an influence on how fathering is conducted because they are the main source of information about children for men. Children's dependence on their mothers can give women a sense of purpose lacking elsewhere in their lives and this can prevent women seeking to share parenting equally with husbands (Coward 1992: 56). The issue of women's collusion with men in maintaining the gender division of domestic childcare has been difficult for feminists to address. Yet it is understandable that women should seek to maintain control of the childrearing and other domestic labour processes in a social context where they lack control in other areas. Even as convenience baby food, easy care children's clothing, disposable nappies and domestic household appliances have reduced some of the physical labour involved in caring for children, there has been an intensification and redefinition of childcare as a labour process. Offsetting some reduction in the physical aspects of the work, there has been an increased emphasis on mothers' responsibility for their children's emotional and intellectual development. The main elements of mothering, as described by Ruddick (1989), have become 'preservative love', 'fostering growth' and 'training'.

In the 1950s and 60s maternal altruism was perceived as a woman giving up her own needs in order to feed, clothe and provide security for children. Simply being present was often enough. Children entertained themselves while mothers got on with the visible, physically demanding tasks of cooking, cleaning and washing. A 1960s survey of young housewives which investigated how they went about domestic tasks and viewed their husbands' participation in these asked about meal preparation, shopping, washing, cleaning, making beds and washing up but did not include childcare (Walter Thompson 1967). By the 1970s and 1980s the demands of maternal altruism had shifted towards much greater responsibility for children's emotional and educational development. By the 1990s lone mothers especially were under attack for providing inadequate standards of parenting. There was also a large expansion of commercially provided leisure opportunities for children at the same time as a widespread decline of street culture as a safe option for children. The responsibility of the household, especially mothers, to manage and pay for increasing standards of entertainment for children increased greatly.

9.4 PARENTHOOD AND FEMALE EMPLOYMENT

Responsibility for children and childcare has become an increasingly complex influence on women's patterns of employment. Motherhood now both marginalises women in the labour market and pushes them into employment, an experience with which black women have been familiar for a much longer period. There have been enormous shifts in patterns of female employment in Britain in the twentieth century with parenthood having an increasingly significant influence relative to marital status. In the 1920s and 1930s in Britain it was normally marriage, rather than the birth of the first child, which led to women's withdrawal from the labour force and marriage bans operated in relation to female employment in many occupations. After the Second World War parenthood, and especially age of children, began to replace marriage as the major determinant of female employment patterns in Britain although, as late as 1980 at least, the presence of a husband made it more likely that women would work part-time, even after allowing for the effects of children and income, reflecting, 'the extra domestic work required to look after the average husband' (Joshi, 1986: 235). By 1992 employment rates (defined as the proportion of women in different groups who were employed either full-time or part-time) were actually slightly higher for married women (68 per cent) than for single women (67 per cent) and lowest for formerly married women (widowed, separated and divorced) at 55 per cent. Labour force participation rates, however, defined as the proportion of the population employed or unemployed, continued to be higher for single women since they had an unemployment rate of 10 per cent in 1992 compared to 5 per cent of married women who were recorded as unemployed (OPCS 1994a: 111). A higher proportion of single women also worked full-time (47 per cent) as compared with married women of whom only 32 per cent worked full-time in 1992.

For about four decades after the Second World War it was the employment rates of married women without dependent children and those with older dependent children that rose most. As late as 1983 only 29 per cent of mothers of children under five and 59 per cent of mothers with youngest child aged 5–9 were in employment. By the same date 70 per cent of women whose youngest child was at least 10 were in employment, comparable to the 72 per cent of women with no dependent children in employment (OPCS 1994a: 112). From the mid-eighties the employment rates of women with young children rose sharply and by 1992 49 per cent of mothers of children aged 0–4 and 72 per cent of those with 5–9 year olds were in employment (OPCS 1994a: 112). Hence, although the age of youngest child continues to have a strong effect on female participation in the labour market its importance has been diminishing.

The 1980s was also a period in which there was a large rise in the proportion of children in lone parent households and lone parenthood had an especially negative effect on female employment, particularly in the presence of children under five, because mothers relying on state benefit were caught in the poverty trap (Metcalf and Leighton 1989: 64). In 1977–79 the proportion of lone mothers with children under five in employment (26 per cent) was very similar to the proportion of married mothers with children in the same age group (27 per cent) By 1991-93, the employment rate for this group of lone mothers had actually declined to 23 per cent less than half that of married mothers with under-fives which was 49 per cent (OPCS 1995: 66). At the same time the proportion of families with dependent children headed by a lone mother increased from 10 per cent in 1979 to 20 per cent in 1993 (OPCS 1995: 19).

Whilst age of youngest child continued to have the strongest influence on women's employment rates, by the late 1980s the second greatest influence was women's educational background (OPCS 1991: 49). Mothers with GCE Advanced level or above were more likely to be in employment than those with fewer qualifications. Women's occupational background also had a strong influence. Employment rates were highest for mothers of pre-school children among professional and managerial occupational groups with as many as 61 per cent of these women in employment by 1992 (32 per cent full-time) (see table 9.1). The next highest employment rates were for skilled manual/own account non-professional mothers at 50 per cent (15 per cent full-time). Unskilled manual mothers were actually more likely to be in employment (48 per cent but only 1 per cent full-time) than those in the semi-skilled manual and personal service group (31 per cent and 7 per cent full-time). The pattern was similar among mothers with youngest child aged 5–9 where the highest rate of employment was among professional and managerial (77 per cent), and skilled/own account non-professional (72 per cent).

There are two conflicting economic pressures affecting the market labour supply decisions of mothers. Whilst the domestic labour associated with children tends to reduce market labour supply, the extra financial cost associated with children tends to enhance it. As children grow older the extra cost becomes a stronger influence pushing mothers into the labour market relative to the pressure of domestic labour pulling them in the opposite direction, especially for women in the lowest income groups. As can be seen in table 9.1, by

Table 9.1 Proportion of women in employment by age of youngest child and own socio-economic group

Women aged 16–59 Great Britain 1990–92

Source: OPCS 1994a: 116

Age of youngest dependent child and employment status	Percentage of women in employment in each socio-economic group					
	Professional, employer or manager	Intermediate and junior non-manual	Skilled manual and own account non-professional	Semi-skilled manual and personal service	Unskilled manual	All
Youngest child 0–4						
All employed	61	46	50	31	48	44
Employed full-time	32	14	15	7	1	13
Youngest child 5–9						
All employed	77	69	72	61	64	68
Employed full-time	51	22	28	14	3	21
Youngest child 10+						
All employed	89	81	76	67	77	78
Employed full-time	64	35	36	23	3	33
All with dependent children						
Employed	75	63	64	49	63	61
Employed full-time	48	23	25	13	2	21
No dependent children						
Employed	88	80	74	66	63	77
Employed full-time	78	59	50	40	13	53

the early 1990s, employment rates were actually slightly higher for women with dependent children aged ten and over than they were for women with no dependent children. This pattern is particularly marked for women in the unskilled manual group where 77 per cent of those with older dependent children were in employment as compared with only 63 per cent of those with no dependent children. Because of these high employment rates for mothers of older children in the unskilled manual group, women with dependent children in this group were just as likely to be in employment as those without them, unlike all the other socio-economic groups.

However the presence of dependent children made it much more likely that women's employment would be part-time. Whilst 13 per cent of women without children in the unskilled group were employed full-time only 2 per cent of those with children were in full-time employment. This pattern was repeated across all socio-economic groups with only 21 per cent of women with dependent children and 53 per cent of women without dependent children in full-time employment (see table 9.1). The difference was least marked for professionals, employers and managers where 48 per cent of those with and 78 per cent of those without dependent children were in full-time employment. Amongst women with children there were very different influences on employment across classes, with relatively high earnings and career opportunities for some and pressures to take low paid part-time jobs to contribute to family income for others. However across classes, mothers increasingly found economic and social benefits from employment and, as discussed below in section 9.6, more would have sought employment if better childcare arrangements were in place.

It remained very uncommon for women and men to reverse their traditional roles within the family. Among couples with a child under ten in 1993, only 1 per cent had a husband economically inactive and a wife working, with a further 2 per cent having an unemployed husband and employed wife (OPCS 1995: 68). The *General Household Survey* in 1991 found that 96 per cent of families with children under 12 (including lone parent families) reported that the children's mother was the person primarily responsible for the care of children and 3 per cent that this was the child's father (OPCS 1993: 131). In the same year 17 per cent of families with dependent children were headed by a lone mother and 1 per cent by a lone father (CSO 1994a: 36). In 1988, 87 per cent of fathers of under-fives were in employment and only 2 per cent were in part-time employment (Cohen 1990: 12). Whilst there were more men with children under five wanting to reduce their hours of work than amongst other groups of men, men with dependent children over five were the most likely to want to increase their hours of work (Horrell, Rubery and Burchell 1994a: 127).

The proportion of women who are married declined – only 61 per cent of women aged 18–49 were married in 1991 as compared with 74 per cent in 1979 – (OPCS 1993: 227), reversing the trend in the 1950s and 1960s, discussed in chapter 8. However about nine tenths of all women born in the middle years of the twentieth century had children by the time they were in their forties. In 1991 only 8 per cent of all women born in 1970–74 expected to have no children (OPCS 1993: 233). The link between marriage and fertility was loosened with 31 per cent of births outside marriage by 1991 as compared with only 8 per cent in 1971 (CSO 1994a: 39). In the mid-1990s the Family Policy Studies Centre found a rise to 20 per cent in the proportion of women who expected to remain childless. Reasons cited by women included poverty, unstable employment, responsibility for the care of a sick or elderly relative, inability to find a suitable partner and growing pressures of work and career (Grant 1995).

The relationship between parenting and marriage had become more complex than before with increased cohabitation, divorce and second marriages. Most births outside marriage were registered by both parents. Legislation was somewhat inconsistent in its treatment of the link between marriage and parental responsibility. The Children Act 1989 (section 2) defined parental responsibility as shared between father and mother in the context of a marriage relationship. Where biological parents were not married, only the mother was held to have parental responsibility, unless an application was made through the courts for the father to be responsible. However subsequent legislation which introduced the Child Support Agency made fathers financially responsible for children, regardless of whether they were married or not to the mother (Whitney 1994).

9.5   CHILDCARE PROVISION

The assumption in Britain that the care of young children is primarily and naturally carried out by mothers at home is so deeply embedded in public policy that a recent survey of day care services for children in England defined these services as 'all the arrangements mothers may make for their children to be looked after when they are absent' including 'care by the father ...when it was done on a regular basis, while mothers were absent' (OPCS 1994b: 1).

In the UK during the last twenty years governments have not seen childcare as an equality issue. Equal opportunities legislation has not been accompanied by any linked pro-gramme of expansion of childcare services. On the contrary, in the words of the Home Office: 'Long-standing Government policy is that public provision of day care (i.e. services pro-vided or funded by local authorities) should be concentrated on those whose need for it is greatest – those families with par-ticular health or social needs' (Home Office 1987: 52). Consequently the provision of publicly funded under-fives childcare in the UK is lower than in any other country in the European Community (see table 9.2).

The different types of formal pre-school childcare provi-sion and usage made of them is summarised in table 9.3. For an explanation of the different types of childcare available see Mottershead (1988), European Commission Childcare Network (1990) and Cohen (1990). Playgroups, which provide part-time sessional care for children from two and a half (averaging five hours per week), are run by the volun-tary Pre-school Learning Association (formerly Pre-school Playgroups Association) and are the most common type of care available, providing places for about a fifth of all under-fives at any one time. Nursery school or class provision is the next most common type of childcare available. In 1992 38 per cent of three year olds and 9 per cent of four year olds in England were in nursery education, mostly part-time provi-sion of two and a half hours a day. Another 47 per cent of four year olds were in school infant classes on a full-time basis (National Commission on Education 1993: 123). There was a sharp increase in the number of private commercially run nursery schools in the 1980s. By 1990 28 per cent of all

Table 9.2 Full-time equivalent places in publicly funded childcare services as percentage of all pre-school children European Community countries 1986–89

	For children aged 0–2 %	For children from 3 to compulsory school age %	Compulsory school age	Length of school day hours
Germany	3	65–70	6–7	4–5 (a)
France	20	95	6	8
Italy	5	85	6	4
Netherlands	2	50–55	5	6–7
Belgium	20	95+	6	7
Luxembourg	2	55–60	5	4–8 (a)
UK	2	35–40	5	6.5
Ireland	2	55	6	4.5–6.5 (b)
Denmark	48	85	7	3–5.5 (a,b)
Greece	4	65–70	5	4–5 (b)
Portugal	6	35	6	6.5
Spain		65–70	6	8

Source: European Commission Childcare Network 1990: 10
(a) school hours vary from day to day; (b) school hours increase as children get older

children attending nursery classes or schools were in the private sector.

The increase in participation rates among mothers of young children in the 1980s was achieved without a major expansion of publicly funded childcare or any great change in the pattern of provision used by employed mothers (see table 9.4). Care by fathers and relatives continued to be the most common pattern of childcare arrangement although there was a reduction in the proportion of women using this family-based care. The 17 per cent of employed mothers of pre-school children using day nurseries in 1990 indicates some expansion of local authority, private and voluntary nursery

Table 9.3   Proportion of pre-school children aged 0–4 using different types of formal education and childcare (Great Britain 1986 and England 1990)

Type of childcare	Great Britain 1986 %	England 1990 %
Registered childminder	4	6
Nanny, mother's help, au pair*	–	3
Playgroup	20	21
Nursery class or school	15	15
Day nursery	6	8

Source: OPCS 1989: 115 and OPCS 1994b: 15
*Data on childcare within the home were not collected in the 1986 survey.

provision during the decade, resulting from national and local childcare campaigns, government funding for voluntary projects in disadvantaged urban areas and the development of a private market in childcare to meet the needs of mothers in professional and managerial occupations. However Cohen's survey of day nursery places in 1988 found that in spite of some expansion, especially in the private and voluntary sector, there were still only enough full-time equivalent nursery places for 2 per cent of all under-fives in the UK (Cohen 1990: 19).

Because of the low level of publicly funded childcare and the associated heavy reliance of employed mothers on informal and market-based childcare, patterns of childcare use varied greatly by social class. Fathers in manual occupations were much more likely to look after children to enable their wives to go out to work than were those in the non-manual groups (see table 9.5). Grandparents were less likely to look after children in professional and managerial households than elsewhere. Registered childminders were more likely to be used by non-manual than by manual households and were responsible for caring for 12 per cent of all the pre-school children of working mothers in England. Nannies looked after 14 per cent of the pre-school children in professional families and 9 per cent of those in employer/manager households. The use of nannies was also a regional and localised phenom-

Table 9.4   *Arrangements made by employed women for care of pre-school children and school age children, GB, 1980 and 1990 and preferred arrangements 1990*

Percentage of employed mothers making different types of childcare arrangement by age of child

Type of arrangement	1980		1990			
	Pre-school children	School children (term time)	Youngest child under 5		Youngest child 5–11	
			Actual arrangement	Preferred arrangement*	Actual arrangement	Preferred arrangement*
Father	47	57	64**	64**	52**	55**
Grandmother	34	25	1	8	16	23
Friend/Neighbour	3	9	17	8	12	10
Childminder	16	6	7	11	2	9
Nanny/Employee in the home	4	3	–	14	1	5
Day nursery: Local Authority	2	–	17	14	–	–
Day nursery Private/Voluntary	1	–	–	20	1	8
Workplace nursery	1	–	–		–	
Mother employed school hours only			8	39	34	64
Mother works from home			5	17	3	19
Children look after themselves			–	–	17	4

Source: Martin and Roberts 1984: 39, Witherspoon and Prior 1991: 139 and 141

*First and second choices given by women employees when asked which type of childcare they would choose if all were available.

**These figures include care by father and relatives, amongst whom the most common provider of care is a grandmother.

enon with 24 per cent of pre-school children of working
mothers cared for by nannies in Inner London, 8 per cent in
outer London and only 4 per cent in England as a whole
(OPCS 1994b: 20). However Gregson and Lowe (1994) found
that nannies were typically employed by dual-career couples
(both partners in full-time employment in professional or
managerial occupations) and that a similar proportion of
these couples employed nannies in the two areas they surveyed (Reading and Newcastle). They concluded that the regional concentration of nannies reflected the regional
concentration of dual-career couples. Day nursery provision
(including private and publicly funded provision) was the
most evenly spread across classes, providing care for 9 per cent
of the pre-school children of professional households and for
12 per cent of those in unskilled manual households.

The survey of provision in England in 1990 confirms the
limited extent to which market or publicly funded childcare
services expanded to support the increased employment of
mothers in Britain in the late twentieth century, as discussed
in chapter 8. Although there had been some increase in the
use of childminders, nurseries and nannies, only about a
quarter of the pre-school children of employed mothers were
covered by these formal childcare services in 1990. Reliance
on fathers, grandparents and other informal care remained
the typical pattern for the vast majority of employed mothers.

9.6   UNMET DEMAND FOR CHILDCARE

Most British mothers express a preference for part-time rather
than full-time employment and for making the necessary
childcare arrangements associated with employment within
the nuclear or extended family (Witherspoon and Prior 1991).
However it is clear that the presence of more extensive afford-
able childcare arrangements and more parent-friendly employment practices would enable many women to pursue
employment aspirations which they are currently unable to
pursue. In addition many women have aspirations for the
future that are likely to be frustrated without major changes
in policy regarding parental employment and childcare
provision.

Table 9.5   *Proportion of preschool children of employed mothers using different types of formal and informal childcare by social class (England 1990)*

Type of care	Social class as measured by occupation of head of household						
	Professional	Employers and managers	Intermediate and junior non-manual	Skilled and self-employed manual	Semi-skilled manual	Unskilled manual	All
	Percentage of children being cared for in the different types of care in the absence of mothers*						
Father	29	27	29	45	50	47	36
Grand-parent	18	25	44	44	35	44	34
Friend or neighbour	14	8	5	11	9	18	10
Childminder	18	16	14	8	6	9	12
Nanny**	14	9	0	0	0	0	4
Day nursery	9	9	11	9	6	12	9

*columns do not add to 100 because some employed mothers do not use any of these forms of childcare and many make use of more than one type of care.
** includes au pair or mother's help
Source OPCS 1994: 18

In 1990 the *British Social Attitudes* survey asked mothers of children under 12 about the childcare arrangements they would like to have and how their decisions about employment would be affected if they could have the childcare arrange-ment of their choice. The answers given by mothers who were in employment confirmed the strong preference amongst a majority for children to be cared for by fathers and relatives and amongst significant minorities for the option to work during school hours only or to work from home (see table 9.4). However other significant minorities would prefer nursery provision, especially in the workplace, to the arrange-ments they currently make. There is a striking contrast between the 20 per cent of mothers of pre-school children who state a preference for a workplace nursery and the lack of such provision. There is an unsatisfied demand at present in Britain for both nursery provision and for employment con-tracts that are more flexible in the sense of taking account of mothers' wish to spend time with their children.

The same survey also asked mothers to consider whether and how the availability of their preferred childcare arrange-ment would affect their decision about employment (Witherspoon and Prior 1991: 143). Two thirds of the women with children under 12 who were not in employment said that they would seek employment, mostly part-time, if suitable childcare provision were available. Of those mothers in part-time jobs, 30 per cent said that they would increase their hours (16 per cent would opt for full-time employment). On the other hand 23 per cent of the smaller group of women working full-time said they would work fewer hours. On balance it is clear that greater availability of the range of pre-ferred childcare services and more opportunities for flexible employment would increase significantly the market supply of female labour. Also the proportion of mothers intending to seek full-time employment when their children reach 12 (48 per cent) is much higher than the current proportion of mothers of children in secondary school in full-time employ-ment (31 per cent). Given the trend in the British labour market for an increased share of part-time jobs, it is question-able whether the opportunities these women seek will be avail-able in sufficient numbers for them (Witherspoon and Prior 1991: 144).

Another survey of children aged 0–7 years in England in 1990 also revealed a large unmet demand among mothers for a range of childcare provision, peaking for children aged 2 but significant for all age groups. Mothers were asked to indicate which type of provision they would prefer for their child at present, taking account of their employment situation and the likely cost but disregarding whether the facility was available in their area. Table 9.6 gives the percentages of mothers of children in particular age groups who stated a preference for particular types of childcare to which they did not have access. It shows that, for example, 20 per cent of mothers of children aged two would prefer a nursery class or school place for their child (and do not have one at present), that 22 per cent of the same group would prefer a playgroup place and that 28 per cent would prefer a day nursery place. Unmet demand for nursery education was also significant for 3 and 4 year olds (29 per cent and 20 per cent respectively). Unmet demand for day nursery places was substantial across the 0–4 age range. Amongst mothers whose children were at school in the 4–7 age group, 22 per cent would have liked alternative after-school arrangements for their children.

In place of the integrated approach to care of young children common elsewhere in Western Europe, which is based

Table 9.6   *Unmet demand amongst mothers of pre-school children for specific types of childcare by age of child (England 1990)*

Type of care preferred	Percentage of mothers with children in each age group (at previous birthday) who do not have a place in their preferred type of childcare				
	0	1	2	3	4
Playgroup			22	3	1
Nursery class or school			20	29	20
Day nursery	23	28	28	20	16

Source: OPCS 1994b: 32, 36, 39

on recognition of the social and educational needs of children and of patterns of parental employment, in Britain childcare provision has evolved along two distinct lines. The increased employment of mothers has led to a class divided pattern of provision in which manual occupational groups rely mainly on informal care (most often by the child's father or grandparents) whilst professional and managerial groups are more likely to employ childminders or nannies. Nonetheless most women across social classes are forced to rely on a complex patchwork of informal and formal provision. Attempts to respond to the social and educational needs of children have resulted in a separate array of play and nursery education provision in which voluntary organisations have played a major part.

The evidence discussed in this chapter suggests that a concerted reappraisal of the organisation of childcare is needed. There is a strong and widespread commitment to the preservation of time and space for domestic childcare but also a growing awareness that current definitions of mothering bring with them unrealistic and burdensome social expectations. State policy has perpetuated the assumption to a greater extent than in most other European countries that women's domestic labour should provide the basic infrastructure of care for young children. Women and men have acquiesced in women assuming a disproportionate share of the most mentally, physically and emotionally demanding aspects of domestic childcare. The enormous human effort and skill involved in rearing children remains largely unrecognised and unresearched. This invisibility has a class as well as a gender dimension. A public policy for childcare is needed in Britain as part of a broader policy for greater social and gender equality.

10 The Political Economy of Care

> In Britain, the interests of women workers are placed within a framework of market-determined priorities...the timing and the nature of the state's response to the concerns of women workers are based on the immediate 'needs' of the economy for women workers and less on the needs and abilities of women workers themselves (Ruggie 1984: 297).

This chapter investigates the prerequisites for developing a public policy for the care of dependent children and adults, starting from an examination of the current policy context in Britain with regard to childcare. Alternative policy proposals, ranging from the provision of publicly funded care services to monetary payments to carers are then discussed. The chapter concludes with a discussion of the preconditions for progress to be made in relation to the development of a public policy for care. The discussion draws mainly on debates about childcare but it is hoped that it will have wider relevance to policy regarding domestic caring work in general.

10.1   THE CHILDCARE POLICY CONTEXT IN BRITAIN

Childcare policy in Britain developed out of four fragmentary sets of influences, namely labour market conditions for women, issues of public finance and spending, campaigns for early childhood education and equal opportunities campaigns. The fragmentation of policy and services for young children has a long history, dating back to 1918 when an Education Act was passed to establish nursery schools and, in the same year, the Maternity and Child Welfare Act made it possible for the Ministry of Health to set up day nurseries.

Fragmentation was further reinforced by the implementation of compulsory education from age five in the 1944 Education Act. Formal education, with its emphasis on reading and writing, starts later in most other European countries (see table 9.2) whilst responsibility for pre-school children normally remains a more integrated aspect of social policy. For example, in Denmark and Sweden childcare policies were integrated with social policies in the 1930s and remained separate from the education system. The early onset of formal education in Britain, without any parallel development of out-of-school and school holiday care, locks parents – particularly mothers – into a highly rigid pattern of care responsibilities.

10.1.1 The labour market context

Interest in childcare to support women's employment has surfaced only occasionally at times of concern about a shortfall in labour supply. The clearest example of this was undoubtedly during the Second World War, when concern about shortages of female labour led to a rapid expansion of nursery provision, from 194 nurseries in 1941 (in England and Wales) to 1450 full-time and 109 part-time nurseries in 1944 (Tizard, Moss and Perry 1976: 72). Serious labour shortages continued after the war ended, in particular industries and services, and a Political and Economic Planning report written in 1948 highlighted these as the primary influence on nursery policy in the immediate post-war period. 'Although it is Government policy that nurseries should be provided to meet the educational, health and social needs of children under five years of age, at present new nurseries are being established only where the Ministry of Labour is satisfied that they are needed to enable mothers to take work of national importance' (Political and Economic Planning 1951: 58). Nurseries, in the immediate post-war years became increasingly the responsibility of private employers, based in mills and factories and tied in with the fluctuating needs of those employers (Riley 1983: 137).

Careful calculations were made during the war period regarding the costs and benefits, from a labour market perspecive, of nursery provision. Its labour intensive nature, especially where babies and under two year-olds was concerned, meant that the extra female labour supply made available by nursery provision would always be partially offset by the additional demand for nursery staff. Mass Observation suggested in 1942 that a mother with several young children should be discouraged from taking on war work on the grounds that another woman would be needed to care for her children in a nursery: 'It may well be that the large familied woman is an "inefficient" subject for Day-nursery attention. The one-child woman provides optimum opportunity' (Mass Observation 1942: 156).

After the war, the tension in public childcare policy between labour market concerns, education commitments and ideas about child health and welfare began to surface. As early as 1945 the Ministry of Health set out the policy which was to set the framework for childcare provision in Britain in the second half of the twentieth century:

> positively to discourage mothers of children under two from going out to work; to make provision for children between two and five by way of nursery schools and classes; and to regard day nurseries and daily guardians as supplements to meet special needs (where these exist and cannot be met within the hours, age, range and organisation of nursery school and nursery classes) of children whose mothers are constrained by individual circumstances to go out to work or whose home conditions are in themselves unsatisfactory from the health point of view, or whose mothers are incapable for some good reason of undertaking the full care of their children. (Ministry of Health circular 221/45 cited Tizard et al. 1976: 73)

The view was thus well established, some years before John Bowlby published his influential report, *Maternal Care and Mental Health* in 1951, that mothers of young children should be responsible for the care of their children, other than during nursery school hours (where such provision was available), or in exceptional circumstances where they were forced into employment or 'incapable' of providing full care themselves. In practice, even less childcare provision was delivered than implied by the policy statement. The promised expansion of nursery schools and classes for three and four year olds failed to take place. In 1964 the Ministry of Education admitted: 'since the war it has not been possible to allow local education authorities to extend their provision for children below compulsory school age in nursery schools and classes, mainly because it was felt that worthwhile provision was bound to absorb teachers badly needed in the primary schools' (Ministry of Education Annual Report 1964, cited Tizard et al. 1976: 75). Even the policy commitment to offer nursery provision to mothers forced by circumstance into employment was gradually eroded. By the 1980s day nurseries had ceased to offer places to mothers in employment and had become a 'social work' service for children 'at risk' (European Commission Childcare Network 1990: 35).

In the economic boom years of the 1950s and 1960s, conservative family policy, based on the model of the male breadwinner and dependent wife and mother, militated against the expansion of public childcare provision as a means of tackling labour shortages and by 1955, half of the wartime nurseries were closed (Lewis 1992: 71). Instead immigration from the New Commonwealth countries of South Asia and the Caribbean was encouraged. There was an implicit racism in this labour market strategy. Whilst white mothers were expected to provide full-time domestic childcare, many Afro-Caribbean women were drawn into jobs which meant long term separation from their children who were left in the care of relatives in their home countries (Bryan, Dadzie and Scafe 1985: 29). As far as white married mothers were concerned, the conclusion drawn by policy makers from the experience of the Second World War was that part-time employment, rather than childcare provision, should be the preferred mechanism for tapping female labour (Summerfield 1984).

It was not until the late 1980s that concern about the supply of indigenous female labour was again expressed by policy makers. At that time there appeared to be an impending labour shortage resulting from low birth rates in the 1970s, the 'demographic time bomb'. However the Conservative Government explicitly ruled out direct state provision of childcare. This response was the result of both the neo-liberal economic philosophy of the Government with its emphasis on leaving the market and employers to determine the pattern of childcare development and the clash of views within the Conservative Party between those traditionalists who believed that mothers should be encouraged to stay at home to look after their children and those who believed in women having freedom of choice and equality of opportunity. In 1989 John Patten, Employment Minister and chair of a newly created ministerial group on women's issues urged employers to develop childcare facilities but offered no support for this to happen. It took another 12 months before the Government bowed to pressure from employers and childcare campaigners to lift the tax charged to parents on employers' subsidies to workplace nurseries. This move benefited the parents of only 5000 children in the 130 workplace nurseries estimated to exist in 1990 (Cole 1990). John Major, then Chancellor of the Exchequer, in announcing the abolition of the tax stated: 'We have always made it clear that it is not for the Government to encourage or discourage women with children to go out to work. But it is undeniable that an increasing number of mothers do want to return to work and many employers in private industry and in public services are keen to encourage them to do so' (Cole 1990). Within a year the economy was moving into another major recession, concern about unemployment re-emerged and the demographic time bomb was quietly defused.

Labour market conditions are only one element of the political and economic context in which childcare policy develops and are, themselves, influenced by other aspects of public policy, as will be discussed below. That having been said, shifts in labour demand and supply during the 1980s and 1990s were not particularly conducive in themselves to the development of a public childcare policy. If the supply of female labour expands in line with labour demand, there is no immediate economic incentive for governments to encourage and support childcare services, even if they were politically predisposed to do so. On the demand side, the growth in employment opportunities for women (measured by an additional 1.7 million women in employment in 1994 compared with 1979 (Sly 1994: 405)) largely consisted of additional part-time jobs (over 1.3 million). During this period the number of men in full–time employment declined by 1.9 million whilst the number of women in full-time employment rose by under 0.3 million, all the increase in female full-time employment taking place in the boom years for the service sector of the late 1980s. Hence the nature of demand for labour was such that it enabled growing numbers of women with children to find employment that dovetailed with childcare responsibilities or to box and cox with partners, relatives or neighbours to provide childcare cover.

On the supply side growing numbers of women with dependent children were seeking employment for social and economic reasons and available to fill the vacancies created by the pattern of labour demand. The greatest increase in labour market participation amongst women was amongst those with children aged under five of whom 52 per cent were economically active in 1994 as compared with only 37 per cent in 1984 (Sly 1994: 403). Another important aspect of labour supply was the expansion of higher education and women's increased share of higher education opportunities. By 1994, 25 per cent of all economically active women with children under five had higher education qualifications. The activity rate for women graduates with children under five was much higher (75 per cent) than for mothers of pre-school aged children in general (52 per cent) and was supported by higher earnings which made it more possible for these women to afford paid childminders, private nurseries or nannies.

From a short-term, Treasury-led, government perspective, the particular interaction of labour demand and supply in the 1980s and 1990s was not conducive to an expansion in the public provision of childcare services. A Treasury perspective would compare the cost of childcare provision with the benefits to the economy of extra women in employment, earning and paying taxes. According to this perspective, any provision which was taken up by parents who were already in employment prior to the childcare services being provided would be of no benefit to the economy representing merely 'dead-weight' costs (Metcalf 1989: 87). The more women are able to find family-based or market solutions to the childcare problems associated with employment, the more the dead-weight costs of childcare provision are likely to rise. Hence the more mothers' economic activity rates rise, unaided by childcare provision, the greater the ultimate costs of introducing state support for childcare would appear to be relative to the benefits of enhanced labour supply.

The above discussion of the labour market is, however, premised on a short-term perspective and one that assumes a minimalist role for the state in terms of human resource development. A more long-term perspective, one which saw labour as an equal partner with employers and the state and a key economic resource, would generate rather different conclusions. If economic success were assumed to be premised on the fullest possible development and utilisation of the skills and abilities of the working age population, the costs of childcare provision could be offset in the long-term, not just by the benefits of additional female labour supply, but also by raising the quality of jobs accessible to mothers and by improving educational opportunities for pre-school children. This alternative perspective will be developed further in sections 10.1.3 and 4. The Treasury driven and free market strategy of the 1980s and 1990s Conservative governments, as reflected in public finance policy, is explored further in the next section.

10.1.2   The public sector finance context

In the late twentieth century the British state paid for childcare in two major ways: payments to single parents for full-time childcare and the collective provision of education and childcare services. Conservative governments in power from 1979, seeking the freeing of markets and privatisation of public providers, pursued the goal of minimising both state intervention and public sector spending. To the extent that mothers managed to find their own solutions to the problem of combining childcare responsibilities with employment, pressure on the state to provide publicly funded childcare services was reduced. The experience of the 1980s and 1990s was reminiscent of the late 1960s when the Pre-school Playgroups Association set up voluntary playgroups to demonstrate to the government the benefits of play provision for children as part of a campaign for nursery education (Orton 1991). Instead of the state responding with an expanded nursery education programme, playgroups were perceived as offering a cheap alternative to local authority nursery provision. Twenty five years on voluntary playgroups still provide for more under-fives than nursery schools and classes, as discussed in chapter 9. Women's creativity and skill in developing their own patchwork of part-time employment and informal childcare arrangements was consistently taken for granted by policy makers.

The growing cost of income support for lone parents, two thirds of whom were dependent on social security by 1990, and the absence of a government equality policy perspective on childcare, meant that public policy focused on finding ways of enabling and encouraging lone mothers, specifically, into employment, rather than offering childcare support as a universal entitlement and various policies were developed to this end. Family credit was introduced, payable to low income families including lone parents who worked for at least 16 hours a week and further encouragement was given to lone parents to come off income support by the introduction of a childcare expenses allowance for those on family credit. The Child Support Agency was also established to secure maintenance payments from absent fathers in place of income support.

These policies had only minimal impact by the mid-1990s on the overall proportion of lone mothers in employment which remained at less than half the level for married mothers (see chapter 9 section 4). Adjustments in the benefit system without a significant expansion of low cost high quality childcare are unlikely to achieve a major increase in the employment of lone parents. Government attempts to facilitate the employment of lone mothers were also opposed by the traditionalist right as anti-family. Any childcare support available to lone mothers but not to married couples is deemed to undermine marriage (Institute of Economic Affairs 1995).

In relation to the direct provision of childcare services, the emphasis within government policy was to encourage the development of private and voluntary alternatives to state provision and to minimise any additional public expenditure. Hence, any public subsidies for childcare or educational provision for young children focused on subsidising parental demand for places (for example tax allowances, or childcare vouchers) rather than on funding the supply of provision by the state. In 1995 the Government announced a pilot project to introduce vouchers for parents of four year old children, redeemable against places in state or private nurseries and schools and voluntary playgroups and to be funded largely by a transfer of existing local authority nursery funding (*Times Education Supplement* 14 July 1995: 4). Although, in theory, subsidising parental demand appears to have the advantage of allowing greater flexibility of provision and parental choice, in practice, because of its reliance on a market supply response, there are serious limitations associated with over-reliance on demand subsidies. Market supply depends on confidence on the part of private providers in there being an adequate rate of return. An infrastructure of education and training for staff also needs to be in place to ensure the quality of service provision. For children under three, services are particularly costly to develop, requiring high ratios of both staff and space to children, which reduce opportunities for profit. Without public support for the supply of these services, market provision is likely to be patchy and particularly inadequate in rural and disadvantaged urban areas (Cohen 1991: 72).

In the United States, where considerable reliance was placed on a market oriented demand-subsidy approach, childcare developed in a very uneven way (Melhuish and Moss 1990). Childcare tax relief systems also tend to favour higher income families rather than targeting subsidy towards those on lower incomes (European Childcare Network (ECCN) 1990: 57). Both the Equal Opportunities Commission (EOC 1990) and the European Childcare Network (1990) rejected demand subsidies as a major long term mechanism for funding childcare services.

Policy makers who lack either a strategic economic or an equality perspective, face a number of dilemmas with regard to childcare. Offering provision to single parents only, to enable them to gain employment, appears to discriminate against married parents. Childcare offered to all parents, on the other hand, will be more costly in terms of public spending since it will substitute for the domestic labour of married women which is not funded by the state as well as for that of lone parents. Also the return from the outlay in terms of extra female labour supply is likely to be lower since a higher proportion of married women with young children are already in employment without the support of publicly funded childcare. (Therefore dead-weight costs will be higher.)

However, as is argued below, an expansion of publicly funded childcare makes economic sense if the context is one of income and employment expansion and political commitment to equality of opportunity and achievement. The economic case is further strengthened when childcare is recognised as an investment in children's learning and development. It is to this aspect that we now turn.

10.1.3 The campaign for nursery education

The child-centred campaign for nursery education proved more politically effective than the childcare for equality lobby in late twentieth century Britain. The greater appeal of education for children, rather than of childcare for mothers, reflects the ideological context in which debates about nursery provision took place in Britain during this period. Nursery education for three and four year olds is known to be a vote winner and is supported unequivocally by research which demonstrates the educational benefits for children. Each of the major political parties in Britain in the 1990s claimed to support the goal of providing part-time nursery education for all three and four year olds whose parents wanted it.

Yet the campaign for nursery education also foundered on the cost implications of under-fives provision and on a lack of consensus on the role the state should play in that provision. In 1993 John Major announced a commitment to universal nursery education but stated that the funds to pay for it were not available. In 1994 the Adam Smith Institute, adopting the demand-subsidy approach discussed above, called for the introduction of vouchers for parents to use in both state and private nursery schools, funded by an increase in income tax. It was very definitely formalised education not play or care that was being proposed. 'We are not talking about child-minding. We are talking about teaching reading, writing and even languages, starting at the age of three' (Pirie 1994, cited *The Guardian* 19 March 1994: 5). Vouchers were also supported by the Centre for Policy Studies (CPS) which perceived them as a means of encouraging lower cost alternatives to state nursery education. Critics argued that the CPS voucher scheme would only be adequate to pay for care, not education (Blackburne 1995). The Royal Society of Arts (RSA) called for universal part-time nursery education based on a high quality nursery curriculum encouraging active learning and 'purposeful play'. The RSA favoured a public funding of supply approach and proposed raising the school starting age to six as a means of financing an expanded nursery education programme (Ball 1994).

None of these approaches addressed the issue of fragmentation of services for under-fives and all implicitly assumed that the interests of children could be tackled without regard for the working lives of mothers. The 1993 Report of the National Commission on Education adopted a more integrated approach, recommending that there should be a national strategy for early childhood education and care and national multi-professional and graduate-level training for all staff working with under-fives whether in education or care settings (National Commission on Education 1993: 133). One way of securing integrated services that had been adopted by several local authorities was to make education departments responsible for all pre-school children's services. The Commission argued for an expansion of publicly funded pre-school provision. This was to be achieved by increasing state expenditure on education as a whole and, within that, refocusing public funding towards pre-school and compulsory education and away from higher education. The proposals of the Commission offer scope for linkage to be made between education and equality policy.

10.1.4   The equality campaign for childcare

The Equal Opportunities Commission (EOC 1986 and 1990) and the European Commission Childcare Network (Cohen 1988, Moss 1988, ECCN 1990) were strong advocates for childcare as an equality issue in the 1980s and 1990s. Their argument was that achieving high levels of economic performance increasingly depended on ensuring equality of opportunity and that equality of opportunity could not be achieved without a major public commitment to childcare provision. Hence childcare was an economic as well as an equality issue.

Cohen and Fraser (1991) suggested the following four elements of provision:

- parental leave entitlements for men and women of between three and six months after the birth of a child;
- expansion of daycare (nursery and childminding services) for 0–2 year olds;
- expansion of nursery education and care for 3–4 year olds;
- out-of-school care for 5–11 year olds.

A range of more or less expansionary models for these four elements were offered, each assuming different levels of take up by parents and different labour supply responses of mothers. To illustrate the argument, the most conservative and least expansionary model, based on the EC Childcare Network minimum five year targets for member states (Moss 1988), is used in this discussion. This model assumed the following pattern of provision (Cohen and Fraser 1991: 97):

- take-up by between 47 per cent and 67 per cent of families of parental leave;
- publicly funded daycare provision (a mix of two thirds day nurseries and centres and one third publicly funded and supported childminders) for 10 per cent of 0–2 year olds;
- nursery education for 70 per cent of 3–4 year olds with supplementary care for 15 per cent of those children;
- out-of-school care for 15 per cent of 5–11 year olds.

The measurable likely benefits in terms of household incomes, alleviation of poverty and government revenue were compared with the capital and running costs of implementing such a programme. Central government taxation was assumed to bear 100 per cent of the costs of parental leave and nursery education and 70 per cent of daycare and out-of-school care with parents meeting 30 per cent of the costs of these latter programmes. Fee relief for parents on low incomes, for daycare and out-of-school care, was assumed within these estimates.

Assuming an adequate growth in job opportunities in the economy as a whole, there would be significant benefits from such a programme of childcare. There would be increased income from additional employment for mothers and their families. This additional employment would also result in increased tax revenue for the government (estimated at 52 per cent of additional earnings). There would be significant benefit savings arising from the increased employment of lone parents. Moreover up to half of children under five currently living in poverty could be brought out of poverty by the programme (32 per cent of all under-fives were estimated to be living in poverty at the time of the research) (Cohen and Fraser 1991: 111–116).

There would also be additional increased income and tax revenue generated by the additional childcare workers and staff employed to train those workers. In the longer term there would be additional income and tax revenue arising from higher lifetime earnings for women in general associated with enhanced skill and career progression, provided this was part of a shift to a general reskilling of the workforce rather than a redistribution of skilled jobs from men to women.

Even excluding the other very important but less easily quantified benefits associated with the enhanced opportunities for children's learning and development (Osborne 1987), the estimated return to the government on its investment, on the least ambitious programme of expansion, would average 5 per cent over a twenty year period whilst the return to society as a whole in terms of extra income would be 24 per cent (Cohen and Fraser 1991: 126). The more expansionary childcare models would result in higher rates of return because the dead–weight costs would be proportionately less. Public childcare programmes emerged as a good investment for both the economy and society. A government department would need to be identified to administer and coordinate the development of a childcare programme. The Children's Act (1989) could be amended to broaden the definition of public responsibility for children. Funding would need to be identified and, to assist in this, European Structural Funds could be tapped. A timetable would need to be set for the expansion to take place with capital spending and training of staff put in place. Local authorities would need to be given responsibility for developing appropriate local development plans consistent with national objectives.

While the economic case for an integrated childcare and nursery education policy is well made by the equality and education lobbies, the adoption of such a policy would require major shifts in economic policy and in perceptions of the role of the British state. There would need to be less emphasis on the creation of low wage jobs and greater commitment to the development of higher level skill and value added employment areas. These policy shifts would require a government commitment to increased public spending on education, especially early childhood education, and the acceptance of a more positive role for the state in the development of the economy's human and physical resources. These points will be discussed further in section 10.3 and in chapter 11. Choices would also have to be made about the nature of state involvement in supporting and substituting for domestic caring labour. It is to these alternative strategies that we now turn.

10.2 ALTERNATIVE STRATEGIES FOR SOCIAL CARE

Debates about different options for public support of domestic caring labour, are concerned with issues of poverty, especially the poverty of families with children, with opportunities for women to make full use of their abilities and skills and have access to financial independence, and with the rights of dependent adults and children to receive the care to which they are entitled. Policy in this area needs to be consistent with patterns of employment and household formation, and with economic performance.

Support for domestic care is closely bound up with the whole question of how society redistributes income from those in employment to those who are not. The Beveridge assumptions underlying the British welfare state were conservative in terms of the roles perceived for men and women, even when it was set up in the 1940s (Lewis 1992). It was assumed that carers were married women who were financially dependent on husbands in employment. Hence Beveridge saw no difficulty in tying benefits to employment rather than to caring responsibilities.

In the latter years of the twentieth century, household structure became increasingly diverse and fluid and employment become less and less secure. For both these reasons, caring responsibilities became a real challenge to the benefit system (Roll 1991: 74). The male breadwinner/dependent wife model of care became unsustainable given the large number of lone parent families, the high level of male unemployment and the increased dependence of households on female earnings from employment.

The divergence between the Beveridge model of care and patterns of household formation and labour market conditions in the 1990s resulted in a complicated and inadequate patchwork of public support for domestic caring labour (Lister 1992). There were three main elements to this pattern of support: support for the direct costs of children and disability, support for the costs of domestic caring and the funding of care services. Support for the direct costs of children and disability takes three forms:

- means-tested benefits (for example income support and family credit payments for children);
- contributory benefits based on employment record (for example invalidity benefit);
- categorical benefits (for example child benefit, one parent benefit, disability living allowance, severe disablement allowance) which are paid without either contribution or means-test towards meeting the living expenses of children and disabled people.

Support for the costs of domestic caring for dependent children or adults consists of income replacement for domestic carers. The two main examples of this type of support which were available in the 1990s were income support for lone parents and invalid care allowance (extended to married women in 1986 in face of a European Court ruling).

The third type of support is the funding of services which provide an alternative to domestic labour and may provide domestic carers with access to employment (for example nurseries or day centres).

This patchwork of support developed in Britain in a piecemeal way, rather than within a strategic framework for social care. In fact there are four different strategic directions which public policy in this area could take and the choices become clearer if these strategies are articulated. The first strategy would be to attempt to reinforce private dependency by public means. The second approach would involve offering carers greater opportunity to gain access to employment and independent earnings and accepting that employment should remain the primary basis of entitlement to benefit. A third approach would be for care responsibilities to provide entitlement to independent state benefits alongside the entitlement to benefits currently provided by employment. An alternative model, involving a complete revision of the system along the lines of a citizen's income, would be the fourth possible approach. This involves the payment of a full or partial basic income to all individuals defined as legally resident in the country. These four strategic approaches are now considered in more detail.

10.2.1 The reinforcement of dependency on the household unit

The first option of increasing the dependency of carers on the household unit would attempt to stem an opposite trend which gained momentum in the 1980s and 1990s towards individual rather than family assessment, as illustrated in the separate taxation of husbands and wives and individual rather than household community charges. In that period there was a developing social consensus that women should be treated as individuals in their own right rather than as dependants. The large expansion of employment amongst married women, especially those with young dependent children (Sly 1994), was a response to the declining success of male workers in securing a family wage and a factor further undermining the legitimacy of the male family wage concept.

However means-tested benefits, which are based on assessments of family income, reinforce individual dependence on the family unit (Roll 1991: 42) and means-testing became an increasingly pervasive aspect of the benefits system in the 1980s. Shifting financial responsibility for the children of lone mothers from the state to fathers provides another example of an attempt to reinforce private dependency.

The serious growth of poverty amongst families with children (Utting 1995) provides disturbing evidence of the results of over-reliance on attempts to reinforce the traditional private dependency model of care. However it would be mistaken to reject all aspects of private relationships of dependency (in the tradition of Kollontai's arguments as discussed in chapter 4) since women who rear children on their own following divorce are the most likely to suffer from such a strategy. The acceptance by the Government in 1995 of a House of Lords amendment to the Pensions Bill to split the main breadwinner's pension between divorced partners is an example of the reinforcement of private responsibility for domestic caring labour that was welcomed as long overdue by divorced women (although there were criticisms of the way the policy was to be implemented) (Hunter 1995). Similarly, lone mothers welcomed, with reservations, the enforcement of maintenance payments through the Child Support Agency as a means of lifting them out of the poverty associated with dependence on the state. The key question would appear to be how to develop greater independence for women without undermining the private responsibility of men. This takes us on to the question of access to employment for carers.

10.2.2 Enhancing access to employment for carers

The second strategic approach, which would enhance domestic carers' access to independent earnings, is consistent with socio-economic trends in Britain in the latter years of the twentieth century and in line with the overall approach to social security in the European Union. Amongst Britain's European partners there is an even stronger tradition of reliance on employment as the basis for social insurance than in Britain (Atkinson 1993: 8). Hence the social protection provisions of the European Social Charter are seen as a two tier structure in which there is entitlement to benefit deriving from employment and a means-tested second tier of benefit for all those excluded from the labour market. Given this European context and the public support for the social insurance principle in Britain, the accrual of entitlement to benefit through paid employment is likely to remain a major element of the UK social security system.

Access to independent earnings for women is, arguably, the most attainable means of securing progress towards gender equality from an economic as well as a political perspective (Coote, Harman and Hewitt 1990). An expansion of publicly funded childcare and education, accompanied by rising employment and incomes, would attract more women into the labour market, as discussed in chapter 9, and could pay for itself in the medium term through increased tax revenues, as discussed in section 10.1.4. Such a strategy would also benefit the economy by enhancing the skill level of women's employment and their lifetime earnings and improving educational opportunities for children across social classes. Improving the access of domestic carers to employment and independent earnings would require a range of different policies. As well as an expansion of childcare and other care services, there would need to be improvements in parental and carers leave schemes. The strategy would imply improved employment rights and social security entitlements for part-time workers (Brown 1994). Earning disregards (the amounts claimants are entitled to earn before benefit is deducted) would also need to be enhanced for parents and carers claiming income support and other means-tested benefits (McLaughlin 1994). In addition, training and education opportunities geared to the needs of people with domestic care responsibilities would be needed.

However, improving women's access to employment and independent earnings, on its own would only partially eliminate the gender inequality associated with the social organisation of care (Lewis 1992: 115). Even with much improved care services and leave entitlements, without other forms of recognition of domestic caring labour and the costs associated with it, women, especially working class women, would continue to find themselves excluded from effective citizenship. There is a risk that policies designed to support the employment of mothers would be of particular benefit to women in the higher income groups, given that, amongst women with dependent children, it is women from a higher education background that are most likely to be in employment and more likely to work full-time than part-time. Without major shifts in the demand for female labour as a whole, opportunities for most women to combine their domestic caring labour with reasonably paid employment would remain restricted. Even if a minimum hourly wage were to be introduced which made it possible for every worker to earn enough to cover basic individual needs by doing paid work for half a week (McLaughlin 1994: 59), without other changes taking place, most women with children would remain relatively poor throughout their working lives and after retirement. Serious consideration would therefore need to be given to the third strategy of benefits for carers.

10.2.3   Benefits for carers

If domestic caring labour is as essential to future prosperity as employed labour, there is a strong case for the entitlement of domestic carers to independent benefits. Such benefits would only be genuinely independent if they did not undermine carers' access to independent earnings. Any benefit which is means-tested, such as a parental care allowance for non-earning mothers (Esam 1991: 46), would continue to re-inforce carers' dependence on their household unit or partner and act as a disincentive for them to find paid employment. However a universal parents' benefit, payable to all those with childcare responsibilities, regardless of employment status, would offer a contribution towards either the time costs of domestic care or towards alternative childcare costs. The benefit could be payable at the highest rate for children under five, at a lower rate for children aged 5–11 and could cease to be paid, once children reached 12, on the grounds that out-of-school childcare ceases to be necessary at this age. Esam and Berthoud (1991: 50) suggested a rate of £20.90 per week for parents of pre-school children reducing to £10.45 for the 5 to 11 age group. This benefit could be taxable and hence of greatest value to those parents on lowest income. It could be funded by an increase of 0.8 per cent in the basic rate of income tax, combined with abolition of the married couple's allowance. Parents would be given the choice of using the benefit to compensate for the loss of earnings associated with their care responsibilities or, alternatively, to contribute to the costs of childcare. Even though the amount of the benefit politically and economically acceptable would be likely to be far less than the actual costs of childcare, it would at least establish the principle of social recognition of domestic caring labour without trapping women in a domestic caring role. It could be administered through the existing child benefit system and hence households could opt for fathers to receive the benefit if they were the primary carer.

A parent's benefit of the type discussed above needs to be distinguished clearly from the concept of a 'parent wage' for parents who opt to stay at home to look after their children, rather than seek employment, as proposed by Young and Halsey (1995). A parent's wage that is conditional on non-employment would preclude access to employment, cutting off opportunities to supplement low income and to have a break from care responsibilities. Such a proposal would serve to tie parents, overwhelmingly mothers, to dependency on the state and to the demanding experience of full-time care-giving work in the isolation of the home. It is reminiscent of the demand for wages for housework that was strongly opposed in the 1970s feminist movement (Malos 1980).

An alternative approach to introducing a benefit entitlement for carers is Atkinson's Participation Income proposal which would extend individual entitlement to benefit to those caring for young, elderly or disabled dependants (as well as certain other groups like voluntary workers) (Atkinson 1993: 10). This proposal was developed in the context of debates about a citizen's income to which we now turn.

10.2.4   Citizen's income

The fourth strategy, that of a basic or citizen's income (CI), would involve all individuals becoming eligible for an independent benefit, or rather a convertible tax credit, in their own right on the basis of residence (Parker 1989). The ultimate goal of supporters of CI is for all benefits and tax allowances to be amalgamated into a minimum income for all that would eliminate the need for means-testing and hence eradicate poverty. However it is generally recognised that such a goal would be politically and economically unattainable in the foreseeable future. Hence debate focuses on alternative models of transitional basic income (TBI) such as that developed by Parker and Sutherland (1994).

There are two main problems with most TBI proposals. The first is that, because the level of basic income would be set well below subsistence standards, and because of enormous variations in housing costs, a range of other benefits would have to be retained. Hence means-testing, although reduced in scale, would continue. The second problem is that all basic income schemes involve increased rates of taxation on earned income, both because tax allowances disappear and because higher rates of taxation are needed to pay for the extra income going to people who are not in employment. Basic income, in whatever form, would involve a reallocation of some of the value of tax allowances from those paying tax to those who do not (Clinton 1994: 38). It therefore risks reducing people's incentive to take paid work. Specifically it would be likely to act as a disincentive for women with domestic care responsibilities to take part-time employment, especially if basic income was introduced as an alternative to improving publicly funded child-care and other care services. There is a risk that women would find themselves trapped, even more than before, in domestic caring roles. This problem is avoided however if, instead of a transitional basic income for all, a full basic income for children and dependent adults were to be introduced, which came closer to meeting the cost of living for these groups. Child benefit in Britain is already a partial basic income for children in the sense that it is a universal contribution to the living expenses of children. Bradshaw (1993) estimated that in Britain child benefit met only 15 per cent of the cost of a child (Hewitt and Leach 1993: 29). Supporters of basic income find common ground with those who are concerned about the employment disincentive effects of basic income for women when they advocate substantial increases in child benefit as a way forward (Parker and Sutherland 1991: 12). A proposal meriting consideration is a European Basic Income for children which would strengthen the political case for child benefit to approximate more closely the living costs of children (Atkinson 1995).

10.2.5   Overview of alternative strategies

Achieving a politically acceptable and economically feasible balance between the four strategies outlined above would depend partly on projections of economic and employment growth rates. If the context were favourable to an expansion of incomes and employment, priority could be given to the expansion of nursery education, childcare and other care provision, linked with a carer's benefit and a substantial increase in child benefit for all dependent children. These strategies would have the advantage of widespread political support and consistency with European Union policy and should not result in intolerable tax burdens for those in employment. They could be financed by a combination of redirected public spending (within the departments of education and social security) and increased tax revenue (abolition of married couple's allowance, the additional tax yield on higher female earnings and a small increase in the basic rate of tax).

Ultimately the choice between a citizen's income and a modified social insurance system, based on domestic caring as

well as employment, depends on the capacity of the labour
market to generate adequate employment and incomes, both
in Britain and the European Union as a whole (Parker 1989:
286). Advocates of CI take the view that full employment (full-
time jobs for all who want them) has gone for ever and that ultimately society will have to respond to this by guaranteeing a
minimum standard of income to everyone regardless of work
record and availability. If the demand for labour is ultimately
finite it makes no sense to pursue policies that push everyone,
however unwilling, into employment. Others would argue
that, although full employment might be much harder to
achieve in future than it was in the 1950s and 60s, it is still attainable and should remain on the policy agenda (Sawyer
1993). Given the relatively low per capita incomes generated
by the British economy in the last decade of the twentieth
century and the need for significant increases in infrastructural and industrial investment, there would appear to be considerable scope for growth in incomes and employment.
Experience in Denmark indicates the feasibility of a different
gender contract in which female and male labour force participation rates are more or less equal (whilst women continue to
be in employment for fewer hours) and there is a generous
contributory social insurance system based on employment.

However no one can be confident about the future and it
seems wise to reserve judgement in the long term about the
direction policy should take. In the words of the Borrie
Commission: 'It would be unwise, however, to rule out a move
towards Citizen's Income in future: if it turns out to be the
case that earnings simply cannot provide a stable income for a
growing proportion of people, then the notion of some guar-
anteed income outside the labour market could become increasingly attractive' (Commission on Social Justice 1994:
263).

10.3   A PUBLIC POLICY FOR DEPENDANT CARE

Dependent children and adults cannot be adequately cared
for given the nature and levels of public support for care provided in Britain in the 1980s and 1990s. Inadequate and inappropriate public policies perpetuate poverty, gender and class

inequality and poor educational and economic performance. The failure of the state even to maintain its support for the costs of children (for example the freeze on child benefit from 1987 to 1991) contributed to the increased incidence of poverty in households with children (Parker and Sutherland 1991: 7).

A lack of public support and funding for childcare, accompanied by inadequate support for parents in employment, also perpetuated gender and class inequality. Although it did not prevent many mothers from getting employment, many others would do so if satisfactory childcare provision were available. Moreover the inadequacy of state support for parenting reduced drastically the employment options and earnings opportunities for mothers. It made access to market childcare alternatives more pressing and reinforced class divisions between women. Most women were forced to compete for low paid part-time jobs consistent with their childcare responsibilities and to forego long-term employment and career opportunities that might otherwise be available to them. This perpetuated gender segregation of jobs, low pay for women and gender inequality in the home, the workplace and public life as a whole. The skills and abilities of women who had children were not used to their full potential. Choice of childcare was restricted by its uneven geographical pattern and by over-reliance on private market-based services which the low pay of most women made inaccessible.

In other countries, notably in Scandinavia, there were much better levels of childcare provision and support for employed parents. This was linked to the nature of the labour market and demand for female labour as well as to the political and cultural traditions in those countries. For example in Sweden, women's fuller integration into the labour market by means of training, childcare and anti-discrimination policies is perceived to reflect a long-standing conception of women as potential or actual workers, in contrast to the traditional conception of women in Britain as mothers, first and foremost (Ruggie 1984: 295). The different policy orientations in the two countries reflect different political cultures in terms of the role of the state in the economy and the status of labour in general. The predominance of a neo-liberal conception of the state in Britain (Marquand 1988) meant that the interests of women and labour in general were placed within the framework of market-determined priorities and hence the immediate 'needs' of the economy, often interpreted in terms of external financial stability rather than domestic welfare and economic growth. In Sweden policies to support women's full participation in the labour market were effective because of a context in which the state was perceived to have a role in enhancing labour productivity and economic growth and labour was accepted as an equal partner alongside employers and the state.

Let us conclude by discussing the preconditions for care to be placed on the political and economic agenda in Britain. The lack of a coherent and comprehensive policy for the care of dependent children and adults reflects, in part, the fragmentation of the various lobbies and interest groups which, in turn reflect the patchwork and fragmented nature of policy and provision in this area. A coalition of political forces around parents, especially mothers of young children, and carers in general would be required to overcome this fragmentation. Women carers, on their own, have little political bargaining power and are confronted with urgent problems they have to solve. Individual and immediate solutions have to be found with whatever resources are to hand. There is no time to develop a political or strategic approach or to wait for the benefits it might bring. Once one set of childcare problems are resolved (pre-school childcare) new ones have to be tackled (after-school and holiday care). Each set of problems affect only a minority of the population at any one time although a majority of women will experience them at some stage in their lives. Most women, by the time they have worked through their years of childcare, either find themselves in positions of economic and political marginality or have to redouble their career building efforts to make up for the childcare years. For many the responsibility for childcare is soon replaced by responsibility for adult dependants.

Political arguments are only effective if they can be translated into economic feasibility. Hence another precondition for a comprehensive care policy is an expectation of sustained growth in real incomes and employment and a restructuring of the labour market towards the expansion of higher skill, higher quality jobs. Such a change in economic performance is unlikely to come about without a major change in the direction of economic policy and perceptions of the economic role of the state. The type of strategic policy for care suggested in the above analysis would imply a developmental role for the state in place of the neo-liberal economics underlying Conservative government policy in the 1980s and 1990s (Marquand 1988: 103).

Developmental states are those like Japan, France and Sweden, which accepted that the abilities of their citizens to compete with those of other nations were enhanced by the state using its power and resources to direct and harmonise the efforts of market actors. In so doing they rejected the orthodox Anglo-American economic tradition in which the atomistic, eighteenth century market economy described by Adam Smith, was still the model for an efficiently working economy. In the post-Second World War settlement, Britain became a welfare state rather than a developmental state, recognising some responsibility for redistributing income and alleviating poverty but not for promoting productivity or growth. Hence the British state adopted the burdens associated with economic adjustment without a clear strategy for steering the processes of adjustment in the interests of its citizens. The British public policy for care in the second half of the twentieth century was squarely within this welfare tradition. What is needed for the twenty-first century is a developmental care policy. The linkages with broader economic development and policy are explored more fully in the final chapter. Without these political and economic shifts it is likely that policy makers will continue to off-load on to women, society's responsibility for the care of dependent children and adults.

11 Towards an Alternative Feminist Economics

> Where our progress hitherto has been warped and hindered by the retarding influence of surviving rudimentary forces, it will flow on smoothly and rapidly when both men and women stand equal in economic relation (Gilman 1905: 340).

The acceptance that economic analysis can and should take account of the social division of labour as a whole, including domestic labour, is an essential aspect of a feminist economics. Households, markets and states should be analysed as interrelated sectors of the economy. Domestic labour, like the market and state sectors of industrial economies, undergoes continuing change and restructuring. An understanding of the internal processes within the three sectors and the linkages between them, is necessary to inform the development of economic policy.

11.1 REVIEWING ECONOMIC THEORIES

This book advocates a refocusing of economics more closely to its original purpose, namely the study of how the material needs of complex industrial societies are met. Mainstream economics in the course of the twentieth century moved away from this agenda towards a more restricted focus on a specific model of human behaviour in which self-interested, self-supporting agents make rational choices and trade with each other. A feminist perspective suggests four radical shifts in the economics paradigm. First it is proposed that the economics agenda is broadened to encompass the study of how material needs and wants are met, rather than the more restricted application of rational choice theory. Second feminism suggests a wider definition of economic well-being than normally assumed in economic discourse. The notion of economic well-being encompasses not just sustainable material consumption and standards of health, environment and housing but also opportunities for leisure, for socially useful work, for personal development, for individual independence and for access to care over the life-cycle. The third element of a feminist perspective is that markets have an important but only partial role to play, alongside households and state institutions, in the provisioning of all of these aspects of economic well-being. Economics therefore needs to embrace the total social division of labour, including domestic labour, not just that proportion of labour which is allocated through the market. The fourth point is that human economic behaviour is more complex and more socially constructed than rational choice theory suggests. Analysis of markets and entrepreneurial contexts, as well as households, would be strengthened by a less restricted view of human nature than that underpinning mainstream economic theory.

The feminist critique of rational choice theory needs to be complemented by critiques of the structural alternative analytical perspectives that have been offered by Marxist and feminist theory. This section offers an overview of the limits in all three theoretical perspectives that have been identified in this book by focusing on three key aspects: assumptions about human behaviour, conceptualisations of households and characterisations of the capitalist economy.

11.1.1 Models of human behaviour

In neoclassical economics economic agents are assumed to be individualistic, materialistic and self-supporting, although, outside market contexts, it is also accepted that people are capable of behaving altruistically, especially within household units. In the absence of regulation and political interference, supply in the labour market and demand in product markets are perceived as aggregations of individual choices. Hence the rational choice of buyers and sellers underpins the allocation of social resources. But free, unregulated markets can never be more than an abstraction. Individual choices may be rational within circumscribed limits, but they are also gendered and socially and economically constructed. The forces of supply and demand are shaped by combinations of cultural identities and ideologies, global capitalist forces, national capitalist and state institutions.

Individual choice has generally been an insignificant factor in Marxist and feminist accounts. Behaviour is constrained and shaped by, respectively, class and gender belonging. The economic structures of capitalism and patriarchy preclude action on the part of the oppressed party (working class/women) other than through collective resistance. Action on the part of the dominant party (capitalist class/men) is also socially structured rather than individually chosen, but also sustained by the material self-interest associated with economic privilege and control. Within Marxist theory, working class people have no choice about economic survival, but are forced to sell their labour power to capitalist employers. In feminist theory patriarchal structures force women into economic dependence on men. In each structural account, bargaining power and dependence are asymmetrical and the scope for individual choice greater for the economically dominant party, but still circumscribed by class and gender allegiance and material interests in the maintenance of the status quo.

Although neoclassical and Marxist paradigms are based on conflicting assumptions about human nature and behaviour, both assume a dualism between the market and the household which has militated against the exploration of gender inequality in either (Folbre and Hartmann 1988). Throughout the history of mainstream economic thought, from Adam Smith through to the New Home Economics, a dualistic conception of market and household behaviour was dominant (see chapters 2 and 3). Altruism in the household was contrasted with self-interest in the market. In the New Home Economics the underlying assumption of a joint household utility function continues to obscure the possibility of conflicts between individuals within the household. In the words of Becker: 'the advantages of altruism in improving the well-being of children and parents are contrasted with its disadvantages in market transactions' (Becker 1981: 1).

Marxism adopted a different but parallel dualistic perspective on working class motivation and behaviour. Class solidarity in the household was contrasted with the pursuit of antagonistic class interests in the market and the workplace. Within Marxism the exclusive focus on the class dimension of people's identity and interests discouraged exploration of difference and conflict within classes, including possible conflicts of interest within the same household although gender inequality and patriarchal relations were acknowledged in propertied middle class households (see chapter 4). The failure of the domestic labour debate to address ways in which men might benefit from women's domestic labour maintained this resistance to tackling gender inequality (see chapter 5).

The traditional dualistic treatment of households and markets as separate spheres, within both mainstream social science and Marxism is therefore problematic from a feminist perspective because it supported the exclusion of households and domestic labour from economic analysis and the neglect of gender inequality. Both market and household behaviour were misrepresented, the former as exclusively individualistic, self-interested and competitive, the latter as exclusively altruistic, harmonious and cooperative.

Market environments are characterised by different patterns of social relationship, not just individualistic competition. They do not always conform to the neoclassical model of human behaviour. Economic life, whether in private companies, public sector organisations or households is pervaded by combinations of self-interested behaviour and cooperative endeavour, by conflict and altruism. Men are encouraged by their socialisation and the market environment to pursue individual self-interest and get rewarded for doing so in organisational contexts where career development is based on individuals promoting their own worth in dialogue with managers. Women find themselves in a more contradictory position in such organisational environments where self assertion is perceived to transgress femininity and yet career progression requires it. Most women, and many men, are more likely to flourish in organisational environments where the emphasis is on identifying organisational needs and tapping and developing the abilities of all employees in meeting those needs, rather than on constructing and rewarding a small elite.

11.1.2 Conceptualising the household

Within the three theoretical perspectives under discussion households are perceived as being either egalitarian and harmonious (neoclassical/Marxist working class) or unequal and conflictual (feminist/Marxist middle class). This polarity is depicted in table 11.1.

In each of these conceptualisations the historical and cultural differentiation of household relationships are ignored. At one end of the spectrum, the New Home Economics characterises the household as an egalitarian, harmonious unit and attempts to explain all variations in household behaviour in terms of rational responses to market prices. At the other polarity the household is characterised as a patriarchal unit in which all women share a common class position in which they are obliged to perform unpaid domestic services for the male head of household. The treatment of the household by neoclassical economists as an unproblematic unity conceals unfounded assumptions about gender relations. However replacing the concept of a harmonious household by the concept of an equally universal and ahistorical patriarchal household ignores the historical and cultural differentiation of households. It is not adequate to assume either 'an undifferentiated autocracy' or 'an undifferentiated communality' (Harris 1981: 57). An approach is needed which takes account of choices and constraints, of common and divergent interests and of difference based on class, race, culture and household composition (see chapter 6). A feminist political economy perspective seeks to investigate and specify the diverse social relationships that actually operate within households and to identify more complex models of cooperative conflict in place of the polar opposites posited above (Sen 1984).

Table 11.1   A comparison of different theoretical perspectives on the household

Theoretical perspective	Conceptualisation of households
Neoclassical Marxist (working class households)	Harmonious, shared interests and resources
Feminist Marxist (middle class households)	Conflictual, unequal power and resources

11.1.3   The nature of the capitalist economy

In spite of their theoretical differences, economists on the
right and on the left have, in practice, often shared similar assumptions about the capitalist economy and the market as an
environment in which economic success thrives on inequality
and conflict. For Marxists, in the world system tradition
(Harris 1988), global capitalism is driven by the search for
profit and the impetus to permanently reduce the costs of reproduction of labour power relative to the production of a
surplus which can be reinvested back into the capitalist accumulation process. Unemployment is the natural product of
this process in which reserve armies of labour need to be
recreated regularly to maintain the profitability of capitalist
expansion. For neoclassical economists unemployment is
mainly the result of a failure of wages to adjust downwards to a
level where labour supply matches labour demand. Attempts
by states to regulate, reform or direct the market economy will
either inhibit economic success (according to neoclassical
theory) or be ineffectual (Marxist world systems theory).
Neither of these theoretical perspectives is particularly helpful
in the task of explaining how particular societies become
economically successful and why some are more successful
than others. A regulationist perspective, or one which recognises the possibility of a developmental role for the state,
offers more insights on these processes. Institutions and political ideas are perceived to play a significant role in the economic performance of different nations (Marquand 1988), as
discussed in chapter 10.

  The centre left current in British politics at the close of the
twentieth century seeks a radical reappraisal of the political
traditions of both left and right, and provides a stimulus and
context for the arguments developed in this book. From this
perspective the economic success of mature industrial
economies and liberal democracies like Britain will in future
be based on the development and full utilisation of human resources, rather than the permanent drive to cheapen the costs
of reproduction of labour. State regulation and institutional
reform are essential ingredients of economic success. The
recognition of diversity in national capitalist institutions is a
necessary step towards developing successful economic strate-

gies (Hutton 1995). The next section sets out the elements of a feminist input into this political economic discourse.

11.2   THE ELEMENTS OF A FEMINIST POLITICAL ECONOMY

It was argued in section 11.1.1 that dualistic perspectives obstructed the integration of gender and households into economic analysis and misrepresented economic behaviour and motivation in both markets and households. Dualism is also associated with the exclusion of inter-generational and intra-generational care from economic analysis and an over-restricted identification of economic well-being with monetised economic activity. Dualistic perspectives legitimise the market undervaluation of skills associated with interpersonal work and the management of social relations.

Rejecting dualism does not mean, however, that households and markets should be equated. For example, merely counting domestic labour into market statistical aggregates, would not significantly advance understanding of gender and care. Households, markets and states are distinctive but linked, complementary and differentiated economic spheres. Some feminists have called for the inclusion of household production in national income accounts (Waring 1989 and Goldschmidt-Clermont 1990). Attempts to measure the value of domestic production are helpful in demonstrating the scale of household economic activity and increasing awareness that economic well-being is a broader concept than Gross National Product. However making the scale of domestic labour more visible through applying some form of market valuation, risks submerging the important distinctions between households and markets (O'Brien 1993). This study of domestic labour suggests an alternative analytical framework is needed that takes account of distinctions and linkages between households and markets. Households and markets are also highly differentiated. Market-based work environments are differentiated by policy and institutional contexts and managerial strategies and cultures. Households are also differentiated by composition, by class, education and access to income, by race and culture, by sexual orientation, by stage in the life-cycle and generation, by degree of isolation from other households. There is a matrix of gender relations and relations between partners within households in which shared interests coexist with divergent interests. The elements of this matrix include the bargaining power of partners, the nature of dependency relations, and types of caring relations.

11.2.1 Households as care providers

Conceptually, domestic labour combines many different roles and social relationships which are both internal and external to the household. Different households demonstrate different combinations of these roles and social relationships including the care and education of dependent children, the care of dependent adults, reciprocal care, self-servicing, personal servicing of men by women and the maintenance of the social relations of the household unit. Domestic labour embodies a complex set of economic and social relationships in which women, men, parents, children, dependent adults, employers and the state all have interests. Analyses which equate domestic labour solely with the reproduction of the capitalist wage labour force and/or with patriarchal exploitation give only a partial picture and are inadequate to the task of explaining the complex relationships between and within households, markets and states. The relations involved in domestic labour change within households over the life cycle and across society over time.

In mature industrial societies, multi-person households are units for the intra-generational and inter-generational care of people and their living environment. There are three important aspects of households as care providers which distinguish the domestic labour process from market-based or public sector labour processes. First, the social relationships between carers and those cared for in a household context are different from the impersonal market relations of buyers and sellers. Second, and linked to this, costs and benefits of household care are shared in a personalised way which is distinct from the allocation and redistribution processes of both markets and public finance. Third, the relations of dependence between households and markets are asymmetrical.

Domestic labour is associated with economic dependency in contexts in which economic independence is based on access to market earnings.

Household care of people and their living environment is provided in a way that is distinct from the market model of buyers and sellers, involving, instead, one or more of the three different types of social relationship between carer and cared for, discussed in chapter 9. These three different types of care relationships are personal service relationships (care relationships which are socially constructed, gendered and associated with social inequality between the parties), care-giving relationships (based on physical dependency associated with age, disability, long-term health problems) and reciprocal care relationships (mutual dependency in emergency and ill health).

Households, whichever type of care relationships are operating, provide highly personalised services of a kind that are distinct in terms of the social relations involved from services that might be provided through the market. In market contexts, economic viability would require the operation of economies of scale and complex divisions of labour. The work involved in care and the management of the social relations of households has proved to be the aspect of domestic labour that is least amenable to market substitution (see chapters 8 and 9). Choice and cost both play a part in the limited marketisation and socialisation of care. Most people prefer to live in households with others and to provide care for and receive care within a family context of emotional relationships. Personalised one-to-one care is also highly labour intensive and therefore costly if that labour has to be paid for. Hence market substitutes for personalised care are expensive and only accessible to high income groups, for example nannies employed by professional dual earner couples (Gregson and Lowe 1994), and even then, only in a labour market context where there are plentiful supplies of personal service labour at relatively low wages. For the state to organise subsidised care services of a comparable quality to those provided on a household basis would be very expensive, hence the attempts made by government in the 1990s to shift the burden of care of the elderly on to individuals themselves, to be financed through their own savings, the sale of their homes or reduced pensions.

The social relationships of carers and those cared for are also qualitatively different as between households and market/public service care contexts. This is because households personalise the costs and benefits involved in care. The costs of care are borne by those with a personal investment in the relationship with the persons needing care. If given a choice, most people would probably prefer a balance in which there were more time to care for their own family members rather than much higher taxes to support social care in general. This personalisation of costs has considerable economic merit in a context in which state spending is constrained.

The third distinguishing feature of domestic labour is the asymmetrical nature of its dependence on the market economy. Domestic labour is highly dependent on the relationship of the household to the market economy and the state, which together influence the resources coming in, the nature of housing and the external environment and the bargaining positions of different household members. Households and markets are, of course, mutually dependent. Markets depend for their success on the human resources reproduced and sustained in households. However this dependence is long-term rather than experienced on a daily and weekly basis and, in contexts in which there are plentiful supplies of labour and skill, the dependence of the market on the domestic labour process can be ignored for long periods by employers and politicians. On the other hand, households depend absolutely and routinely on a regular flow of income from the market or the state to support domestic labour. Whilst wage labour generates an independent income to sustain the worker, domestic labour and care responsibilities limit access to independent income. Wage labour is a source of individual independence and domestic caring labour a source of dependence on other household members or the state in the context of the type of welfare system that operated in Britain in the second half of the twentieth century.

The experience of industrial societies like Britain in the twentieth century suggests that domestic labour has been extraordinarily resistant to processes of market substitution. The limits to market substitution are different as between those groups who benefited from rising material standards in the second half of the twentieth century and those who experienced persistent poverty. For the former group, domestic labour was sustained as a means of supporting rising standards of living, particularly housing ownership and the rise of consumerism. There was limited scope for market substitution for caring work which remained highly gendered. Women in full-time employment did not significantly reduce the time they spent on domestic labour, between the 1960s and the 1980s, even though the husbands of some of these women took a greater share of domestic labour (see chapter 7).

However domestic labour was sustained even more by poverty than by rising standards of living. In the 1980s in the UK there was an increase in the proportion of households with dependent children on low incomes. In 1992, 32 per cent of dependent children (4.1 million children) were in households receiving less than half average income as compared with 10 per cent (1.4 million) in 1979 (Utting 1995). By 1992, 20 per cent of families with dependent children were headed by a lone parent compared with 8 per cent in 1971. These figures suggest that, in the latter years of the twentieth century a growing proportion of Britain's domestic labour was carried out in households with very poor access to independent income and market substitutes. In such households much more time has to be spent to stretch very limited resources and to deal with the larger and endemic problems that arise in poor living environments. By the end of the twentieth century, full-time domestic labour, originally a symbol of affluence and social status, had become, typically a mark of poverty. The chance of women being full-time houseworkers was greatest for non-married mothers and the wives of unemployed men.

In the last three decades of the twentieth century, care-giving work became an increasingly significant component of domestic labour. The rise in divorce and growth of lone parent families, headed by women, reflected a decline in the patriarchal, personal service aspect of domestic labour relative to the care-giving work aspect. The gender division of domestic labour is increasingly explained by the gendered nature of care, by women's commitment to the care of dependent children and other relatives, and by the lack of social support for care. However households in which women service male partners, with or without other care relationships, remain a significant proportion of all households. The concentration of married women in part-time employment and men in long hours full-time employment sustained these traditional gender relations.

11.2.2 Linkages between households and markets

All people with a home and some income move between households and markets, usually on a daily basis. They combine the roles of household members, buyers, sellers, employees or managers, and their identity and motivation is influenced in a complex way by these distinct experiences. Experience of household relations will influence identity and behaviour in the workplace and vice versa. For example single women and lesbian women experience a particular pressure in the workplace to assert their need for financial independence. They also benefit from the autonomy which comes with a domestic life not organised around supporting men. Asserting self-interest is more possible in this context but it carries the risk of transgressing femininity (Gardiner and O'Rourke 1996). Men who have wives who are willing and able to provide the domestic services which enable them to work long hours away from home, have more opportunities to demonstrate their individual dedication to their employing organisation and hence to advance their career. Experience of gender relations in the household is likely to influence the perceptions men and women have of colleagues and job applicants in the workplace, legitimising implicit and explicit gendered job descriptions. Personal service relations learned in patriarchal household contexts are replicated and given new life in the workplace. More research of the kind pioneered by Cockburn (1985) is needed on the linkages between experience and motivation in households and workplaces.

Skills and experience acquired in the market economy are transferred to the household and vice versa but these transfers are not recognised or valued in most market contexts. Domestic labour is viewed as disinvestment, not investment, in human capital. Care-giving work is seen to detract from performance at work, instead of enriching it, and the interpersonal skills developed through it are viewed as natural, undervalued attributes, not as skills acquired through a complex learning process. Women's low pay is related to the undervaluation of the skills required for the jobs in which they are concentrated, as well as to under-representation in skilled occupations, especially amongst part-time employees (Horrell, Rubery and Burchell 1994b). The value of skills which domestic labour processes develop, such as communication skills and the ability to manage social relations are not given recognition equivalent to comparable skills developed through formal training (England 1992). The valuation of skills also depends, not just on supply and demand in the labour market, but also on the style and culture of management, on whether individual competitiveness or team work and cooperation are favoured and rewarded.

11.3   AN EQUALITY ECONOMIC STRATEGY

There are three key levels of economic decision-making that are particularly relevant to this study, namely households, employing organisations and government. Socio-economic change depends on actions at all three levels. Strategies for change will only be effective and meaningful if they engage with all three levels. Action at each level is linked with and influences what happens at the other levels.

Economics is about social choices and trade-offs as well as individual choices. Social choices, determined through political processes and regulatory systems, set the boundaries within which individual choices are made. The key social choices often involve trade-offs between the present and future, between short-term and long-term objectives. Examples are those between the consumption standards of the current generation and investment for future generations, between current utilisation of resources and conservation for the future, between minimising the cost of reproduction of human resources and maximising the development and future use of human resources. Short-termism has been identified as a particularly British problem, present in the financial and legal structure of companies, the adversarial two party system of government and the Treasury dominated approach to public finance. The corporate and financial institutions of

British capitalism have been criticised for favouring short-term profitability over long term investment and economic development (Hutton 1995). The absence in the UK in the 1980s and 1990s of a strategic policy for care and pre-school education, as discussed in chapter 10, and the emphasis on achieving competitiveness through labour market flexibility and a low wage economy were both reflections of short-termism. Levels of investment have been historically low in Britain by comparison with successful industrial competitors and the investment that has taken place has often not been directed to areas that enhance productive capacity or human resources. For example in the 1980s investment was concentrated in financial services and retail distribution rather than manufacturing industry and education (Glyn 1992: 85).

A central aspect of an egalitarian feminist economic strategy would be to secure a shift away from policies which emphasise the short-term cheapening of the costs of reproduction of labour towards those which facilitate the development and full utilisation of society's human resources. Such a shift in policy would involve major changes in political and economic direction at a national level and also cultural and organisational changes in private companies and public sector organisations. It would mean moving away from the concept of labour as a factor of production to employees as stakeholders in the company.

Key elements of such a shift in policy would be raising the level of investment and redirecting it in ways that enhanced productive capacity and human capability, tackling family poverty, developing an infrastructure of care services, shifting the balance of power from company owners to other stakeholders, improving employment opportunities for people with disabilities. At the level of the enterprise and workplace, key changes would be the skilling of part-time work, the development of career break schemes and bridges between full-time and part-time employment, leave for care and personal development purposes, the democratising of company management.

Higher levels of investment in manufacturing industries would raise the productivity of the workforce and make it possible for full-time working hours to be reduced without lowering take-home pay. Raising productivity throughout the economy is the key to reducing the differential between male and female employment hours. This would offer the possibility of reducing two structural constraints on women's participation in the labour market: men's household absenteeism and the difficulties faced by women with care responsibilities, in full-time jobs, in attempting to compete with men. Parallel investment in education and care services would raise the quality of labour supply, in line with the developing demands of industry and generate itself a large demand for skilled labour.

Access to jobs and care services is vital for families living in poverty. It is in the long-term interests of society as a whole for both lone and married parents to have access to a combination of earnings, care services and benefits which support the living costs of children and parenting. Social security support for care involving enhanced child benefit and the possibility of carers benefits, as discussed in chapter 10, would be needed to complement access to employment and care services.

The creation of more high quality jobs could be accompanied by the skilling of part-time employment, by the expansion of career break schemes and an expansion of the number of jobs which enable people to work at home for part of their contracted time, to facilitate combining employment with care responsibilities. This type of flexibility could be available at different levels of organisational hierarchies, not just in the highest level jobs. Movement from full-time to part-time, and part-time to full-time could be a much more readily accepted and implemented process, allowing employees to take time out, not just for domestic caring responsibilities but for training and study, and other personal and career development purposes, so that all staff had the opportunity of benefiting from the increased flexibility of employment contracts. As more men in this way gained the experience of periods of part-time employment, individual choice could begin to have a greater influence on the organisation of care and changes in the gendered nature of care-giving work would become more possible. Workplace and household environments could be adapted to reduce disablement, to improve access to independent living and earnings for people with disabilities, and reduce their dependency on household and state care.

Such shifts in the political and economic culture would represent a major break with Britain's particular blend of neo-liberal economics, welfare statism and conservative gender contract. A more egalitarian gender contract would be based on a strategy of support for domestic care and would close the gap in bargaining power between men and women. Whether or not support for such changes develops will depend on individuals' experiences and aspirations and the future they see for households and for gender relations. How much support would there be for a model of household relations based on reciprocal care and the sharing of care-giving work? Such a model for heterosexual household relations would involve radical shifts in gender identities. Are men willing to engage more fully with the care-giving labour process and to learn new interpersonal and social skills? Are women willing to relinquish control of this process? Traditional gender relations in which men command and women obey, men provide income and women provide personal services, are in disarray. As the new millennium approaches, it is time to rethink gender, care and economics.

Bibliography

Allen J. (1988) 'Towards a Post-industrial Economy?' in Allen and Massey (eds): 91–135.

Allen J. and Massey D. (eds) (1988) *The Economy in Question* (London: Sage).

Alwin D., Braun M. and Scott J. (1992) 'The Separation of Work and the Family: Attitudes Towards Women's Labour-Force Participation in Germany, Great Britain and the United States', *European Sociological Review*, Vol. 8 No. 1, May: 13–37.

Amos V. and Parmar P. (1984) 'Challenging Imperial Feminism', *Feminist Review*, No. 17: 3–20.

Amsden A. H. (1980) *The Economics of Women and Work* (Harmondsworth: Penguin).

Anderson M., Bechhofer F. and Gershuny, J. (eds) (1994) *The Social and Political Economy of the Household* (Oxford: Oxford University Press).

Appelbaum E. and Schettkat R. (1991) 'Employment and Industrial Restructuring in the United States and West Germany' in Matzner and Streeck (eds): 137–58.

Aspromourgos T. (1986) 'On the Origins of the Term "Neoclassical"', *Cambridge Journal of Economics*, Vol. 10, No. 3, September: 265–270.

Atkinson A. B. (1993) 'Participation Income', *Citizen's Income*, No. 16, July: 7–10.

Atkinson A. B. (1995) 'Susan Raven Talks to Two Members of the Borrie Commission', *Citizen's Income*, No. 19, February: 11.

Backett K. C. (1982) *Mothers and Fathers* (Basingstoke: Macmillan).

Baldwin S. (1985) *The Costs of Caring: Families with Disabled Children* (London Routledge and Kegan Paul).

Ball C. (1994) *Start Right: The Importance of Early Learning* (Coventry: Royal Society for the Encouragement of Arts, Manufactures and Commerce).

Barclay P. (1995) *Joseph Rowntree Foundation Inquiry into Income and Wealth* (York: Joseph Rowntree Foundation).

Barrett M. (1980) *Women's Oppression Today* (London: Verso).

Barrett M. and McIntosh M. (1980) 'The Family Wage: Some Problems for Socialists and Feminists', *Capital and Class*, No. 11: 51–72.

Barrett M. and Phillips A. (eds) (1992) *Destabilizing Theory* (Cambridge: Polity Press).

Baxandall R., Ewen E. and Gordon L. (1976) 'The Working Class has Two Sexes', *Monthly Review*, Vol. 28, No 3: 1–9.

Bebel A. (1910) *Women under Socialism* (New York: Socialist Literature Co.) cited Diamanti (1993): 9.

Bebel A. (1971) *Women under Socialism* (New York: Schocken Books).

Becker G. (1965) 'A Theory of the Allocation of Time', *Economic Journal*, Vol. 75, No 299, Sept.: 493–517.

Becker G. (1976) *The Economic Approach to Human Behaviour* (Chicago: The University of Chicago Press).

249

Becker G. (1980) 'A Theory of the Allocation of Time' in Amsden (ed.): 52–81.

Becker G. (1981) *A Treatise on the Family* (Cambridge: Harvard University Press).

Becker G. (1985) 'Human Capital, Effort and the Sexual Division of Labour' *Journal of Labor Economics*, Vol. 3, No 1, Part 2, January Supplement: S33–58.

Beechey V. (1987) *Unequal Work* (London: Verso).

Beechey V. (1979) 'On Patriarchy', *Feminist Review*, No. 3: 66–82.

Begg D. (1994) *Economics* (London: McGraw-Hill).

Bell C. S. (1974) 'Economics, Sex and Gender' *Social Science Quarterly*, Vol. 55, No. 3: 615–31.

Bell D. (1973) *The Coming of Post-industrial Society* (London: Heinemann).

Bell D. (1980) 'The Information Society' in Forester T. (ed.) *The Microelectronics Revolution* (Oxford: Basil Blackwell).

Beneria L. (1979) 'Reproduction, Production and the Sexual Division of Labour', *Cambridge Journal of Economics*, Vol. 3, No. 3, September: 203–225.

Benston M. (1969) 'The Political Economy of Women's Liberation' *Monthly Review*, 21, September, reprinted in Malos (ed.) (1980): 119–29.

Bereano P., Bose C. and Arnold E. (1985) 'Kitchen Technology and the Liberation of Women from Housework', in Faulkner W. and Arnold E. (eds) *Smothered by Invention* (London: Pluto Press): 162–81.

Bhopal K. (1993) 'Asian Women within the Household; Domestic Labour: His, Hers or Theirs?' Paper presented to the Conference: *The Family, Minorities and Social Change in Europe* (University of Bristol, Department of Sociology).

Bielby D. T. and Bielby W. T. (1988) 'She Works Hard for the Money: Household Responsibilities and the Allocation of Work Effort', *American Journal of Sociology*, Vol. 93 No. 5, March: 1031–59.

Blackburne L. and Hackett G. (1995) 'Right Praises Under-five Vouchers' *Times Education Supplement*, 17 March: 8.

Blau F. D. and Ferber M. A. (1986) *The Economics of Women, Men and Work* (New Jersey: Prentice-Hall).

Bodichon B. L. S. (1859) *Women and Work* (New York: C. S. Francis).

Bonney N. and Reinach E. (1993) 'Housework Reconsidered: The Oakley Thesis Twenty Years Later', *Work, Employment and Society*, Vol. 7, No. 4, December: 615–27.

Boralevi L. C. (1987) 'Utilitarianism and Feminism' in Kennedy and Mendus (eds): 159–78.

Borchorst A. (1990) 'Political Motherhood and Childcare Policies: A Comparative Approach to Britain and Scandinavia' in Ungerson (ed.): 160–78.

Boulton M. G. (1983) *On Being a Mother* (London: Tavistock).

Bradshaw J. (1993) *Household Budgets and Living Standards* (York: Joseph Rowntree Foundation).

Brannen J. and Moss P. (1991) *Managing Mothers: Dual Earner Households After Maternity Leave* (London: Unwin Hyman).

Braverman H. (1974) *Labor and Monopoly Capital* (New York: Monthly Review Press).

Braverman H. (1976) 'Two Comments', *Monthly Review*, Vol. 28, No 3: 119–24.

Brown C. V. (1980) *Taxation and the Incentive to Work* (Oxford: Oxford University Press).

Brown C. V. (1988) 'Will the 1988 Income Tax Cuts either Increase Work Incentives or Raise More Revenue?' *Fiscal Studies*, Vol. 9. No. 4, November: 93–107.

Brown J. C. (1994) *Escaping from Dependence* (London: Institute for Public Policy Research).

Brownmiller S. (1975) *Against Our Will: Men, Women and Rape* (New York: Simon and Schuster).

Bryan B., Dadzie S. and Scafe S. (1985) *The Heart of the Race* (London: Virago).

Buckley M. (1989) *Women and Ideology in the Soviet Union* (Hemel Hempstead: Harvester Wheatsheaf).

Bullock A. A. (1974) *A Language for Life, Committee of Enquiry* (London: HMSO).

Burns S. (1977) *The Household Economy: Its Shape, Origins and Future* (Boston: Beacon Press).

Byers A. (1981) *Centenary of Service: A History of Electricity in the Home* (London: Electricity Council).

Carby H. V. (1982) 'White Woman Listen! Black Feminism and the Boundaries of Sisterhood' in Centre for Contemporary Cultural Studies, *The Empire Strikes Back* (London: Hutchinson): 212–35.

Central Statistical Office (CSO) 1992, *Social Trends 22* (London: HMSO).

Central Statistical Office (CSO) 1994a, *Social Trends 24* (London: HMSO).

Central Statistical Office (CSO) 1994b, *Family Spending 1993* (London: HMSO).

Chadeau A. (1985) 'Measuring Household Activities: Some International Comparisons', *Review of Income and Wealth*, Vol. 31, No. 3, September: 237–53.

Clinton D., Yates M. and Kang D. (1994) *Integrating Taxes and Benefits?* (London: Institute for Public Policy Research).

Cockburn C. (1983) *Brothers* (London: Pluto Press).

Cockburn C. (1985) *Machinery of Dominance* (London: Pluto Press).

Cockburn C. and Furst-Dilic R. (eds) (1994) *Bringing Technology Home* (Buckingham: Open University Press).

Cockburn C. and Ormrod S. (1993) *Gender and Technology in the Making* (London: Sage).

Cohen B. (1988) *Caring for Children* (London: Family Policy Studies Centre).

Cohen B. (1990) *Caring for the Children: the 1990 Report* (Edinburgh: Family Policy Studies Centre).

Cohen B. and Fraser N. (1991) *Childcare in a Modern Welfare System* (London: Institute for Public Policy Research).

Cole R. and Whitfield M. (1990) 'Childcare Move will Help a Few' *The Independent*, 21 March: 22.

Collins P. H. (1990) *Black Feminist Thought* (New York: Routledge).

Commission on Social Justice (1994) *Social Justice: Strategies for National Renewal* (London: Vintage).

Conference of Socialist Economists (1976) *On the Political Economy of* Women, Pamphlet No. 2 (London: Conference of Socialist Economists).

Coole D. H. (1988) *Women in Political Theory* (Sussex: Wheatsheaf Books).

Coote A., Harman H. and Hewitt P. (1990) *The Family Way* (London: Institute for Public Policy Research).

Coulson M., Magas B. and Wainwright H. (1975) 'The Housewife and her Labour under Capitalism–a Critique' *New Left Review*, No. 89, January-February: 59–71.

Cowan R. S. (1974) 'A Case Study of Technological and Social Change: the Washing Machine and the Working Wife', in Hartmann M. and Banner L. W. (eds) *Clio's Consciousness Raised: New Perspectives on the History of Women* (New York: Harper & Row): 245–253.

Cowan R. S. (1983) *More Work For Mother* (New York: Basic Books).

Coward R. (1992) *Our Teacherous Hearts* (London: Faber and Faber).

Craig C., Rubery J., Tarling R. and Wilkinson F. (1982) *Labour Market Structure, Industrial Organisation and Low Pay* (Cambridge: Cambridge University Press).

Dalla Costa M. (1973) *The Power of Women and the Subversion of the Community* (Bristol: Falling Wall Press).

Davis A. (1982) *Women, Race and Class* (London: The Women's Press).

Delphy C. (1977) *The Main Enemy: a Materialist Analysis of Women's Oppression* (London: Women's Research and Resources Centre Publications).

Delphy C. (1984) *Close to Home: a Materialist Analysis of Women's Oppression* (London: Hutchinson).

Delphy C. and Leonard D. (1992) *Familiar Exploitation: a New Analysis of Marriage in Contemporary Western Societies* (Cambridge: Polity).

Department of Employment (1993) *New Earnings Survey 1993* (London: HMSO).

DeVault M. L. (1991) *Feeding the Family* (Chicago: University of Chicago Press).

Devine F. (1994) 'Segregation and Supply: Preferences and Plans among "Self-Made" Women', *Gender, Work and Organisation*, Vol. 1, No. 2, April: 94–109.

Dex S. (1985) *The Sexual Division of Work* (Brighton: Wheatsheaf Books).

Diamanti F. (1993) 'Marxism, A Viable Alternative', paper presented to the Conference *Out of the Margin – Feminist Perspectives on Economic Theory* (Amsterdam: University of Amsterdam).

Dobb M. (1973) *Theories of Value and Distribution since Adam Smith* (Cambridge: Cambridge University Press).

Dodge N. T. (1966) *Women in the Soviet Economy: Their Role in Economic, Scientific and Technological Development* (Baltimore: John Hopkins Press).

Draper H. and Lipow A. G. (1976) 'Marxist Women versus Bourgeois Feminism' in Miliband R. and Saville J. (eds) The Socialist Register 1976 (London: Merlin Press): 179–226.

Edgeworth F. Y. (1881) *Mathematical Psychics: an Essay on the Application of Mathematics to the Moral Sciences* (London: Kegan Paul, reprinted London School of Economics 1932).

Edholm F., Harris O. and Young K. (1977) 'Conceptualising Women', *Critique of Anthropology*, Vol. 3: 101–30.

Elson D. (ed.) (1979) *Value: The Representation of Value in Capital* (London: CSE Books).

Engels F. (1969) *The Condition of the Working Class in England* (London: Panther).

Engels F. (1972) *The Origin of the Family, Private Property and the State* (London: Lawrence and Wishart).

England P. (1992) *Comparable Worth* (New York: Aldine de Gruyter).

England P. (1993) 'The Separative Self: Androcentric Bias in Neoclassical Assumptions' in Ferber and Nelson (eds): 37–53.

Equal Opportunities Commission (EOC) (1986) *Childcare and Equal Opportunities: Some Policy Perspectives* (Manchester: Equal Opportunities Commission).

Equal Opportunities Commission (EOC) (1990) *The Key to Real Choice and Action Plan for Childcare* (Manchester: Equal Opportunities Commission).

Esam P. and Berthoud R. (1991) *Independent Benefits for Men and Women* (London: Policy Studies Institute).

European Commission Childcare Network (1990) *Childcare in the European Community 1985–1990* (Brussels: Commission of the European Communities).

Farnsworth B. B. (1978) 'Bolshevik Alternatives and the Soviet Family' in Atkinson D. et al. (eds) *Women and Russia* (Hassocks: The Harvester Press).

Ferber M. A. and Birnbaum B. G. (1977) 'The "New Home Economics": Retrospects and Prospects', *Journal of Consumer Research*, Vol. 4, June: 19–28.

Ferber M. A. and Nelson J. A. (eds) (1993) *Beyond Economic Man* (Chicago: University of Chicago Press).

Ferguson A. and Folbre N. (1981) 'The Unhappy Marriage of Patriarchy and Capitalism', in Sargent L. (ed.): 313–38.

Finch J. and Groves D. (1983) *A Labour of Love* (London: Routledge and Kegan Paul).

Firestone S. (1970) *The Dialectic of Sex* (New York: Bantam Books).

Fleming S. (1973) *Women in Rebellion-1900: Two Views on Class, Socialism and Liberation* (Leeds: Independent Labour Party).

Folbre N. (1982) 'Exploitation Comes Home: A Critique of the Marxian Theory of Family Labour', *Cambridge Journal of Economics*, Vol. 6, No. 4, December: 317–29.

Folbre N. (1983) 'Of Patriarchy Born: The Political Economy of Fertility Decisions', *Feminist Studies*, Vol. 9, No. 2, Summer: 261–84.

Folbre N. (1991) 'The Unproductive Housewife: Her Evolution in Nineteenth Century Thought', *Signs*, Vol. 16, No. 3, Spring: 463–84.

Folbre N. (1993) 'Socialism, Feminist and Scientific' in Ferber and Nelson (eds): 94–110.

Folbre N. (1994) *Who Pays for the Kids?* (London: Routledge).

Folbre N. and Hartmann H. (1988) 'The Rhetoric of Self-interest: Ideology of Gender in Economic Theory' in Klamer A., McCloskey D. N. and Solow R. M. (eds) *The Consequences of Economic Rhetoric* (Cambridge: Cambridge University Press): 184–203.

Fonda N. and Moss P. (eds) (1980) *Work and the Family* (London: Temple Smith).

254 *Bibliography*

Frederick C. (1920) *Scientific Management in the Home: Household Engineering* (London: Routledge).

Freely M. (1995) 'Left Holding the Baby', *The Guardian 2*, 23 January: 4–5.

Galbraith J. K. (1973) 'The Economics of the American Housewife', *Atlantic Monthly*, Vol. 232, August: 78–83 (reprinted as chapter 4 in Galbraith 1975).

Galbraith J. K. (1975) *Economics and the Public Purpose* (Harmondsworth: Pelican).

Gallie D. and White M. (1994) 'Employer Policies, Employee Contracts, and Labour Market Structure' in Rubery and Wilkinson (eds): 69–110.

Game A. and Pringle R. (1983) *Gender at Work* (Sydney: George Allen & Unwin).

Gardiner J. (1975) 'Women's Domestic Labour' *New Left Review*, No. 89, January–February: 47–58.

Gardiner J. (1976a) 'Political Economy of Domestic Labour in Capitalist Society' in Barker D. L. and Allen S. (eds) *Dependence and Exploitation in Work and Marriage* (London: Longman): 109–20.

Gardiner J. (1976b) *A Case Study in Social Change: Women in Society* (Milton Keynes: Open University Press).

Gardiner J. and O'Rourke R. (1996) 'Less Lucky, Less Stroppy or What?' in Taylor R. (ed.). *Beyond the Walls: 50 Years of Continuing Education at the University of Leeds* (Leeds: University of Leeds Series in Continuing Education).

Gardiner J., Himmelweit S. and Mackintosh M. (1975) 'Women's Domestic Labour', *Bulletin of the Conference of Socialist Economists*, Vol. 4, No. 11, June: 1–11.

Gardiner J., Himmelweit S. and Mackintosh M. (1976) 'Women's Domestic Labour', in Conference of Socialist Economists (1976): 3–16.

Gavron H. (1968) *The Captive Wife* (Harmondsworth: Pelican).

Gershuny J. (1978) *After Industrial Society* (Basingstoke: Macmillan).

Gershuny J. (1983) *Social Innovation and the Division of Labour* (Oxford: Oxford University Press).

Gershuny J. (1985) 'Economic Development and Change in the Mode of Provision of Services', in Redclift N. and Mingione E. (eds) *Beyond Employment: Household, Gender and Subsistence* (Oxford: Basil Blackwell): 128–64.

Gershuny J. (1992) 'Change in the Domestic Division of Labour in the UK, 1975–1987: Dependent Labour versus Adaptive Partnership', in Abercrombie, N. and Warde, A. (eds) *Social Change in Contemporary Britain* (Cambridge: Polity Press): 70–94.

Gershuny J. and Jones S. (1987) 'The Changing Work/Leisure Balance in Britain, 1961–1984', *Sociological Review Monographs* No. 33.

Gershuny J. and Robinson J. P. (1988) 'Historical Changes in the Household Division of Labour', *Demography*, Vol. 25, No. 4, November: 537–52.

Gershuny J. and Thomas G. S. (1980) *Changing Patterns of Time Use: Data Preparation and Some Preliminary Results UK 1961–1974/5*, Science Policy Research Unit Occasional Paper No. 13 (Brighton: University of Sussex).

Gershuny J., Godwin M. and Jones S. (1994) 'The Domestic Labour Revolution: a Process of Lagged Adaptation?', in Anderson et al. (eds): 151–97.

Gershuny J., Miles I., Jones S., Mullings C., Thomas G. and Wyatt S. (1986) 'Time Budgets: Preliminary Analyses of a National Survey', *The Quarterly Journal of Social Affairs*, Vol. 2, No. 1: 13–39.

Gilligan C. (1982) *In a Different Voice: Psychological Theory and Women's Development* (Cambridge: Cambridge University Press).

Gilman C. P. (1898) *Women and Economics* (Boston: Small, Maynard & Company).

Gilman C. P. (1905) *Women and Economics*, fourth edition (Boston: Small, Maynard & Company).

Gilman C. P. (1971) *The Man-Made World or Our Androcentric Culture* (New York: Johnson Reprint Corp.) cited Waring (1989): 354.

Glucksmann M. (1990) *Women Assemble:Women Workers and the New Industries in Inter-war Britain* (London: Routledge).

Glyn A. (1992) 'The "Productivity Miracle", Profits and Investment' in Michie (ed.): 77–88.

Goldschmidt-Clermont L. (1982) *Unpaid Work in the Household* (Geneva: International Labour Office).

Goldschmidt-Clermont L. (1990) 'Economic Measurement of Non-market Household Activities: Is it Useful and Feasible?', *International Labour Review*, Vol. 129, No. 3: 279–99.

Gorz A. (1982) *Farewell to the Working Class* (London: Pluto Press).

Gough I. R. (1972) 'Marx's Theory of Productive and Unproductive Labour', *New Left Review*, No. 76, November–December: 47–72.

Graham H. (1985) 'Providers, Negotiators and Mediators: Women as the Hidden Carers', in Lewin E. and Olesen V. (eds) *Women, Health and Healing* (London: Tavistock): 25–52.

Graham H. (1991) 'The Concept of Caring in Feminist Research: the Case of Domestic Service', *Sociology*, Vol. 25, No.1, February: 61–78.

Grant L. (1995) 'No Kids on the Block', *The Guardian 2*, 11 April: 2–3.

Green F. (1991) 'The Relationship of Wages to the Value of Labour-power in Marx's Labour Market', *Cambridge Journal of Economics*, Vol. 15, No. 2, June: 199–213.

Gregg P. and Wadsworth J. (1994) 'More Work in Fewer Households?', mimeo (London: National Institute for Social and Economic Research) cited Barclay (1995): 58.

Gregson N. and Lowe M. (1994) *Servicing the Middle Classes* (London: Routledge).

Hakim C. (1991) 'Grateful Slaves and Self-made Women: Fact and Fantasy in Women's Work Orientations', *European Sociological Review*, Vol. 7, No. 2, September: 101–21.

Hakim C. (1992) 'Explaining Trends in Occupational Segregation: The Measurement, Causes, and Consequences of the Sexual Division of Labour', *European Sociological Review*, Vol. 8 No. 2, September: 127–52.

Hakim C. (1993) 'The Myth of Rising Female Employment', *Work, Employment and Society*, Vol. 7, No. 1, March: 97–120.

Hardyment C. (1990) 'Rising out of the Dust', *The Guardian*, 11–12 August: 8.

Harris L. (1988) 'The UK Economy at the Crossroads' in Allen and Massey (eds): 7–44.

Harris O. (1981) 'Households as Natural Units' in Young, Wolkowitz and McCullagh (eds): 49–68.

Harris O. and Young K. (1981) 'Engendered structures: some problems in the analysis of reproduction' in Kahn J. S. and Llobera J. R. (eds) *The Anthropology of Pre-capitalist Societies* (London: Macmillan): 109–47.

Harrison J. (1973a) 'Productive and Unproductive Labour in Marx's Political Economy', *Bulletin of the Conference of Socialist Economists*, Autumn: 70–82.

Harrison J. (1973b) 'The Political Economy of Housework' *Bulletin of the Conference of Socialist Economists*, Winter: 35–52.

Harrod R. F. (1958) 'The Possibility of Economic Satiety–Use of Economic Growth for Improving the Quality of Education and Leisure' in *Problems of United States Economic Development*, Vol. I (New York: Committee for Economic Development): 207–13.

Hartmann H. (1974) *Capitalism and Women's Work in the Home, 1900–1930*, PhD Dissertation, Yale University.

Hartmann H. (1979a) 'Capitalism, Patriarchy and Job Segregation by Sex', in Eisenstein Z. R. (ed.) *Capitalist Patriarchy and the Case for Socialist Feminism* (New York: Monthly Review Press): 206–47.

Hartmann H. (1979b) 'The Unhappy Marriage of Marxism and Feminism: Towards a More Progressive Union', *Capital and Class*, No. 8, Summer: 1–33.

Hartmann H. (1981) 'The Family as the Locus of the Gender, Class and Political Struggle: The Example of Housework', *Signs*, Vol. 6, No. 3: 366–94.

Hawrylyshyn O. (1976) 'The Value of Household Services: A Survey of Empirical Estimates', *Review of Income and Wealth*, Vol. 22, June: 101–31.

Hayden D. (1982) *The Grand Domestic Revolution: A History of Feminist Designs for American Homes, Neighbourhoods and Cities* (Cambridge: The MIT Press).

Heitlinger A. (1979) *Women and State Socialism: Sex Inequality in the Soviet Union and Czechoslovakia* (London: Macmillan).

Hewitt P. (1993) *About Time* (London: Rivers Oram Press).

Hewitt P. and Leach P. (1993) *Social Justice, Children and Families* (London: Institute for Public Policy Research).

Higgs E. (1987) 'Women, Occupations and Work in the Nineteenth Century Censuses', *History Workshop*, No. 23: 59–80.

Hill T. P. (1979) 'Do-It-Yourself and GDP', *Review of Income and Wealth*, Vol. 25, No. 1, March: 31–39.

Himmelweit S. and Mohun S. (1977) 'Domestic Labour and Capital', *Cambridge Journal of Economics*, Vol. 1, No. 1, March: 15–31.

Hirsch F. (1976) *The Social Limits to Growth* (Cambridge: Harvard University Press).

Holt A. (ed.) (1977) *Selected Writings of Alexandra Kollontai* (London: Allison and Busby).

Home Office (1987) *The Nairobi Forward Looking Strategies for the Advancement of Women–A Review* (London: HMSO).

Hooks B. (1982) *Ain't I a Woman* (London Pluto Press).

Hooks B. (1984) *Feminist Theory: From Margin to Center* (Boston: South End Press).

Horrell S. (1994) 'Household Time Allocation and Women's Labour Force Participation', in Anderson et al. (eds): 198–224.

Horrell S., Rubery J. and Burchell B. (1994a) 'Working Time Patterns, Constraints and Preferences', in Anderson et al. (eds): 100–32.

Horrell S., Rubery J. and Burchell B. (1994b) 'Gender and Skills' in Penn R., Rose M. and Rubery J. (eds) *Skill and Occupational Change* (Oxford: Oxford University Press): 189–222.

Howard K. (1986) *Managerial Skills: Yes They Can be Developed in the Home* (Linlithgow: Howard Affiliates).

Humphries J. (1977) 'Class Struggle and the Persistence of the Working-class Family' *Cambridge Journal of Economics*, Vol. 1, No. 3, September: 241–58.

Humphries J. and Rubery J. (1984) 'The Reconstitution of the Supply Side of the Labour Market: the Relative Autonomy of Social Reproduction', *Cambridge Journal of Economics*, Vol. 8, No. 4, December: 331–46.

Humphries J. and Rubery J. (1992) 'The Legacy for Women's Employment: Integration, Differentiation and Polarisation' in Michie (ed.): 236–55.

Hunt A. (1968a) *A Survey of Women's Employment, Vol. 1: Report* (London: HMSO).

Hunt A. (1968b) *A Survey of Women's Employment, Vol. 2: Tables* (London: HMSO).

Hunter T. (1995) 'Divorced Women Step Closer to Justice' *The Guardian Outlook* March 11: 31.

Hutton W. (1995) *The State We're In* (London: Jonathan Cape).

Institute of Economic Affairs (1995) *Farewell to the Family?* (London: Institute of Economic Affairs) cited *The Guardian* 3 January 1995.

Jevons S. (1965) *The Theory of Political Economy* (New York: Augustus M. Kelley).

Joshi H. (1986) 'Participation in Paid Work: Evidence from the Women and Employment Survey' in Blundell R. and Walker I. (eds) (1986) *Unemployment, Search and Labour Supply* (Oxford: Oxford University Press): 217–242.

Joshi H. (1987) 'The Cost of Caring' in Glendinning C. and Millar J. (eds) *Women and Poverty in Britain*, (Brighton: Wheatsheaf Books): 112–33.

Joshi H. (1991) 'Sex and Motherhood as Handicaps in the Labour Market' in Maclean M. and Groves D. (eds) *Women's Issues in Social Policy* (London: Routledge).

Kaluzynska E. (1980) 'Wiping the Floor with Theory–a Survey of Writings on Housework', *Feminist Review*, No. 6: 27–54.

Kapp Y. (1979) *Eleanor Marx Vol.1 Family life 1855–1883* (London: Virago).

Kennedy E. and Mendus S. (eds) (1987) *Women in Western Political Philosophy* (Brighton: Wheatsheaf).

Knights D. and Wilmott H. (1986) *Gender and the Labour Process* (Aldershot: Gower).

Kollontai A. (1977a) 'Communism and the Family' in Holt (ed.): 250–60.

Kollontai A. (1977b) 'Theses on Communist Morality in the Sphere of Marital Relations' in Holt (ed.): 225–31.

Kollontai A. (1977c) 'Prostitution and Ways of Fighting it' in Holt (ed.): 261–75.

Kollontai A. (1977d) 'Marriage and Everyday Life' in Holt (ed.): 300–11.

Kollontai A. (1977e) 'The Labour of Women in the Revolution of the Economy' in Holt (ed.): 142–9.

Krouse R. W. (1982) 'Patriarchal Liberalism and Beyond: from John Stuart Mill to Harriet Taylor' in Elshtain J. B. (ed.) *The Family in Political Thought* (Amherst: University of Massachusetts Press): 145–72.

Kurz H. D. (1994) 'Value' in Arestis P. and Sawyer M. (eds) *The Elgar Companion to Radical Political Economy* (Aldershot: Edward Elgar): 462–7.

Laidler D. and Estrin S. (1989) *Introduction to Microeconomics*, third edition (London: Philip Allan).

Land H. (1978) 'Who Cares for the Family?' *Journal of Social Policy*, Vol. 7, No. 3: 257–84.

Laslett P. (ed.) (1949) *Patriarchia and Other Political Works of Sir Robert Filmer* (Oxford: Oxford University Press).

Leigh A. and Butler L. (1993) *Unpaid Work: What People Do in the Home, Community and Voluntary Work* (Ashbourne: Butler Miles Leigh).

Lenin V. I. (1965) *On the Emancipation of Women* (Moscow: Progress Publishers).

Lewis J. (1992) *Women in Britain since 1945* (Oxford: Blackwell).

Lewis J. and Meredith B. (1988) *Daughters Who Care* (London: Routledge).

Linder S. B. (1970) *The Harried Leisure Class* (London: Columbia University Press).

Lister R. (1992) *Women's Economic Dependency and Social Security* (Manchester: Equal Opportunities Commission).

Luxemburg R. (1963) *The Accumulation of Capital* (London: Routledge and Kegan Paul).

Luxemburg R. (1976) 'Women's Suffrage and Class Struggle' in Draper and Lipow (1976): 210–16.

Luxton M. (1980) *More than a Labour of Love* (Toronto: The Women's Educational Press).

Mackintosh M. (1977) 'Reproduction and Patriarchy', *Capital and Class*, No. 2, summer: 119–27.

Mackintosh M. (1979) 'Domestic Labour and the Household' in Burman S. (ed.) *Fit Work for Women* (London: Croom Helm): 173–191.

Mackintosh M. (1981) 'Gender and Economics: The Sexual Division of Labour and the Subordination of Women' in Young, Wolkowitz and McCullagh (eds): 1–15.

Mackintosh M. (1988) 'Domestic Labour and the Household', in Pahl (ed.): 392–406.

Malos E. (ed.) (1980) *The Politics of Housework* (London: Allison and Busby).

Manwaring T. (1984) 'The Extended Internal Labour Market', *Cambridge Journal of Economics*, Vol. 8, No. 2, June: 161–187.

Marglin S. A. (1978) 'What Do Bosses Do?' in Gorz A. (ed.) *The Division of Labour* (Brighton: Harvester Press): 13–54.

Marquand D. (1988) *The Unprincipled Society* (London: Jonathan Cape).

Marsh C. (1991) *Hours of Work of Women and Men in Britain*, Equal Opportunities Commission Research Series (London: HMSO).

Marshall A. (1959) *Principles of Economics* (London: Macmillan, reprint of eighth edition 1920).

Martin J. and Roberts C. (1984) *Women and Employment a Lifetime Perspective* (London: HMSO, Department of Employment/Office of Population Censuses and Surveys).

Marx K. (1961) *Capital: Volume One* (London: Lawrence and Wishart).

Marx K. (1969) *Theories of Surplus Value: Part One* (London: Lawrence and Wishart).

Marx K. and Engels F. (1967) *The Communist Manifesto* (Harmondsworth: Penguin).

Marx K. and Engels F. (1976) *Collected Works: Volume Five* (London: Lawrence and Wishart).

Mass Observation (1942) *People in Production* (Harmondsworth: Penguin).

Matzner E. and Streeck W. (1991) 'Introduction: Towards a Socio-Economics of Employment in a Post-Keynesian Economy' in Matzner and Streeck (eds): 1–18.

Matzner E. and Streeck W. (eds) (1991) *Beyond Keynesianism* (Aldershot: Edward Elgar).

McCrone D. (1994) 'Getting By and Making Out' in Anderson et al. (eds): 68–99.

McLaughlin E. (1994) *Flexibility in Work and Benefits* (London: Institute for Public Policy Research).

Meillassoux C. (1975) *Femmes, Greniers et Capitaux* (Paris: Librairie Francois Maspero).

Melhuish E. C. and Moss P. (eds) (1990) *Daycare for Young Children: International Perspectives, Policy and Research in Five Countries* (London: Tavistock/Routledge).

Menasco M. B. and Curry D. J. (1989) 'Utility and Choice: An Empirical Study of Wife/Husband Decision Making' *Journal of Consumer Research*, Vol.16, No.1, 254 June: 87–97.

Metcalf H. and Leighton P. (1989) *The Under-Utilisation of Women in the Labour Market* (Brighton: Institute of Manpower Studies).

Michie J. (ed.) (1992) *The Economic Legacy 1979–1992* (London: Academic Press).

Mies M. (1986) *Patriarchy and Accumulation on a World Scale* (London: Zed Books).

Mill J. S. (1865) *Principles of Political Economy* (London: Longman).

Mill J. S. (1935) *Autobiography* (1873) (Oxford: Oxford University Press).

Mill J. S. (1970) 'The Subjection of Women' in Rossi (ed.): 123–242.

Millett K. (1971) *Sexual Politics* (London: Rupert Hart-Davis).

Mincer J. (1962) 'Labor Force Participation of Married Women' in Lewis H. G. (ed.) *Aspects of Labor Economics* (Princeton: Princeton University Press): 63–105.

Mincer J. (1980) 'Labor Force Participation of Married Women: A Study of Labor Supply' in Amsden (ed.): 41–51.

Ministry of Agriculture, Fisheries and Food (1974) *Household Food Consumption and Expenditure: 1972 – Annual Report of the National Food Survey Committee* (London: HMSO).

Mitchell J. (1975) *Psychoanalysis and Feminism* (Harmondsworth: Penguin).

Molyneux M. (1979) 'Beyond the Domestic Labour Debate', *New Left Review*, No. 116, July–August: 3–27.

Morris L. (1993) 'Domestic Labour and Employment Status among Married Couples: A Case Study in Hartlepool', *Capital and Class*, No. 49, Spring: 37–52.

Morton P. (1971) 'Women's Work is Never Done', in Altbach E. and H. (eds) *From Feminism to Liberation* (Cambridge: Schenkman), reprinted in Malos (ed.) (1980): 130–57.

Moss P. (1988) *Childcare and Equality of Opportunity* (London: Commission of the European Communities).

Mottershead P. (1988) *Recent Developments in Childcare: A Review*, Equal Opportunities Commission Research Series (London: HMSO).

Myrdal A. and Klein V. (1956) *Women's Two Roles: Work and Home* (London: Routledge and Kegan Paul).

National Commission on Education (1993) *Learning to Succeed* (London: Heinemann).

Nelson J. A. (1993) 'The Study of Choice or the Study of Provisioning? Gender and the Definition of Economics' in Ferber and Nelson (eds): 23–36.

New C. and David M. (1985) *For the Children's Sake* (Harmondsworth: Penguin).

Newell S. (1993) 'The Superwoman Syndrome: Gender Differences in Attitudes Towards Equal Opportunities at Work and Towards Domestic Responsibilities at Home' *Work, Employment and Society*, Vol. 7, No. 2, June: 275–89.

Nissel M. and Bonnerjea L. (1982) *Family Care of the Handicapped Elderly: Who Pays?* PSI Report No. 602 (London: Policy Studies Institute).

O'Brien D. P. (1975) *The Classical Economists* (Oxford: Clarendon Press).

O'Brien E. S. (1993) 'Putting Housework in the GNP: Towards a Feminist Accounting?', paper presented to the Conference *Out of the Margin-Feminist Perspectives on Economic Theory* (Amsterdam: University of Amsterdam).

Oakley A. (1974) *The Sociology of Housework* (London: Martin Robertson).

Office of Population Censuses and Surveys (1989) *General Household Survey, 1986* (London: HMSO).

Office of Population Censuses and Surveys (1991) *General Household Survey, 20, 1989* (London: HMSO).

Office of Population Censuses and Surveys (1992a) *General Household Survey, 21, 1990* (London: HMSO).

Office of Population Censuses and Surveys (1992b) *1991 Census* (London: HMSO).

Office of Population Censuses and Surveys (1993) *General Household Survey, 22, 1991* (London: HMSO).

Office of Population Censuses and Surveys (1994a) *General Household Survey, 1992* (London: HMSO).

Office of Population Censuses and Surveys (1994b) *Day Care Services for Children* (London: HMSO).

Office of Population Censuses and Surveys (1995) *General Household Survey, 1993* (London: HMSO).

Organisation for Economic Cooperation and Development (1994) *Women and Structural Change* (Paris: OECD).

Ormrod S. (1994) 'Let's Nuke the Dinner': Discursive Practices of Gender in the Creation of a New Cooking Process', in Cockburn and Furst-Dilic (eds): 42–58.

Orton C. (1991) 'Working in Partnership? Voluntary Sector Child Care', *Women's Studies International Forum*, Vol. 14, No. 6: 573–5.

Osborne A. and Milbank J. (1987) *The Effects of Early Education: A Report from the Child Health and Education Survey* (Oxford: Oxford University Press).

Ott N. (1992) *Intrafamily Bargaining and Household Decisions* (New York: Springer).

Owen S. J. (1987) 'Household Production and Economic Efficiency: Arguments For and Against Domestic Specialisation', *Work, Employment and Society*, Vol. 1, No. 2, June: 157–78.

Pahl J. (1989) *Money and Marriage* (Basingstoke: Macmillan).

Pahl R. E. (ed.) (1988) *On Work: Historical, Comparative and Theoretical Approaches* (Oxford: Basil Blackwell).

Parker G. (1985) *With Due Care and Attention: A Review of Research on Informal Care* (London: Family Policy Studies Centre).

Parker H. (1989) *Instead of the Dole* (London: Routledge).

Parker H. and Sutherland H. (1991) 'Child Benefit, Child Tax Allowances and Basic Incomes: A Comparative Study', *BIRG Bulletin*, No. 13, August, 6–12.

Parker H. and Sutherland H. (1994) 'Basic Income 1994: Redistributive Effects of Transitional BIs', *Citizen's Income*, No. 18, July, 3–8.

Pearce D., Markandya A. and Barbier E. B. (1989) *Blueprint for a Green Economy* (London: Earthscan Publications).

Piachaud D. (1984) *Round About Fifty Hours a Week: the Time Costs of Children* (London: Child Poverty Action Group).

Picchio A. (1992) *Social Reproduction: the Political Economy of the Labour Market* (Cambridge: Cambridge University Press).

Pigou A. C. (1929) *The Economics of Welfare* (London: Macmillan).

Pigou A. C. (1956) *Memorials of Alfred Marshall* (New York: Kelly and Millman).

Pirie M. (1994) *20–20 Vision* (London: Adam Smith Institute).

Polanyi K. (1957) *The Great Transformation* (Boston: Beacon Press).

Political and Economic Planning (1945) *Report on the Market for Household Appliances* (London: Political and Economic Planning).

Political and Economic Planning (1951) *Manpower* (London: Political and Economic Planning).

Pujol M. A. (1984) 'Gender and Class in Marshall's Principles of Economics', *Cambridge Journal of Economics* Vol. 8, No. 3, September; 217–34.

Pujol M. A. (1992) *Feminism and Anti-feminism in Early Economic Thought* (Aldershot: Edward Elgar).

Ravetz A. (1965) 'Modern Technology and an Ancient Occupation: Housework in Present-day Society', *Technology and Culture*, Vol. 6, No. 2, Spring: 256–60.

Reid M. G. (1934) *Economics of Household Production* (New York: John Wiley).

Rendall J. (1987) 'Women in the Making of Adam Smith's Political Economy' in Kennedy and Mendus (eds): 44–77.

Ricardo D. (1966) *The Works and Correspondence of David Ricardo Vol. 1*, Sraffa, P. (ed.) (Cambridge: Cambridge University Press).

Riley D. (1983) '"The Serious Burdens of Love?" Some Questions on Childcare, Feminism and Socialism' in Segal L. (ed.) *What is to be Done about the Family?* (Harmondsworth: Penguin): 129–56.

Riley D. (1983) *War in the Nursery* (London: Virago).

Robbins L. (1962) *The Nature and Significance of Economic Science* (London: Macmillan).

Roberts B., Finnegan R. and Gallie D. (eds) (1985) *New Approaches to Economic Life: Economic Restructuring, Unemployment and the Social Division of Labour* (Manchester: Manchester University Press).

Robinson J. (1964) *Economic Philosophy* (Harmondsworth: Penguin).

Robinson J., Converse P. and Szalai A. (1972) 'Everyday Life in the Twelve Countries' in Szalai (ed.).

Roll J. (1991) *What is a Family* (London: Family Policy Studies Centre).

Ross C. E. (1987) 'The Division of Labor at Home', *Social Forces*, Vol. 65, No. 3, March: 816–33.

Rossi A. S. (ed.) (1970) *Essays on Sex Equality* (Chicago: Chicago University Press).

Routh G. (1989) *The Origin of Economic Ideas*, second edition (Basingstoke: Macmillan).

Rowbotham S. (1974) *Hidden from History* (London: Pluto Press).

Rowbotham S. (1982) 'The Trouble with "Patriarchy"', in Evans M. (ed.) *The Woman Question* (London: Fontana).

Rowbotham S. (1990) *The Past Is Before Us* (Harmondsworth: Penguin).

Rowe M. (1917) 'The Length of a Housewife's Day in 1917', *Journal of Home Economics*, December, reprinted Vol. 65, October 1973.

Rowthorn B. (1974) 'Neo-classicism, Neo-Ricardianism and Marxism', *New Left Review*, No. 86, July–August: 63–87.

Royal Commission on Population (1949) *Report* (London: HMSO, Cmd. 7695).

Rubery J. (1988) *Women and Recession* (London: Routledge and Kegan Paul).

Rubery J. and Wilkinson F. (eds) (1994) *Employer Strategy and the Labour Market* (Oxford: Oxford University Press).

Ruddick S. (1989) *Maternal Thinking* (London: The Women's Press).

Ruggie M. (1984) *The State and Working Women: A Comparative Study of Britain and Sweden* (Princeton: Princeton University Press).

Sargent L. (1981) *The Unhappy Marriage of Marxism and Feminism* (London: Pluto Press).

Sawhill I. V. (1980) 'Economic Perspectives on the Family' in Amsden (ed.) 125–39.

Sawyer M. (1989) *The Challenge of Radical Political Economy* (Hemel Hempstead: Harvester Wheatsheaf).

Sawyer M. (1993) 'Working for a Return to Full Employment', *Centre for Industrial Policy and Performance Bulletin*, No. 1, Spring: 1–2.

Scott H. (1984) *Working Your Way to the Bottom: the Feminization of Poverty* (London: Pandora Press).

Seccombe W. (1974) 'The Housewife and her Labour under Capitalism', *New Left Review*, No. 83, January–February: 3–24.

Seiz J. (1991) 'The Bargaining Approach and Feminist Methodology', *Review of Radical Political Economics*, Vol. 23, Nos 1 and 2: 22–9.

Sen A. (1984) *Resources, Values and Development* (Oxford: Basil Blackwell).

Sharpe S. (1984) *Double Identity* (Harmondsworth: Penguin).

Siltanen J. and Stanworth M. (1984) *Women and the Public Sphere: A Critique of Sociology and Politics* (London: Hutchinson).

Silver H. (1987) 'Only So Many Hours in a Day: Time Constraints, Labour Pools and Demand for Consumer Services', *Service Industries Journal*, Vol. 7, No. 4, October: 26–45.

Sly F. (1993) 'Women in the Labour Market' *Employment Gazette* November: 483–93.

Sly F. (1994) 'Mothers in the Labour Market', *Employment Gazette*, November: 403–13.

Smart C. (1983) 'Patriarchal Relations and Law: an Examination of Family Law and Sexual Equality in the 1950s' in Evans M. and Ungerson C. (eds) *Sexual Divisions: Patterns and Processes* (London: Tavistock): 174–196.

Smeds R., Huida O., Haavio-Mannila E. and Kauppinen-Toropainen K. (1994) 'Sweeping Away the Dust of Tradition: Vacuuming as a Site of Technical and Social Innovation', in Cockburn and Furst-Dilic (eds): 22–41.

Smith A. (1976) *An Inquiry into the Nature and Causes of the Wealth of Nations*, edited by Campbell R. H. and Skinner A. S. (Oxford; Clarendon Press).

Smith J. (1928) *Woman in Soviet Russia* (New York:) cited Heitlinger (1979): 226.

Social and Community Planning Research (1988) *British Social Attitudes: the 5th Report* (Aldershot: Gower).

Social and Community Planning Research (1991) *British Social Attitudes: the 8th Report* (Aldershot: Dartmouth).

Social and Community Planning Research (1992) *British Social Attitudes: the 9th Report* (Aldershot: Dartmouth).

Sokoloff N. J. (1980) *Between Money and Love: The Dialectics of Women's Home and Market Work* (New York: Praeger).

Steuernagel G. A. (1990) '"Men Do Not Do Housework": The Image of Women in Political Science' in Paludi M. and Steuernagel G. A. (eds) *Foundations for a Feminist Restructuring of the Academic Disciplines* (New York: The Haworth Press): 167–84.

Strassman D. (1993) 'Not a Free Market: the Rhetoric of Disciplinary Authority in Economics' in Ferber and Nelson (eds): 54–68.

Strober M. H. and Weinberg C. B. (1980) 'Strategies Used by Working and Nonworking Wives to Reduce Time Pressures' in *Journal of Consumer Research*, Vol. 6, No. 4, March: 338–48.

Strumilin S. G. (1926) 'Natsional' nyi Dochod v SSSR', *Planovoe Khoziastvo*, No. 8, cited Heitlinger (1979): 226.

Summerfield P. (1984) *Women Workers in the Second World War: Production and Patriarchy in Conflict* (London: Croom Helm).

Szalai A. (ed.) (1972) *The Use of Time* (Hague: Mouton).

Taylor B. (1983) *Eve and the New Jerusalem* (London: Virago).

Taylor H. (1970) 'Enfranchisement of Women' in Rossi (ed.): 91–121.

Thomas G. and Zmroczek C. (1985) 'Household Technology: the "Liberation" of Women from the Home?', in Close P. and Collins R. (eds)

(1985) *Family and Economy in Modern Society* (Basingstoke: Macmillan): 101–28.

Thompson W. (1825) *Appeal of One-half of the Human Race, Women, against the Pretensions of the Other Half, Men, to Retain Them in Political, and Hence in Civil and Domestic, Slavery* (New York: Burt Franklin, reprinted 1970).

Tizard J., Moss P. and Perry J. (1976) *All Our Children* (London: Temple Smith).

Tronto J. (1993) *Moral Boundaries* (London: Routledge).

Ungerson C. (1990) *Gender and Caring* (Hemel Hempstead: Harvester Wheatsheaf).

Utting D. (1995) *Family and Parenthood: Supporting Families, Preventing Breakdown* (York: Joseph Rowntree Foundation).

Vanek J. (1974) 'Time Spent in Housework', *Scientific American*, Vol. 231, November: 116–20.

Vickery Brown C. (1982) 'Home Production for Use in a Market Economy' in Thorne B. with Yalom M. (eds) *Rethinking the Family* (New York: Longman): 151–67.

Vickery C. (1979) 'Women's Economic Contribution to the Family' in Smith R. (ed.) *The Subtle Revolution: Women at Work* (Washington D.C.: Urban Institute).

Wadel C. (1979) 'The Hidden Work of Everyday Life' in Wallman S. (ed.) *Social Anthropology of Work* (London: Academic Press): 365–84.

Waerness K. (1984) 'Caring as Women's Work in the Welfare State' in Holter H. (ed.) *Patriarchy in a Welfare Society* (Oslo: Universitetsforlaget): 67–87.

Wajcman, J. (1991) *Feminism Confronts Technology* (Cambridge: Polity Press).

Walby S. (1990) *Theorizing Patriarchy* (Oxford: Basil Blackwell).

Walby S. (1986) *Patriarchy at Work* (Minneapolis: University of Minnesota Press).

Walker K. and Woods M. (1976) *Time Use: A Measure of Household Production of Family Goods and Services* (Washington: American Home Economics Association Center for the Family).

Walkerdine V. and Lucey H. (1989) *Democracy in the Kitchen* (London: Virago).

Walter Thompson J. (1967) *The New Housewife* (London: J. Walter Thompson).

Warde A. (1990) 'Household Work Strategies and Forms of Labour: Conceptual and Empirical Issues', *Work, Employment and Society*, Vol. 4, No. 4, December: 495–515.

Warde A. and Hetherington K. (1993) 'A Changing Domestic Division of Labour? Issues of Measurement and Interpretation', *Work, Employment and Society*, Vol. 7, No. 1, March: 23–45.

Waring M. (1989) *If Women Counted* (London: Macmillan).

Watson G. and Fothergill B. (1993) 'Part-time Employment and Attitudes to Part-time Work', *Employment Gazette*, May: 213–20.

Wells J. (1989) 'Uneven Development and De-industrialisation in the UK since 1979', in Green F. (ed.) *The Restructuring of the UK Economy* (Hemel Hempstead: Harvester Wheatsheaf): 25–64.

Wheelock J. (1990) *Husbands at Home* (London: Routledge).

Whitney B. (1994) 'Whatever Happened to "Parental Responsibility"?', *Childright* No. 112, December: 4–5.

Wicksteed P. H. (1910) *The Common Sense of Political Economy* (London: Macmillan).

Witherspoon S. and Prior G. (1991) 'Working Mothers: Free to Choose?' in Social and Community Planning Research: 131–54.

Yanagisako S. J. (1979) 'Family and Household: The Analysis of Domestic Groups' *Annual Review of Anthropology*, Vol. 8: 161–205.

Yeandle S. (1984) *Women's Working Lives* (London: Tavistock).

Young K. and Harris O. (1978) 'The Subordination of Women in Cross Cultural Perspective', in Patriarchy Conference London 1976, *Papers on Patriarchy* (Brighton: Women's Publishing Collective): 38–55.

Young K., Wolkowitz C. and McCullagh R. (eds) (1981) *Of Marriage and the Market* (London: CSE Books).

Young M. and Halsey A. H. (1995) *Family and Community Socialism* (London: Institute for Policy Research) cited *The Guardian Society*, 31 May 1995: 2.

Index

Index

time
  economics of, 45, 54
  see also opportunity cost
time budget studies, 128, 175–6

unemployment, 127, 134, 139, 146,
  149, 221, 238, 243
United Nations system of accounts,
  77
United States of America, 30, 39, 41,
  43, 58–9, 97, 157–8, 165, 216
universalistic assumptions, 10, 15, 37
Union of Soviet Socialist Republics
  (USSR), 4, 72–77, 79
utilitarianism, 27
utility
  interpersonal comparison of, 36,
    55
  joint, 45–6
  measurement of, 32, 36
  see also household as a
    decisionmaking unit

value, concept of, 10, 62
  see also domestic labour, value of,
    labour theory of value
Vanek, Joann, 168
variable capital, 61

wages for housework, 6, 86, 89, 184,
  227

wages
  general, 26, 31, 53–4, 62, 70,
    90–1, 108
  and labour supply, 40–43
  women's, 28, 34, 42, 46, 48,
    50, 53, 144, 146,
    158
Walby, Sylvia, 87–8, 90, 102, 103,
  109–12
Wealth of Nations, 1, 21, 24–5
  see also Smith, Adam
welfare state, 232
  Beveridge, 221
welfare, economic, 35–36, 37, 46,
  233–4
Women's Liberation Movement,
  see feminist movement
  1960s–80s
Women's Two Roles: Work and Home,
  185
work
  commitment, 154–5
  concept of, 2, 6–7, 13, 47, 57,
    80
  feminist redefinition of, 6
  interpersonal, 167, 175–6,
    179–80
  leisure choices, 40–3
  unpaid, *see* domestic labour
working time, 41–4, 128–35, 157,
  246–7